The Hatherleigh Guide

to

Psychotherapy

The Hatherleigh Guides series

The Hatherleigh Guide

to

Psychotherapy

■ Hatherleigh Press • New York

The Hatherleigh Guide to Psychotherapy

Cover photo: Christopher Flach, PhD
Production Editor: Joya Lonsdale
Indexer: Angela Washington-Blair, PhD
Cover Designer: Gary Szczecina

© 1996 Hatherleigh Press
A Division of The Hatherleigh Company, Ltd.
420 East 51st Street, New York, NY 10022

This book is printed on acid-free paper.

Compiled under the auspices of the editorial boards of *Directions in Mental Health Counseling, Directions in Clinical Psychology,* and *Directions in Rehabilitation Counseling.*

Library of Congress Cataloging-in-Publication Data

      Includes bibliographical references and index.
      ISBN 1-886330-04-2

The Hatherleigh Guide to Psychotherapy

First Edition: January 1996

10 9 8 7 6 5 4 3 2 1

About the photograph and the photographer

Lily Pads, 1994
The tranquil subject of this image captures the essence of nature's patience and sublime beauty, expressed in the delicate placement of the lily pads on the pond's surface.

Christopher Flach, PhD, is a psychologist in private practice in southern California. An avid photographer for more than 20 years, his favorite subjects include people and nature. He has studied photography with Ansel Adams, and his work has been on display in public galleries and in private collections.

Table of Contents

Illustrations

Introduction

The Hatherleigh Guide to Psychotherapy has been conceived and structured to meet the unique needs of the professional who regularly is engaged in carrying out psychotherapy with clients. The chapters, prepared by experienced psychotherapists, are not only designed to convey practical information in a lucid and useful manner, but the topics selected reflect some of the most crucial and problematic aspects influencing the nature of the therapeutic alliance and the eventual outcome of treatment.

This book is truly a guide. It is not meant to be read from cover to cover on a cold winter's night or sitting in the shade on a warm summer's day. The information is designed to answer specific questions that arise in a variety of clinical settings. How often have you asked yourself: "Is it my job to help relieve a client of the distressful and limiting symptoms for which he or she has consulted me?" or "Should I also be encouraging the client to utilize the experience of therapy in a positive way, learning new coping skills, becoming more aware of hidden aspects of personality, moving toward a higher level of maturity?" or "How can I accomplish this within the framework of managed care, in which more of the responsibility for personal growth through therapy lies in the hands of my clients than ever before?" Paul L. Adams's chapter, "'Repair' Versus 'Growth' Approaches to Therapy," addresses this question.

Other concerns will arise. You have a client who appears to be extremely resistant to change. Is this classical resistance, or is it an inherently human situation that requires special understanding and management? Turn to the chapter by James and Elizabeth Bugental, "Resistance to and Fear of Change." Or you have a client who is obviously disinclined to cooperate with the therapeutic process. What steps can you take to deal with such issues as cynicism about the value of talk in solving problems, a client's unwillingness to forfeit control, or a client who is convinced that all of his or her problems are caused by forces entirely outside himself or herself? How do you deal with a client whose sense of futility about therapy stems from treatment failures with other therapists in the past? These issues are addressed by Dr. George A. Harris in his chapter, "Dealing with Difficult Clients." Dr. Lynn Loar offers sound theoretical and practical guidelines for treating such clients on a time-limited basis in "Brief Therapy with Difficult Clients."

Do you have a client in individual therapy for whom you might consider the addition of group therapy or marriage and family therapy? How would you recognize such a need and what can you expect of such modalities? Do you have one or more elderly clients, and, if so, what special approaches can you use to make your therapy with such clients more effective? Do you or any of your clients question the efficacy of the therapeutic process? Would it help to know what studies exist that clarify and support psychotherapy as a powerful instrument?

Or perhaps an attractive client begins to dress in a slightly seductive fashion. With some reluctance, he or she slowly tells you of sexual feelings and wishes, which you shortly discover are directed toward you. What do you do? As Michael Perlin points out in "Power Imbalances in Therapeutic Relationships," you could be at high risk for a personal boundary violation and, if your best judgement should fail you, for charges of malpractice. Do you assume that the client's erotic feelings are being stirred by you? Do you assume that they are arising from transference issues, past experiences that may or may not be primarily sexual in character? Dr. Glen O. Gabbard, in his chapter "Therapeutic Approaches to Erotic Transference," offers you clear and invaluable answers.

I've been practicing psychotherapy myself for more than 40 years. Like most of you, I was trained in a particular approach to therapy, in my case psychodynamic psychotherapy shaped by the psychobiological school of Adolf Meyer. To this, I added my own classical psychoanalysis with Lawrence Kubie and Bertram Lewin, five times a week for 3 years, on a couch of course. As the years went by, I incorporated aspects of existential and Jungian psychology into my practice. I attended special experiential seminars with Fritz Perls and Alan Watts, and, more recently, took a hard look at cognitive, behavioral, and interpersonal therapeutic approaches. I was especially influenced by Dr. Jerome Frank's analysis of therapy in which he concluded that the two fundamental aspects of all successful therapy were the relationship between therapist and client and restoration of the client's morale. By now, I have constructed a philosophy of psychotherapy that seems to work for me and my patients, shaped, in no small part, by my own experiences on the front lines of treatment.

Looking back, I wish I had had the kind of information contained in *The Hatherleigh Guide to Psychotherapy* readily available to me when the special treatment situations these authors address arose in my own practice. Even now, as chairman of the editorial team that worked with them to develop this guide, I'm still learning, still discovering viewpoints and strategies that are extremely useful.

I think you'll agree. So, now, review the clients under your care. Who among them poses you with therapeutic challenges discussed in this book? Turn to the appropriate chapters and see what special insights you may come upon to help you in your therapeutic endeavors. And keep this guide readily available, because you never know what serious challenges will face you with each new client you see.

Frederic Flach, MD
New York

Dr. Flach is Adjunct Associate Professor of Psychiatry, Cornell University Medical College, New York; and Attending Psychiatrist at Payne Whitney Clinic of the New York Hospital and St. Vincent's Hospital and Medical Center, New York.

1

"Repair" Versus "Growth" Approaches to Therapy

Paul L. Adams, MD

Dr. Adams, Emeritus Professor of Child Psychiatry, University of Texas Medical Branch, Galveston, TX, and Visiting Professor of Child Psychiatry, University of Tennessee Center for Health Sciences, Memphis, TN, maintains a private practice in Louisville, KY.

KEY POINTS

- Although substantial differences exist between repair and growth approaches to psychotherapy, the dialectic process between the two can lead to a new synthesis.

- The main goal of repair therapy is to reduce symptoms of distress such as fear, loneliness, dysphoria, emptiness, and pointlessness.

- Nine characteristics of repair therapy are discussed: fault-centered, limit-setting and controls, postulated homeostasis, change viewed as realignment, use of a mechanistic paradigm, variety of views about humankind, realis-

tic goals and standards, aims of social acceptability, and regularized training for its practitioners.

- In contrast to repair therapy, growth therapy focuses on the client's potential for self-actualization and ability to relieve suffering.

- Growth therapy accentuates the positive aspects of clients, emphasizes openness and flexibility, and focuses on vital change rather than mechanic change. However, it can carry a risk of glorifying the "self" and tends to be iconoclastic about training.

INTRODUCTION

Psychotherapy is best understood today as one of several modalities that can help our clients. Wondrous claims made for psychotherapy are more modest today than they were a half-century ago. Today our outlook is more pragmatic and realistic. As a vital part of a multimodal treatment regimen, psychotherapy can make valued, unique contributions to the overall program, but psychotherapy today is only part of the entire therapeutic spectrum.

Those who deny that psychotherapy may play an important role appear to have become less strident and less numerous. Many honest and effective clinicians now acknowledge the efficacy of psychotherapy in helping their clients alleviate personal distress, restoring their morale, improving their interpersonal relations, and adding a worthwhile dimension of personal growth. Little remains, apparently, for serious debate on this score by those who adopt a biopsychosocial model.

REPAIR VERSUS GROWTH

The debate within psychotherapy and among psychotherapists over symptom removal versus personal reorientation or recommitment may endure, however, and this debate merits our consideration in this chapter. The person who adopts the client role appeals to a therapist for help in solving a variety of problems — in changing what they do, think, or feel — and the therapist aims to aid them in functioning better. For most, a reduction of their symptoms of distress, such as fear, loneliness, dysphoria, emptiness, or pointlessness, is what they long for. Freud, therefore, held the sensible opinion that any treatment that left a person feeling better was good treatment.

Certainly, symptom reduction, if only by reframing the problem, is also the intent of all forms of psychotherapy, whether cognitive, behavioral, or expressive. Viewed mechanistically, symptom reduction is a repair job. The quicker, the better. There is a place for this in the general scheme of psychotherapy.

If we see the repair and growth poles at opposite ends of a psychotherapy spectrum, we may view the situation aright. But we should not forget that there is a possibility that the relationship between repair and growth is not a linear and bipolar one, but rather a circular and spiralling spectrum, with the seeming contraries encircling and overlapping each other at the very moment that they may strain to be most distinct and differentiated. Hence, Jung could try to snap his clients back to reality at the very moment that, with his encouragement, his clients had taken flight into the highest excesses of fantasy. Such ascensions and descents are built into many psychotherapies. There may be no sharp demarcations between repair and growth as goals in psychotherapy.

REPAIR THERAPY

Nine characteristics of repair therapy can be distinguished: fault-centered, limit-setting and controls, postulated homeostasis, change viewed as realignment, use of a mechanistic paradigm, variety of views about humankind, realistic goals and standards, aims of social acceptability, and regularized training for its practitioners.

Fault-centered:

Repair therapy is fault-centered or problem-oriented. People with human troubles, like those with malfunctioning automobiles, have a place to go when something needs to be fixed — in this case a therapist, who can make a sensible evaluation of what needs fixing, and then proceed with rational steps to solve the identified problem. The auto mechanic does focused work, usually leaving undone whatever is extraneous to the problem at hand; perhaps even peripheral work is omitted or neglected as a result of task-centering, of the focal scrutiny being directed exclusively on what needs to be fixed. A good auto mechanic may warn of other observed difficulties but will let them go until later.

The repair therapist, taking a problem-oriented approach to a client, would attempt to size up the problems and weaknesses rather quickly to identify the main difficulties the client has, and then would work in the sector of those problems as expeditiously as possible.

Psychiatrist and anthropologist Arthur Kleinman (1988) has criticized the current-day therapeutic preference for observable behavioral *signs*, while neglecting *symptoms*. He notes that neo-Kraepelinians, the biological therapists of today, posit that whereas signs will point the faithful to a disease in its biological substrate, symptoms only point to sociocultural idioms of distress and are regarded as more subjective and less "real." Kleinman knows that an illness is often present when no disease exists; he writes about psychotherapy cross-culturally, and he largely employs a "growth" perspective.

The repair-oriented therapist gives top concern or priority to those problems that could be called "signs," but does not balk at putting some subjective symptoms onto the work list.

Limit Setting and Controls:

Repair therapy is cognizant of, and uses, limits and controls. It seeks brevity rather than interminability, so it can stop at less than a thorough overhaul. Repair work sets realistic goals, gets on with what is called for, and takes periodic stock of the progress made. Repair work is usually cogent, accountable, and cost-effective.

Postulated Homeostasis:

Repair therapy shares a widely held and widely revered view of humankind in which a person is, as the automobile he or she drives, a generally sufficient homeostatic system — a vital balance — that goes through unbalancing crises at times but returns then to a steady state, or at least a *steady-enough* state. The repair therapist's only metaphor is of a slightly haywire machine that lives nearest its essence when not a bit haywire or worn, but nearly perfect and running smoothly. The repair therapist would not be restrained in taking a history of the onset of the disorder, in examining the chronology of the symptom progression, and in exploring with the client what the meaning might be. However, if the picture was of recent onset, a new episode of disorder rather than chronic, the repair therapist might hope that the disorder would resolve quickly. Indeed, many human stresses and strains (crises) can be reequilibrated over a 5- or 6-week period, provided clients have a chance to spill out their anguish to a good listener, one who is expert in crisis intervention. If the symptoms worsen and the time of crisis runs out, as often occurs when a repair therapist is optimistic about quick relief, the repair therapist would begin to have reservations about the prognosis; but in his or her higher moments, the repair therapist would be optimistic that a timely rebalancing and repair could be effected.

Change Viewed as Realignment:

Repair therapy has one particular outlook toward change. It considers all change to be more apparent than real, a reshuffling of the same old deck of cards. Repair therapy subscribes to a philosophy of gradualism, which rejects conversion, sudden rebirth, or profound and enduring change. What is envisaged is basically the notion of change on a continuum. Indeed, Freud condemned therapeutic zeal —*furor sanandi* — and preferred dull, habitual reasonableness. In the repair approach, not much change is called for and change, after all, is not a dangerous swaying; it is a waxing and waning, certainly, but never very radical. Changes are said to be made always according to a prescribed and predictable pattern. If a client can become a mite better, losing the more florid signs and symptoms even if retaining character or personality problems, that may be sufficient progress in the opinion of a repair therapist.

Use of a Mechanistic Paradigm:

Repair has a preference for interactions that fit a mechanistic, morbidly rational, and highly cognitive paradigm. It is almost as if a little science can be made to appear formidable by the choice of a vocabulary derived from rational mechanics. Insight is often the goal in one major school of repair therapy, but insight-seeking therapy will seldom specify how insight betokens a personal change, a reorientation of the person. Indeed, well-treated, insightful people are rarely made more loving than, or otherwise very different from, their pretherapy state because a hard core narcissism endures, an "unlived life that kills," as the poet Rainer Maria Rilke termed it. The repair approach may content itself with seeing alterations only in the realm of the intellect and reasoning.

In the 1940s, a reconciliation between behaviorism and psychoanalysis was thought to be imminent. John Dollard, Franz Alexander, and many other therapists and behavioral scientists participated in that hope. Truly, both schools held to a common mechanistic-materialistic base, so why should they not join together and integrate? But why the hurrah? In both behavioral and psychoanalytic therapy, the therapist is steeped in insight and filled with notions, but only in psychoanalysis is the client expected to partake of the therapist's ideologic feast. It was only during the 1960s that humanistic psychotherapy began to call down a pox on both their houses and declare itself a "third force." Of course, there were forerunners, and Bruno Bettelheim even declared Freud to be more humanistic than his translators, the Stracheys, wanted him to be. Surely, Adler, Jung, and especially Otto Rank, foreshadowed humanistic psychotherapy by decades.

Variety of Views About Humankind:

Repair therapists do differ among themselves about the nature of knowing the human machine. One school, behaviorism, claims the knowable machine is completely and exquisitely bound to its surroundings and to environmental contingencies. Behavior, says the behaviorist, is so governed by its environment that only a fool would attempt to speculate about what occurs within the black box attached to the machine. A second school, psychoanalysis, says, "Nay, brothers, the machine's very controls are in the black box!" To psychoanalists, the machine as a whole, including the part boxed off from awareness, is fully comprehensible; it follows laws, it is preprogrammed; it is impelled by Eros and Thanatos. It is an all orderly arrangement—of id, ego, and superego—of basic conflicts and defensive maneuvers. Self-concept and self-system receive nods of approval, perhaps, but self-transcendence warrants only a perplexed look from many psychoanalysts.

Realistic Goals and Standards:

Repair therapy does have some realistic goals and standards that are distinctive to it as "scientific" work. Its first rule is to do no harm as it goes about diminishing abnormal signs and painful symptoms. A second rule is to immunize or protect the client against future outbreaks of the disorder. A third rule or goal is to bring about a genuine reorganization or recommitment of the personality. Behavior therapy, by contrast, pooh-poohs the very idea of undertaking all that work because, behaviorists insist, symptomatic relief is good enough. Or, symptomatic relief has ramifications that may bring about considerable restoration of morale, as evidenced by positive self-evaluations once the symptoms are gone.

How one gets from immunization to genuine personal reconstruction in the repair approach is usually not specified.

Oftentimes, the ideal of profound personal change is not even explicitly sought; an overhauling and reconditioning is good enough, ambitious enough. A good overhaul readies the machine for effective performance, for a better adjustment to conventional life with fewer pangs from both inner suffering and being different. Some people who have undergone repair therapy with either a psychoanalyst or a behaviorist actually view the whole process as a kind of spectator sport: it is interesting but not very engaging or upsetting.

Aims of Social Acceptability:

An eighth feature of repair therapy is that it aims for the client's greater acceptability and, as a corollary, for the client's greater sense of belonging—with heightened sociability and Adlerian *Gemein-schaftsgefuehl*, a feeling of sociability. Group therapy often expresses this last characteristic most fully among the repair therapies. Nathan Ackerman was the first of the family group therapists to set up the aim of an augmented capability for loving relations, thereby enshrining intimate sociability. To give it its due, such a repair therapy approach does restore some sense of "roots" to the alienated, downtrodden, exploited, and lonely people of this world. Not a bad attainment.

Regularized Training for its Practitioners:

Reparative therapy, being rationally problem-oriented, has a ninth and vital trait: it leans toward disciplined, regularized training for its practitioners. Discipleship and sturdy apprenticeship are stressed as the ways to become professional, which means that therapy training inculcates knowledge, skills, attitudes, minimum standards of good practice, and a code of ethics to govern its practitioners both while they are in training and later when they are full-fledged, "qualified" professionals. The entire repair outlook diminishes "wildness" and to some may seem overly rational, reminiscent of a guild-doctrine or a bureaucratic style.

Clients need whatever advocacy might be accomplished in their behalf, whatever protection, whatever security. They certainly should not be exposed to charismatic quackery by someone who is not rather stably situated in the local community and thus held to the canons of accountability. Because repair therapy claims to be scientific, it is probably more cautious and thus more likely (than some of the fly-by-night growth therapies) to provide that kind of consumer protection.

GROWTH THERAPY

In contrast to repair therapy, growth therapy emphasizes the client's potential for self-actualization and the ability to work towards relief from suffering.

Accentuating the Positive:

Growth therapy underlines the positive aspects of clients, as exemplified by Frederick H. Allen, a Rankian child psychiatrist who never dwelled on the snags and setbacks. The assessment of strengths and coping skills is stressed in growth therapy. Assets are ferreted out as much as weaknesses or liabilities. Even contained in neurosis, say the existentialists and Rankians, we can find some constructive or healthy tendencies that just missed the mark and so became crystallized as neurotic formations.

In emphasizing the positive attributes of a client, the first growth therapy postulate is not too unlike a major tenet of one of the repair therapies, namely behavior therapy, which asserts that it is easier to reinforce preferred behavior than to extinguish undesirable habits. This seems to be a sound psychotherapeutic doctrine in many schools of psychotherapy.

Some clients' assets are so numerous that they easily come to dominate the clinical picture. Intelligence, good ego strengths, a basically favorable picture of self, and very zesty fantasies, dreams, imagery, and appetites—"id strengths"—

awaiting liberation, are all delightful client assets that make most therapists happy in their work.

Openness and Flexibility:

Growth therapy is rather hesitant to aim for cures, to project a goal of results that are analogous to recovering from a bacterial disease. Indeed, all charting and planning may be rejected. The medical aspect of psychotherapeutic work is minimized.

Some of Rank's technical contributions, such as seeking brevity or setting up an endpoint in advance in order to establish bounds and limits for the work to be done, were not in the spirit of growth therapy, but rather in the spirit of repair therapy. The range of reactions to Rank's end setting has been interesting: Alexander and others gave Rank a favorable review on these innovations (of course, only after Rank had died). Clara Thompson, however, doubted that such technical novelties would be a lasting part of the Rankian heritage. Many today agree that contractual and brief therapy is here to stay. A purer growth therapy attitude would not have preconceptions about endpoints and schedules, but instead would nonchalantly see the needed work as requiring from 3 to 4 hours to 700 or 800 hours — showing a Zen-like indifference to time and effort.

An Open System:

Growth therapy has its own specific anthropology. Therapists who take this approach view the human condition as an open system — either as a system that is blown open or as a system that is hardly a system at all, because of its extreme openness. Growth therapists conceive of the human being as capable both of steady habit-forming *and* of unequilibrated flukes, surprises, and *satori*. A growth approach makes room for the universe to be made of cinders, not geometric patterns, and makes allowances for cataclysm, not gradualism. Growth therapy respects the language of myth as well as the language of games and propositions and commitments. Growth therapy, as described by Maslow, sees the human being as a pilot, not a robot. Many growth therapists, from Horney to Rogers to Maslow — but not including Rank or Adler — subscribe to a Rousseauan belief that there is something basically good within us all that impels us toward the fulfillment that a therapist merely facilitates.

The attitude of growth therapy toward a client tends to be highly empirical, relying on experience alone, working out no preconceived formulas. Instead, it waits only for a "holy spirit" to guide the transactions of the precise moment then and there. In actuality, such an approach is often difficult to attain. Yet adopting some growth therapy views makes it possible for a therapist to react at some moments in ways that hold important meaning for both client and therapist.

Vital Instead of Mechanical Change:

Psychotherapy with a growth perspective rejects mechanism and leans toward vitalism. It dispenses with counting and quantifying, and it has no affinity for positivist notions or petty science. The growth perspective is more functional, asking not "What was it?" but "To what ends was it done?" The growth perspective is much more centered on the feelings themselves than on any rational summations about feelings. The growth perspective values understanding more than knowledge.

A true hazard is present when the growth perspective inclines therapists toward mindlessness or demeans the import of hard work and serious application. A Rankian social worker once told me that a supervisor had warned her, "Don't assume that you can feel your way through life!" Since we do, in many ways, feel our way through life, her supervisor was mistaken, of course, but correct in advocating that many faculties other than feelings have some uses as well. The growth perspective's emphasis on guts, or emotions and unvarnished will, might overlook elements of no less critical value.

Danger of Solipsism:

Still another hazard of the growth emphasis needs to be discussed: its risk in what Benjamin deMott called "a glorification of a particular view of the self." He referred to the view of the self as not just the final arbiter on truth and reality but as the only arbiter. The self may come to be quite narcissistic, grandiose, overriding, and negating history, sin, or any previous moral learnings. The comments of another person are discredited by such a view of the self: "For you are not me and therefore cannot begin to understand what I perceive."

Value of the True Self and Self-Transcendence:

The growth emphasis in psychotherapy seems most salutary when it accepts the power of feelings and fantasies and the forcefulness of verbal constructs on human living but also moves onward to penetrate to the depths of selfhood so as to confront one's true self. In those depths of authenticity, a person can move beyond roles to self-transcendence, and not bask in the delights of self-centeredness.

A Goal of Profound Change:

A growth emphasis in psychotherapy seeks all the goals of symptom reduction, immunization, interpersonal aliveness, and personal reorientation adopted by repair therapy but adds to it self-actualizing transcendence. Growth therapy might ignore the supposed hierarchy or sequential arrangement of goals that some repair therapies advocate strongly. As an example, a growth focus may lead to an exploration of character prior to unearthing a neurosis and not hold that character analysis has to wait until neurosis analysis has been completed. Both Adler and Rank, later joined by Reich and Horney, asserted that matters of character (even narcissistic character trends) need not await the resolution of neurotic problems; if longings and cravings are clearly identified, character blocks may be tackled head on, early, and boldly. A person's will can produce powerful changes, when it is not other-directed or in the service of subordination or domination of fellow beings, but rather achieves good attunement with the deeper longings of one's true self.

Focus Toward Individuation:

The growth therapy emphasis shows a greater concern for individuality and uniqueness than for sameness. Growth therapy does not question the fact that we are all alike in important respects, and that we are united by cultural ties to a subspecies of people who are very like ourselves. Still, growth therapy chooses to dwell on the issue of individual differences and the ways in which individuated beings conduct a struggle as each grows and changes. Because the matter of struggle is seen as a needed ingredient of change, experienced growth therapists are not all fatuously optimistic.

A shadow, in the Jungian sense, does accompany the individualistic growth emphasis: a sentimental romanticism vaunting Faustian man so torn and so pathetic, so pathos-riddled. That can easily become absurd and banal. Another human pitfall besets growth therapy: the tendency for people who are not widely experienced and widely read to feel that their discoveries are unique, original, and creative. Only naïveté gives such pseudo-originality the room it needs for staying alive. If we overdo the uniqueness of each of us, we can begin to disrespect differences and even adopt authoritarian attitudes.

Tendency Toward Iconoclasm About Training:

The growth emphasis, whether it is in behavioral or holistic medicine, Gestalt therapy, or encounter groups, unfortunately leans toward iconoclasm about the training required of its practitioners, facilitators, or consultants. The growth focus belittles formal training and sometimes calmly tries to reassure us that wildness in a therapist is a real boon. If we worry about therapeutic casualties from est or Esalen or Rolfing, we are told that going mad can exert a cleansing influence on a rigidly armored character.

For both the guru and the disciple in some of the pop-growth therapies, there is a risk of escalated shopping for a series of weekend marathon encounters to revitalize oneself, rejuice one's life, and recharge one's batteries. Why do some growth movement enthusiasts get locked into a compulsion to repeat their contrived growth weeks or weekends? Because, I think, they burn out quickly and often. An old-fashioned psychoanalysis may do them more good, one surmises.

Sacha Nacht (1962, p. 208), the Parisian psychoanalyst, knew that training and discipline were essential for, not obstacles to, real growth. The analyst can be authentic without being crazy, Nacht wrote, in a spirit that made his psychoanalysis closely akin to some more moderate growth therapies:

> And it can only be so if the analyst possesses an open-heartedness as nearly perfect as possible, arising above all from his unconscious, enabling him to be spontaneously and intuitively what he should be at any given moment in the actual analytical situation. His attitude should respond to the immediate ongoing process, then, and should not have been premeditated. It is in this regard so necessary that the analyst, himself the sole instrument of his technique, should possess a disposition of openness and flexibility. This will enable him to work within the indispensable framework of technical principles and yet create from the analyst/analysand dialogue a living relationship between one particular person and other.

IS SYNTHESIS POSSIBLE?

Repair and growth can coexist peacefully. To say that they can

can work together does not deny, however, that they are different. The dialectic process can lead to new syntheses. I prefer growth as the major thrust, with an emphasis on discovering the true self. But I believe that some of the excesses of growth therapy can be nicely countervailed by some of the rationality of repair therapy. For one thing, it does not escape me that the world's children have a great need for simple repair. Repair is a good beginning and it may be "good enough" for huge masses of children. No therapy by itself is ever enough. As Maslow said, better nutrition and housing must precede self-actualization. Furthermore, the world's children have a crying need for security, sociability, and acceptance or belonging—for communion. In addition, repair work may be a valid precondition for growth in many individuals. The polarized approaches can be conjoined.

Would it not be a felicitous conclusion, for all of our clients, if the two poles (of growth and repair) should wind up harmonized, converged, and overlapped. . . if the dialectic of repair versus growth should play itself out and emerge into a new synthesis? That might make the ways of growing more assured, more predictable, more easily taught and transmitted.

REFERENCES

Kleinman, A. (1988). *Rethinking psychiatry*. New York: The Free Press.

Nascht, S. (1962). The curative factors in psychoanalysis. *International Journal of Psychoanalysis, 43*, 206-211.

FOR FURTHER READING

Bugental, J. F. T. (1967). *Challenges of humanistic psychology*. New York: McGraw-Hill.

Bugental, J. F. T. (1987). *The art of the psychotherapist.* New York: W. W. Norton.

Maslow, A. (1962). *Toward a psychology of being.* New York: Van Nostrand.

Rank, O. (1958). *Beyond psychology.* New York: Dover Publications.

2

Listening Processes in Psychotherapy and Counseling

Fraser N. Watts, PhD

Dr. Watts is at the Medical Research Council's Applied Psychology Unit, Cambridge, England.

KEY POINTS

- Therapists can take an active or a passive approach to listening to their clients. The active approach employs "working models," which are effective in encapsulating information that has been acquired about a particular topic; in a passive approach, which lends itself to distortion, the therapist applies "evenly suspended" or "free-floating" attention to what a client is saying.

- Clients' speech is frequently ambiguous. Factors that compound this lack of clarity include clients' attempts to verbalize something on the boundaries of their conscious awareness, their inability to grasp the significance of important aspects of their experience, and the ambivalence of

their motivations to communicate.

- It is important to make a distinction between the manifest content and the latent content of a client's language. Therapists should strike a balance between listening for both kinds of content.

- Certain cues signal that the client may be saying something of particular importance: voice quality, movement and posture, moments of unintelligibility, sequence, slips of the tongue, novel metaphors, assumptions of preoccupations, conjunctions of adjectives, evaluative terms, frequency of topics and words, and particular content categories.

INTRODUCTION

How psychotherapists listen to their clients has attracted surprisingly little attention in the extensive literature on psychotherapy. Theodor Reik's *Listening with the Third Ear* (1948) is still a classic, yet the time may now be ripe to progress with this important topic. Major recent advances in cognitive psychology concerned with general processes involved in understanding language and acquiring knowledge (Bransford, 1979) provide the framework for a formulation of listening skills of the psychotherapist. A number of authors (Peterfreund, 1975; Spence & Lugo, 1972; Watts, 1983) have recently approached psychotherapeutic listening from this point of view. The cognitive processes involved in this form of listening are very complex, and very little direct research has been done on them.

CLIENTS' LANGUAGE

Before considering how psychotherapists should listen to clients, it will be helpful to note the properties of clients' speech. Like most impromptu spoken language, it will frequently be unclear or ambiguous; however, particular difficulties may also arise in understanding clients in psychotherapy for several reasons.

First, clients will try, at least at times, to express things that are resting upon the boundaries of their conscious awareness and which they have little previous experience articulating.

Second, some clients will systematically lack the concepts necessary to grasp the significance of important aspects of their experience. Psychosomatic clients, for example, have been said to have poorly developed emotional concepts.

Third, the clients' motivations to communicate may be ambivalent. Important personal information may be embarrassing to disclose, and the clients' attitudes about disclosure may fluctuate depending on the state of their relationships with the therapist. Last, the material that eventually needs to be presented (the linking of current relationships and concerns, an autobiography from infancy onwards, and the therapeutic relationship) is extremely complex. Information hinted at can only be properly understood in light of other material, which often will not have been presented at all.

At other times, the therapist will need to relate a single statement of the client to a great deal of scattered material that was previously revealed in order to make sense of the statement. This point is underscored in a masterly study of therapeutic disclosure (Labov & Fanschel, 1977), in which one of the principal methods discussed was how a single remark of the client needed to be expanded to include extensive material from many other statements if its implicit meaning was to be fully explicated.

This emphasizes the difficulty of comprehending the psychotherapeutic client. The main factor to set against this is that the client normally has a basic need and wish to be understood. Partly because of this, and partly through involuntary processes, important material is likely to be repeated. Clients usually give their therapists more than one chance to grasp an important point.

MANIFEST AND LATENT CONTENT

To what extent should a therapist accept at face value what the client says? Psychotherapists have often made a distinction between the manifest content of what the client says (i.e., its ostensible, surface meaning) and its latent content (i.e., the unconscious themes that can be discerned beneath the surface meaning). How should therapists divide their attention between manifest and latent content?

Attending to Manifest Content:

Attending accurately to manifest content is not as easy as

many assume. Shapiro (1979), in an important paper on assessment interviewing, has provided an excellent exposition of the problems. The most substantial body of relevant empirical information comes from studies of listening deficiencies in opinion survey interviews. It confirms that the expectations of interviewers determine what they think they have heard. Particularly interesting are some of the factors that affect interviewers' errors in accurately recording responses. Ambiguous statements present particular problems and are likely to be either omitted or distorted in the interviewers' accounts of what was said. Another finding, which will not surprise psychotherapists, is that behavior stressful to interviewers results in their making more listening errors. However, it may also be salutary for psychotherapists to know that errors are high among interviewers who are oriented toward creating a good interpersonal relationship rather than addressing the task in hand.

We do not know how far such findings of inaccuracies in nonclinical interviews are paralleled by similar deficiencies in psychotherapists. How much the progress of psychotherapy is impeded if a therapist misunderstands what the client has said is an open question. However, the provisional conclusion must be that errors in listening to surface content are easy to make and are probably quite common.

Reading Between the Lines:

It is not sufficient in psychotherapy simply to attend to the manifest content of what clients say. This follows from the assumption that material that is central to the client's problem and that is associated with particular anxiety is unlikely to be produced easily. So, if the therapist is not to miss issues that are really important to a client, he or she will need to learn to "read between the lines" of what is actually said.

Spence (1980) has provided some very elegant evidence that illustrates one way in which the clients' underlying concerns may be revealed under camouflage. In studying the words used by clients suspected of cancer, he found that the word "death" was commonly heard among clients whose diagnosis of cancer was subsequently confirmed. Many uses of the word occurred in contexts that had no obvious connection with illness (e.g., "I was tickled to death"), and such usages would have been missed by a therapist attending only to manifest content. Spence coined the term *lexical leakage* to describe this phenomenon. We do not know how common it is, but it is only one of many ways in which unconscious concerns emerge in camouflaged ways in clients' speech.

Risks in Listening Strategies:

Before looking in further detail at other ways in which latent material can manifest itself and the strategies psychotherapists can use in listening for it, we must consider the different kinds of risks associated with attending to manifest and latent content. Exclusive attention to manifest content may result in the therapist's missing important material. On the other hand, an overeager search for latent content carries with it an opposite risk: the therapist may think he or she has identified important unconscious themes that are not actually present (Rice, 1980). The possibility of such an error occurring, and the difficulty of checking for it, seem to have been seriously underestimated by psychotherapists.

For example, a therapist may pick up a range of cues that could indicate hostility. Sometimes the cues discerned will really represent hostility, other times they will not. It is rather like listening to a poor quality radio and trying to distinguish between real signals and background noise. This analogy with signal detection, which has been extensively used in psychology, will help us here. Two very different factors can result in a listener picking up genuine signals of hostility more often. One is a real improvement in acuity, that is, in his or her capacity to distinguish between genuine hostility and misleading "noise" that does not indicate hostility. The other possible factor is simply that the listener has lowered the criterion for what he or she accepts as a signal of hostility. He may simply have decided to accept almost anything as a signal of hostility. This would result in picking up more correct signals of hostility, but at the cost of more "false alarms," too — cases in which he thinks he or she has detected hostility, but is actually mistaken.

Some disturbing, albeit inconclusive, evidence (Watts, 1980) suggests that as psychotherapists improve their ability to detect signals of hidden themes, such as hostility, the improvement might be done partly by lowering their criterion for what they accept as a signal rather than by improving their ability to distinguish true signals from background noise. This problem arises because psychotherapists tend to base confidence in their judgment on the number of times they are right and take little notice of the number of times they are wrong. In the example of hostility, therapists' confidence may be inflated by the increasing number of times they correctly recognize hostility, but may not be correspondingly deflated by the number of mistakes they make.

Listening for Latent Content:

Most psychotherapists develop rules, often only implicit, to help them listen for important concerns of clients that may be only latent. Such rules fall into two main groups. Some simply alert the therapist to moments in therapy when important material may be close to the surface. Others can be used as a more direct guide to the clients' assumptions and preoccupations. The next two sections contain an illustrative list of such implicit rules, largely drawn from papers by Peterfreund (1975), Rice (1980), and Watts (1983). It should be noted, however, that in many cases we have no scientific evidence to indicate whether or not these are good rules for psychotherapists to follow.

IMPORTANT MOMENTS IN THERAPY

Several cues can alert therapists that the client may be touching on something of particular importance. They are not infallible, but they indicate moments when the therapist should listen with unusual care.

Voice Quality:

The tone of voice that clients use is one of the best indicators of how emotionally involved they are at any particular point in a therapy session. Rice and Wagstaff (1967) have reported important research findings on voice quality as an indication of productive periods in a psychotherapy session. Rice (1980) describes the kind of "focused" voice involved, as follows:

> There is a kind of voice quality that seems to indicate an inner focus on something that is being seen or felt freshly. Sometimes in the midst of a long client discussion expressed in a highly externalizing voice quality, one hears just a small blip of focused voice. The voice slows, softens without losing energy, pauses, and loses the "premonitored" quality of the externalizing voice. This should be an indicator to the therapist that this part must be heard and responded to.

Movement and Posture:

Related aspects of posture and movement can help alert the therapist to important material, including shifts in body posture, sudden changes in direction of gaze, and signs of increased physical tension.

Moments of Unintelligibility:

The therapist should be alert for things the client says that the therapist does not understand. This may be a cue that the client is struggling to articulate something of emotional significance that is difficult to grasp consciously. The same cue applies when the client's affect is not appropriate to what he or she says.

Sequence:

In addition to attending carefully to things he or she does not understand, the therapist should note carefully abrupt changes of topic in which no logical connection exists.

Slips of the Tongue:

Freud's classic monograph on the psychopathology of everyday life (1958a) drew attention to the significance of slips of tongue. They help to alert the therapist to topics that may be emotionally important. Peterfreund (1975) gives an example of a client who had had a vasectomy speaking first of being "still sterile," then correcting it to "again sterile," when he actually meant "now sterile."

Novel Metaphors:

Important moments in therapy are associated with the client's use of novel or unusual metaphors. Pollio and colleagues (1977) have provided convincing evidence that moments of insight are associated with the use of novel metaphors, though trite or "frozen" metaphors are hardly ever used at such moments. Rice (1980) has drawn attention, for example, to the unusual use of sensory words such as a client speaking of a "stretched" smile on the face.

Assumptions and Preoccupations

Some of these listening rules also help therapists grasp important themes in clients' material. The sequence in which topics are raised can be an important clue to their significance. Slips of tongue may reveal unconscious thoughts. Novel metaphors, besides alerting the client to important moments in therapy, can reveal idiosyncratic concepts that may be important in understanding the clients' experience and psychopathology. There are other aspects of the clients' language that reveal such concepts.

Conjunctions of Adjectives:

The conjunctions that link the adjectives used in describing an important person are often revealing. Listen, for example, to whether a client talks about people being "strong and loving" or "gentle and loving" and one can see what assumption he or she makes about how these qualities are related. Kelly (1955) has convincingly argued for the importance of such "personal constructs" in explaining personal development.

Evaluative Terms:

Evaluations — favorable or unfavorable — expressed by a client often reveal important assumptions and personal needs. Expressions of criticism are often richer in content than are expressions of approval.

Frequency of Topics:

Topics that the client uses frequently are also likely to be important. Therapists, therefore, listen carefully to the frequency with which a topic comes up, as well as what is said. For example, if a client frequently raises the topic of hostility, but denies that it is a problem, the therapist would begin to suspect otherwise.

Frequency of Words:

In addition to topics, the therapist will attend to what words are used with unusual frequency. The previously described research on lexical leakage by Spence (1972) makes the point that important concerns can manifest themselves in frequent use of a word such as "death."

Particular Content Categories:

Areas of content that are particularly important probably vary from one kind of presenting problem to another, and from one stage of therapy to another. The therapist may, therefore, adopt a strategy of attending very closely to material of a certain kind. Hedges (1983) published a survey of four therapeutic approaches in terms of the listening focus on which they are based. The listening perspectives she considers correspond roughly to the psychotic, borderline, narcissistic, and neurotic categories of clients. The experienced therapist develops an ability to focus on material that is believed to be relevant to a particular kind of psychological problem.

ACTIVE VS. PASSIVE LISTENING STRATEGIES

What is perhaps the most fundamental issue about listening in psychotherapy has been left until last: should the therapist be active in listening selectively for certain kinds of material and relate it to his or her emerging formulation of the client or should he or she simply maintain what Freud called "evenly-suspended" or "free-floating" attention?

Working Models:

Peterfreund (1975) has provided a statement of the active approach to psychotherapeutic listening, centered around the concept of a "working model." Working models encapsulate information that has been acquired about a particular topic, shape our perceptions by sensitizing us to some events rather than others and giving form and structure to our perceptions; they also guide our responses, making possible predictions, actions, and other adaptive functions. Working models are continually updated as new information becomes available. Such a concept is an accepted feature of contemporary cognitive psychology (Bransford, 1979), though it goes under a variety of names ("schema" being one of the most common) and is defined in a variety of ways. However, researchers generally agree that an important aspect of the comprehension of linguistic material is its relationship to internal cognitive structures such as "working models."

With this in mind, Peterfreund proposes that the analyst develop a series of working models to underpin his or her professional work, one of these being the model of the individual client (though this would be based in part on more general models of the development of psychopathology, etc.). Once a model of a client has begun to develop, it can be used to structure the listening process.

One simple use is to distinguish old material that has already been incorporated into the model from new material that may require a revision of the model. Information will also be categorized according to its relevance to the model, and irrelevant information will be ignored. In general, material that is consistent with internal models is better remembered than incongruent information, though there may be exceptions to this rule (Watts, 1983). This is worrisome because it may result in the therapist's clinging to a prematurely formulated model of the client's pathology when an open-minded and unselective evaluation of the material available would lead to its being rejected or radically modified.

Finally, material tends to be distorted so that it better agrees with the model, which may account for many mistakes that were noted in the discussion of listening to manifest content. All these consequences of working models, or schemata, for the perception and comprehension of linguistic material have been well established as general principles (Bransford, 1979). So far no satisfactory empirical investigation of whether they apply to listening processes in psychotherapy has been conducted, though it seems reasonable to assume that they do.

"Evenly-suspended" Attention:

It is an interesting fact that Freud anticipated many of these issues, even though they had not yet been demonstrated by modern scientific methods, and he discussed their consequences for psychotherapy. In the series of lectures known as "Recommendations to Physicians Practising Psychoanalysis," (1958b) he said:

> For as soon as anyone deliberately concentrates his attention to a certain degree, he begins to select from the material before him. . . and in making this selection he will be following his expectations or inclinations. . . . In making the selection, if he follows his expectations he is in danger of never finding anything but what he already knows; and if he follows his inclinations he will certainly falsify what he may perceive.

Equally interesting is Freud's solution to this problem, which is that the therapist should adopt a style of "evenly-suspended" or "free-floating" attention, which "consists simply in not directing one's notice to anything in particular and maintaining the same 'evenly suspended attention' (as I have called it) in the face of all that one hears" (1958b). He adds that "...this rule of giving equal notice to everything is the necessary counterpart to the demand made on the client that he should communicate everything that occurs to him without criticism or selection."

This concept of evenly-suspended attention has been discussed at length by Reik (1948). The contemporary psychoanalytic theorist, Bion (1970), has developed a similar concept of attention "without memory or desire."

Clearly, the evenly-suspended attention strategy has a number of advantages. One advantage that Freud does not explicitly mention is that it might help reduce the impossible cognitive burden that would fall on a therapist who tried, in an open-minded way, to consider all possible formulations of the available material and the implications of everything the client said. Attempts to do this consciously and rationally would

simply break down, because the amount of information processing required could quickly exceed capacity. Freud's concept of evenly-suspended attention probably involves processing much material "preconsciously" rather than consciously, thus bypassing the point (i.e., consciousness) at which
constraints on processing capacity are most severe.

However, it is questionable whether adopting this kind of
rather passive, unselective processing strategy in fact reduces
selections and distortions due to "expectations" and "inclina-
tions." Although it may, it is also possible that evenly-suspended attention would increase the amount of distortion of
material that emerged. It may do nothing to prevent distortion
to accord with the therapist's working model of the client, but
instead could simply reduce the level of conscious vigilance
against such distortion.

Finally, it is doubtful whether it is realistic for a psychotherapist to follow Freud's advice, or indeed whether Freud himself
did so. Evenly-suspended attention would make it very difficult for the therapist to develop a coherent formulation of the
client's psychopathology or even to remember the material,
because memory is largely dependent on contact between
incoming material and mental "working models." Later in the
same lecture to physicians, Freud acknowledges the difficulty
a psychotherapist encounters when recalling at will a client's
material. However, he argues that the material that arises
serves to aid recall of related material revealed previously, a
process now known as "cued" recall.

Two Stages:

Freud's declared strategy of evenly-suspended attention
does not carry conviction if taken to extremes or used as a sole
listening strategy, though most would agree that it has a place
alongside a more active approach to listening. The relative
importance of the two concepts may depend in part on the
stage of therapy, and many would accept the suggestion (made,
for example, by Langs, 1968) that psychotherapeutic listening

goes through two phases. In the first phase, evenly-suspended attention has its place, and the psychotherapist needs to be unguarded in his or her receptiveness to primary processes and to make full use of his or her unconscious sensitivities. However, this approach needs to be superseded by a second phase which, while retaining a degree of unguardedness, relies fundamentally on cognitive efforts at organization and formulation.

REFERENCES

Bion, W. R. (1970). *Attention and interpretation.* London: Tavistock.

Bransford, J. D. (1979). *Human cognition: Learning, understanding and remembering.* Belmont, CA: Wadsworth.

Freud, S. (1958a). The psychopathology of everyday life. In J. Strachey (Trans.), *Standard Edition, Volume VI.* London: Hogarth.

Freud, S. (1958b). Recommendations to physicians practicing psychoanalysis. In J. Strachey (Trans.), *Standard Edition, Volume XII.* London: Hogarth.

Hedges, L. E. (1983). *Listening perspectives in psychotherapy.* New York: Jason Aronson.

Kelly, G. A. (1955). *The psychology of personal constructs.* New York: Norton.

Labov, W., & Fanschel, D. (1977). *Therapeutic discourse: Psychotherapy as conversation.* New York: Academic Press.

Langs, R. (1968). *The listening process.* New York: Jason Aronson.

Peterfreund, E. (1975). How does the analyst listen? On models and strategies in the psychoanalytic process. In Spence, D. P. (Ed.), *Psycho-analysis and contemporary science, Volume IV.* New York: International Universities Press.

Pollio, H. R., Barlow, J. M., Fine, H. J., & Pollio, M. R. (1977). *Psychology and the poetics of growth*. Hilsdale, NJ: Erlbaum.

Reik, T. (1948). *Listening with the third ear*. New York: Farrar Strauss.

Rice, L. N. (1980). A client-centered approach to the supervision of psychotherapy. In Hess, A. K. (Ed.), *Psychotherapy supervision: Theory, research and practice*. New York: John Wiley & Sons.

Rice, L. N., & Wagstaff, A. K. (1967). Client voice quality and expressive style as indices of productive psychotherapy. *Journal of Consulting and Clinical Psychology, 31*, 557-563.

Shapiro, M. B. (1979). Assessment interviewing in clinical psychology. *British Journal of Social and Clinical Psychology, 18*, 211-218.

Spence, D. P. (1980). Lawfulness in lexical choice—a natural experiment. *Journal of the American Psychoanalytic Association, 28*, 115-132.

Spence, D. P., & Lugo, M. (1972). The role of verbal cues in clinical listening. In R. R. Holt & E. Peterfreund (Eds.), *Psychoanalysis and contemporary science* (vol. I). London: Macmillan.

Watts, F. N. (1980). Clinical judgment and clinical training. *British Journal of Medical Psychology, 53*, 95-108.

Watts, F. N. (1983). Strategies of clinical listening. *British Journal of Medical Psychology, 56*, 113-123.

3

Resistance to and Fear of Change

James F. T. Bugental, PhD, and Elizabeth K. Bugental, PhD

Dr. James Bugental is Rockefeller (Teaching) Scholar at the California Institute of Integral Studies, Emeritus Professor of the Saybrook Institute, and Emeritus Clinical Faculty of the Stanford University Medical School. Dr. Elizabeth Bugental was formerly Assistant Director of Inter/Logue and now serves as a board member and consultant to several community agencies.

KEY POINTS

- Human beings fear change because it appears to threaten the structures that we take to comprise our lives. Clients seek therapy when these structures are not sufficiently satisfying their existential needs.

- Five "conditions of being" form the parameters of being human: embodiment (we have physical bodies), finitude (we are limited in what we can do and know), action (we are active agents in making what is potential, actual), choice (we have free will), and separateness-but-relatedness (though separate from other individuals, we are never wholly isolated from them). These conditions form the underlying life

motivations that animate our actions, most of them unconscious.

- Therapists' perceptions that their clients' fear of change or "resistance" is an opposition to therapy, neurotic, or something that must be overcome are contratherapeutic. Such perceptions undermine the therapeutic alliance and prolong the therapeutic course.

- The therapist should accept resistance to change as appropriate. To be perceived as an ally, he or she should identify what is being threatened, then assure the client that he or she can change what needs to be changed while protecting those fundamental aspects of the self worth preserving.

INTRODUCTION

The fear of change is familiar in psychotherapeutic and psycho-analytic literature, where it is called the "resistance." Freud was not the first to point out what each therapist discovers: the client who comes desperately seeking help soon seems to try to defeat help being given.

When therapists begin their careers, they are apt to see this resistance as directed against them personally and against their efforts. As they mature in their craft, they come to recognize how much more significant this apparent obstinacy is. It turns out to be the way clients act in their lives at large. Indeed, therapists soon realize that this resistance is com-posed of the very patterns that disrupt the clients' lives and are the core of the problems or neuroses that bring them to therapy. It is this keystone recognition that gives therapy the power to affect clients' lives. (Thus Freud insisted that there is no existing psychoanalysis that is not the analysis of the resis-tance.)

Astonishingly, this is still not the end of the chain of signifi-cance. It is this further importance of the resistance that is the point of this presentation.

In brief, we propose that the resistance is not solely that which blocks our clients' full living; it is also what makes it possible for them to have the lives they do lead. Admittedly this is not the traditional view of the resistance, but we will show the values of operating on this hypothesis. In short, we propose:

> In order to live out one's life, one must come to some kind of definition of who one is and what one's nature is, and one must similarly define or structure the nature of the world in which one lives. These same definitions or structures that make life possible also limit it and keep one in self-defeating, repetitive patterns of being.

A parable will convey more graphically what is proposed here. In shock, a man wakes to find himself swimming in the sea. As far as he can see in any direction there is no land or vessel to guide his efforts. Anxiety enters his veins. He treads water, tries to swim in one direction, but fears he may be only circling. He begins to tire; no relief seems likely. Fear mounts toward panic.

Then a blessed sight: a more solid shape close by. Renewed, he swims to a plank and grasps it. Gratefully, he half-rides, half-swims, looks for more flotsam, and ties a hatch cover to the plant. Slowly — with great struggle at times, with fortuitous ease at others — the man collects and puts together what he finds until eventually he can climb out on his raft and rest.

When a squall hits, parts of the raft are swept away, but as the squall passes new gifts arrive from the sea. Now the man builds a more stable vessel.

In time, other castaways float by on their rafts, and they merge constructions until the vessel becomes larger and more dependable. Great storms occasionally wreck it, but it is possible to rebuild adequately.

As days turn into years, the children of the raft laugh at legends of how the rafts came to be. They are sure they know reality: the big raft on which they live is "the world," and they are certain that their lives on it are the way lives are really meant to be.

STRUCTURING OUR LIVES

The allegory reminds us that the structures within which we live our lives are, at root, our own constructions. They have been assembled from whatever was at hand, they sustain us with varied effectiveness, and they remain vulnerable to stresses that may come from any quarter. Characterizing them by no means indicates that they are without significance. Quite the contrary, this structuring of ourselves and our world is one of the astonishing and unique expressions of human capacity. Humans create an overworld of meaning, which is superimposed on the world of direct experience in which other animals apparently dwell. From this meaning world, we transform the immediate world — for good or for ill.

A CLINICAL EXAMPLE

A case synopsis illustrates how threats to our self-and-world structures may bring about excessive fear of change.

Todd is 53 years old, has an advanced degree in electronic engineering, is married, and has two children, ages 18 and 23. He is section chief in a middle-sized but quite successful research and development company. He has been in therapy twice a week for 8 months. In an exchange with his therapist, he tells of driving aimlessly and carelessly on the freeways the previous evening.

"I'm not sure why, but I think I just kind of flipped out. I know I wasn't really there. Shouldn't drive when I'm like that. Though I don't know whether I've ever been like that before. Anyway, I was shut down on all systems — or at least, most all. Some way I kept enough going not to kill anybody or. . . ."

"Or. . . ?" (softly).

"Or myself," (flatly).

"Mm-hmmm."

"It was kind of like being dead, or partly dead."

"Like being dead."

"Yeah, but not really that either. At one point on the freeway I thought of just shutting my eyes and letting the car go without looking, but it was just a thought. I mean, I don't think I would really do that."

"Not really."

"But driving the way I was. . . . That was sort of. . . . Well, I remember thinking, 'It's up to fate.' It was like being partly asleep but still sort of awake."

So why is Todd playing Russian roulette on the freeway? In simplest terms, Todd is fighting off the awareness that he is changing. He believes that if he lets that awareness really take hold, he will cease to be. Within his own experience, Todd is fighting for his life, yet he considers killing himself. What a paradox! Still, that is just what Todd is doing, and it is what many of us do — although, to be sure, not always as overtly and explicitly. Todd is acting out his fear of changing. Yet, ironically, he entered therapy in order to change. When one feels that identity and the known world are in danger of being swept away, it is truly terrifying. The price of preserving the familiar world and one's place in it may be literal and physical death, but that price has been paid repeatedly by men and women throughout human history.

THE NATURE OF LIFE STRUCTURES

We will describe one way of conceiving the nature of the life structures that constitute our identities and our environment. How we interpret the amazing and embracing fact of being is inevitably a product of who and where we are at the moment of interpretation.

The flotsam from which we build our rafts consists of what Rollo May (1981) calls our "destiny": the particular epoch, culture, family, and other conditioning and forming influences of our birth and life span. These provide materials from which we create the structures to meet the ontological circumstances of being human.

That formidable phrase, "the ontological circumstances of being human," means that we have come into different worlds depending upon our *destinies* (as we have just defined that term). Yet behind these differences lie certain constants or "givens" which all humans must deal with in some fashion. These are the ontological givens of being human.

It is convenient to identify five "givens" of being (Bugental, 1981) that each person must take into account in some way:

1. We are embodied. Our lives are expressed in physical bodies.

2. We are finite. We are limited in what we can do, what we can know, how long we will live, and in all dimensions.

3. We are capable of acting or of not acting. We are not passive observers but are, rather, active agents in the creation of the actual from the potential (Bugental & Bugental, 1984).

4. We have choice. Unlike the tropism- and instinct-governed species, we have the capacity to select from repertoires of possible responses.

5. We are each separate from but related to all other humans. Never are we wholly isolated, never wholly in union.

THE PARAMETERS OF BEING HUMAN

These five conditions of being — embodiment, finitude, action, choice, and separate-but-relatedness — form the parameters of our being human. Although it is helpful to distinguish them as in Table 3.1, it is also essential to recognize that in reality they are five aspects of a unity. Thus, for example, finitude is a necessary condition for each of the other four: Our lives are expressed in or through bodies that will live but a time. We can act or not act, but only within certain limits. While we have choice, there is much that we cannot choose. Love may bring us close, but oneness eludes us; hate may divide us, but we can never, if we are truly aware, deny all kinship with our enemy. In the same way, each of the five parameters is interwoven with each of the others.

Table 3.1		
THE EXISTENTIAL CONDITIONS OF BEING		
"Given"	Confrontation	Needs/Values
Embodied	Change	Spiritedness
Finite	Contingency	Identity
Actionable	Responsibility	Potency
Choiceful	Relinquishment	Meaningfulness
Separate-but-related	Apartness*	Relatedness

*in the sense of being a part of, yet apart from.

In some fashion — more implicitly than consciously — each person interprets the meaning of these givens of being. These interpretations are implicit, lived-out patterns. For example, we have no alternative but to be embodied if we are to be physically alive (although Todd is beginning to question whether he will continue to accept that equation). Some center their attention on this dimension, as in those preoccupied with having a "glamour" image; some ignore it, as does the stereotypic successful businessman who drives himself to a heart attack before he is 50; and some attack the body, as do the ascetics who practice mortification of the flesh.

The existential parameters not only set the stage upon which we play out the dramas of our lives, but also form the underlying life motivations that animate our actions. This comes about because each of these givens confronts us with a life issue with which we must continually deal in some fashion. Similarly, each requires us to form certain perceptual structures in order to maintain and live out our lives. Table 3.1 offers estimates of these confrontations and their parallel existential needs.

THE EXISTENTIAL CONFRONTATIONS

In a crude way, the confrontations that arise from these conditions are equivalent to the waves that both support and threaten the riders on the rafts. From them emerge the possibilities of constructing our lives. As we construe the fact of being able to act, for instance, we deal with the issue of being responsible for what we do or do not do and discover our own powers and their limits.

Now, what is the point of all of this? The point is that these needs are truly existential and are as vital to life as safety from threats, food, drink, and reasonable protection from excesses of heat and cold. Unless we have some degree of spiritedness, identity, potency, meaningfulness, and relatedness in our lives, we literally grow weak as persons, and we are likely to go crazy, get sick, or even die.

Our clients come to us because the life structures they have created—the timbers, rudders, and sails of their rafts—are not sustaining them, are not sufficiently satisfying their existential needs. These structures are how they view themselves in their worlds, the patterns they have developed for seeking satisfactions and avoiding harms, and the expectations they evolve for how their lives should be.

This last point is so important to the understanding of the resistance to change that it must be emphasized that we are not using metaphor or hyperbole when we speak of a "death." When one has lived until the present moment with certain images of who one is and what one may expect in life, then the realization that these images are false and will never be realized is a "killing" recognition.

THE NEED/VALUE STRUCTURES OF BEING

The existential issues with which our being confronts us require some response. These are termed *needs/values* in Table 3.1. It is necessary to examine these more fully. Each of us needs a degree of spiritedness, energy, and drive or motivation, and that need, rooted in our bodily being, is evoked as we confront the ever-changing world.

We live in a contingent universe in which we are affected by events beyond our anticipation or control. Our best efforts may succeed or fail; our deepest fears may be realized or not. We are so clearly finite in the midst of infinity, and how we deal with that fact constitutes much of our inner sense of identity. "I am a Christian. . . an atheist. . . a hard worker. . . a physician. . . ." All such statements tell how a person sees himself or herself and something of how that person meets the circumstances of life.

The sense of potency is vital to our sanity. The person who feels totally impotent is the one who may go on an insane shooting spree. We insist on having some power in our lives, and we will do anything necessary to get it. To be able to act is to have responsibility for our actions.

Choice, the miracle of our evolved consciousness, inflicts the endless burden of relinquishment, of having to say "no" to possibilities, of having to kill possible selves. Out of our choices we create meaning, and our meanings guide our choices. Meaninglessness is more fearful than the emptiness of space.

Finally, we need a network of relationships with others. Human beings are as much social organisms as they are physical organisms. Solitary confinement is one of the most dreaded punishments, and extended, unsought solitude can lead to madness or death. Even those who choose to be alone soon populate their isolation with fantasied others — real persons to whom they write, imagined persons who torment or support them, divine persons whom they serve. We are each inexorably separate from others but equally unredeemably bonded to others.

A return to Todd will illustrate these points. Todd learned in his early years that he was brighter than most of his schoolmates, that learning came easily, and that recognition and rewards followed promptly. He learned to expect that he could continually advance in any competitive situation. Although he probably would never have said it aloud even to himself, he anticipated attaining the very top ranks in his profession and the very fullest satisfactions in his personal life. Over the past 5 years, however, the realization has been seeping into Todd's awareness that he is probably at or near the high point of his career, that others are able to go further, that his marriage and family are not exceptional, and that he, while certainly competent and a good friend and family member, is not the special person he had secretly thought himself to be. In short, Todd is on the verge of discovering that the person he has believed himself to be does not—and never did—exist. This is, in subjective terms, a kind of death.

IMPLICATIONS FOR THERAPY

The most important implication of what is being advanced is also the most difficult to convey, because in a way it is something that is already familiar. The point is that perceptions of the client's "resistance" as opposition to therapy, neurotic, or something which must be overcome, analyzed away, or circumvented are themselves countertherapeutic. Such perceptions of what is undoubtedly one of the most central and universal phenomena of therapy repeatedly confound the therapeutic work, undermine the therapeutic alliance, and prolong the therapeutic course.

For many therapists, this will not be a surprising statement. They have known that the old way of conceiving our task has been faulty. Yet we who write this after many years of immersion in our work know that implicitly we also often still tend to cast the therapist as the opponent of a negative force in the client.

Our well-being requires that we maintain a measure of continuity in our way of living in the world and that we develop a repertoire of skills for responding to our existential needs. We cannot do so, we cannot remain sane, if we do not modulate our accessibility to the countless injunctions, seductions, inducements, invitations, and teachings of family and friends, the media, pulpit, and classroom, and every other facet of our lives. Therapists must find ways of supporting their clients' capacity to maintain continuity and must avoid efforts to undermine it.

POINTS FOR THERAPISTS TO PONDER

We offer three observations that therapists may consider as they engage in their work.

1. When the client resists change, he or she is demonstrating that a threat to being is experienced. With this understanding, we need to accept the appropriateness of the client's defense and to join him or her in seeking to identify what is being threatened. Although the words will be unique to the individual, the five existential needs described above offer useful directions for exploration.

2. The stance that the therapist takes in displaying to the client how the latter wards off change is, in itself, exceedingly important. If it is evident that the therapist is not invested in the client's giving up what he or she feels strongly that he or she must have, then the therapist is experienced as an ally rather than an opponent.

3. It is important for the therapist continually to demonstrate to the client the professional's genuine conviction that the client can protect what is truly needed while relinquishing what threatens or cripples the client's life. This strong affirmation of the client's potency does much to support the latter's own readiness to move toward change.

It is evident that the three suggestions are basically directed toward how the therapist conceives his or her role in relation to the life structures and their persistence. Far beyond any techniques or stratagems, the crucial contribution of the therapist resides in his or her attitudes, empathy, and faith in the client's own latent ability to grow.

SUMMARY

We humans fear change because it appears to threaten the very structures that we take to *be* our lives, rather than simply the structures that we think *support* our lives. Because we see these structures in this way, the possibility of their changing is the possibility of death. And there is truth in this apprehension.

To change is to kill, to die. To change is to relinquish one way of being — one identity, one life that might have been. To relinquish is to kill one possible self.

We are confronted with small choices of this type nearly every day. For example, because one of the authors chose to write this chapter at a particular time, he was not able to attend a professional meeting to which he had been invited. On the scale of a day's activities, it is an all-too-familiar and not particularly threatening choice, although, even in such matters, consequences remain unknown and unimaginable.

But larger changes — to change one's way of being alive, one's concept of who and what one is, one's view of the world — can be more sweeping and more frightening, inevitably involving potentially serious relinquishments. And relinquishments are deaths. For example, because one of the authors chose to become a psychotherapist, she did not have the large family she had once dreamed of mothering. Because of an earlier choice, certain roads are forever closed.

Relinquishing the self one has always thought oneself to be is a kind of suicide. If one is strongly invested in that identity — as most of us surely are — physical death may not seem to be too high a price to pay to preserve (or to seem to preserve) who one thought one was.

George A. Kelly (personal communication, c. 1987) once commented, "The key to human destiny is the ability to reconstrue what cannot be denied." When we therapists come to consider changing our way of regarding our clients' fears of and resistance to change, we may find that we, too, are confronted with our own fear of change.

REFERENCES

Bugental, J. F. T. (1981). *The search for authenticity* (Enlarged ed.). New York: Irvington.

May, R. (1981). *Freedom and destiny*. New York: Norton.

FOR FURTHER READING

Becker, E. (1961). *The denial of death*. New York: Dial.

Bugental, J. F. T. (1980). *Intimate journeys: Stories from life-changing therapy*. San Fransisco: Jossey-Bass.

Bugental, E. K., & Bugental, J. F. T. (1984). Dispiritedness: A new perspective on a familiar state. *Journal of Humanistic Psychology, 24*, 49-67.

Bridges, W. E. (1980). *Transitions: Making sense of life's changes*. Reading, MA: Addison-Wesley.

Bugental, J. F. T. (1976). *The search for existential identity*. San Francisco: Jossey-Bass.

Bugental, J. F. T. (1978). *Psychotherapy and process*. Reading, MA: Addison-Wesley.

Bugental, J. F. T. (1987). *The art of the psychotherapist*. New York: Norton.

Fried, E. (1981). *The courage to change: From insight to self-innovation*. New York: Grove Press.

Kubler-Ross, E. (1969). *On death and dying*. New York: Macmillan.

Levenson, E. A. (1983). *The ambiguity of change: An inquiry into the nature of psychoanalytic reality*. New York: Basic Books.

Marris, P. (1975). *Loss and change*. Garden City: Anchor.

Schachtel, E. G. (1959). *Metamorphosis*. New York: Basic Books.

Schneider, K. J., & May, R. (1995). *The psychology of existence: An integrative, clinical perspective*. New York: McGraw-Hill.

Tannenbaum, R., & Hanna, R. W. (1985). Holding on, letting go, and moving on: A neglected perspective on change. In R. Tannenbaum, et al. (Eds.), *Human systems development* (pp. 95-121). San Fransisco: Jossey-Bass.

Wheelis, A. (1973). *How people change*. New York: Harper & Row.

Yalom, I. D. (1980). *Existential psychotherapy*. New York: Basic Books.

4

Dealing with Difficult Clients

George A. Harris, PhD

Dr. Harris is a psychologist in private practice in Kansas City, MO, and formerly a therapist in both vocational rehabilitation and corrections.

KEY POINTS

- Therapists may disagree on what characterizes a "difficult" client; however, it is possible to identify some common causes of problems in treatment such as resistance to change, to the therapist, and to therapy itself.

- Clients resist treatment due to mistrust or cynicism about the value of talk in solving problems, the psychological reaction to a perceived loss of freedom, and the belief that the problem is external to the self.

- The therapist's job is not to remove resistance to change, but only those resistances that are dysfunctional for the client.

- Therapists' counterproductive responses to difficult clients include: authoritarian behavior;

fear of violence or intimidation; deception; hopeless optimism about change; misunderstanding; cynicism; and unconscious encouragement of acting out, rebellion, or misbehavior.

- Three counseling approaches to dealing with difficult clients are discussed: emotive approaches, cognitive therapy, and the strategic or paradoxical approach.

- Managing difficult clients involves: establishing an environment in which communication can occur, identifying the client's problem, understanding and responding to the impediments to change, and developing methods to approach the client's tactics of resistance.

INTRODUCTION

Every therapist encounters clients who are difficult, although what one therapist finds difficult another may not. The psychology literature is replete with discussion of "resistance," but as Anderson and Stewart stated, resistance is often defined as whatever clients do that therapists don't want them to do (Anderson, 1983).

Despite disagreements in defining difficult clients and in resistance, it is possible to identify some common causes of problems in treatment. These causes can be observed by looking at resistance to change, to the therapist, and to therapy itself. This chapter will also discuss: the reactions that therapists have to clients that may impede treatment, client accessibility to treatment, general approaches to working with difficult clients, and points to consider when treating difficult clients.

RESISTANCE TO CHANGE

Most theories of therapy have an explanation of resistance to change. Behaviorists identify the cause of resistance as inadequate reinforcement; family therapists see resistance as a function of the system's efforts to maintain homeostasis and keep the status quo; rational-emotive therapists view resistance as the product of irrational beliefs; psychodynamic theories hold that the unconscious prevents awareness of material that would cause psychic distress.

It is important not to view all resistance as bad. Ellis (1985) pointed out that our clients may resist their therapists' suggestions because the suggestions are sometimes simply wrong. Ansbacher (1981) argued that resistance can be a necessary result of stability and integrity of personality; after all, if a person never resisted change, he or she would never settle on a career, a spouse, or even an opinion. The therapist's job is not to remove resistance to change, but only those resistances that are dysfunctional for the client.

RESISTANCE TO THE THERAPIST

Many theories of psychotherapy consider transference issues appropriate for the therapy process. During the course of therapy, the client may have a reaction to the therapist that seems to be based on imagined rather than actual truths about the relationship that has developed. The client confuses the therapist with someone else — often a parent or authority figure, sometimes a sibling, or occasionally someone who just looks like the therapist. Understanding those reactions is an important tool for helping the client learn to deal with people objectively rather than as mirages and reminders of unrelated past encounters.

Transference issues are especially important when working with clients who have been *coerced* into therapy. Such clients come from correctional, substance abuse, and many other rehabilitation programs. Meloy and associates (1990) argued that the involuntary client has special transference issues because the therapeutic encounter mirrors the early parent/child relationship, which was biologically an involuntary one for the client. Most therapists overlook or minimize the problem of involuntariness in therapy (Harris & Watkins, 1987). In their zeal to begin talking about the client's "problem," therapists may not spend enough time dealing with the resistance to the therapist that is created by the mere fact that therapy was required rather than chosen. As a result, the client's view of the therapist as an agent of coercion is never challenged.

RESISTANCE TO THERAPY

Most theories of psychotherapy assume the therapeutic relationship is voluntary and treatment cannot be initiated ethically until permission to counsel is granted (Shertzer & Stone, 1974). In reality, thousands of clients every day are counseled without consent in prisons, drug programs, and even in private practice. Thus, it is useful to consider resistance to therapy as separate from resistance to change and to the therapist.

Many behavior problems and psychological disorders, such as substance abuse, are accompanied by intense denial, and clients with such problems and disorders do not seek treatment until they are forced. Even in marriage therapy, it is common for one spouse to be eager for therapy while the other resists. The therapist may wish to differentiate "therapy" from "preparing the client for therapy," as a way out of an ethical quagmire. In a sense, the client needs to be sold on the value of therapy. He or she needs to be convinced that therapy can help in some way. It is not unethical to help clients discuss their feelings, objections, and concerns about being coerced into treatment. Such discussion is the beginning of the formation of a therapeutic relationship, though the specific reason why the client was referred may hardly be mentioned. After thoroughly exploring the issues related to participation in therapy, *either therapist or client* may elect not to continue.

Most theories of therapy have an explanation of resistance to change and resistance to the therapist, some in more detail than others. However, few theories directly address or give recommendations for resolving the resistance to therapy *per se* that many clients demonstrate. Therefore, it may be helpful to explore our understanding of why clients object to therapy.

Why do clients resist therapy? There are may practical reasons, including expense and inconvenience. Other reasons are related to the resistance to change. Attending therapy represents change, which the client fears. Clients resist entering treatment for three primary reasons: (a) mistrust or cynicism about the value of talk in solving problems, (b) the psychological reaction to a perceived loss of freedom, and (c) the client's belief that the problem is external to the self and therefore cannot be solved by personal initiative.

Mistrust:

Mistrust of therapy and therapists is understandable when one considers how often people feel that they have been deceived by promises from authority in their lives. That feeling of having been misled leads to cynicism, pessimism, and, therefore, reluctance to participate in therapy. They just don't believe therapy can be trusted. Many clients mistrust themselves and their own capacity to change. They've told themselves before that they would change and didn't, so they don't understand how therapy could help. Thus, not only people but language itself is doubted Therapy is dismissed as only talk, and "talk is cheap."

Loss of Freedom:

The second reason clients resist therapy is they object to any kind of coercion and restriction of freedom (Dowd & Seibel, 1990). Their fears of coercion can sometimes be allayed if the therapist portrays therapy as an opportunity to *increase* freedom by pointing out that the process is designed not to restrict but to increase alternatives. This may be difficult for clients to understand abstractly; nevertheless, it is a point worth making. Therapists can try to give clients as many choices as possible in scheduling appointments, topics to discuss, and even seating arrangements. Such attention to choices *demonstrates* rather than merely *describes* the nonrestrictive nature of the process.

Externality of the Problem:

The final major cause of resistance to therapy is the client's belief that his or her problems are external to himself or herself. After all, if the problems are the fault of parents, schools, spouses, or society in general, why would clients think anything they could change would make a difference? Clients often say, "You've got the wrong person in here. You should fix _____."

Of course, it is often difficult to convince people of their responsibility for their own dilemma. Most therapy theories assume not only a voluntary relationship between therapist and client but also the client's perception of personal responsibility for the problem. Such personal responsibility

would be accompanied by anxiety or guilt, whereas external-
izing responsibility is accompanied by anger or blame. Anger
and blame are emotions that are less likely to evoke sympathy
in therapists and more likely to elicit rejection and distancing
from the client, which clearly makes treatment more difficult.

THERAPIST REACTIVENESS TO DIFFICULT CLIENTS

When clients react negatively, the therapist's response will, of
course, affect the progress of treatment. There are several
frequent and understandable therapist responses or countertransference reactions: authoritarian behavior; fear of violence
or intimidation; deception; hopeless optimism about change;
misunderstanding clients; and unconscious encouragement of
acting out, rebellion or misbehavior.

It must be expected that clients who view therapists as
authority or parent figures and act rebelliously will sometimes
elicit authoritarian, critical parent-like behavior from therapists. It is often hard not to have punishing or rejecting feelings
toward clients who act out their dislike of authority, *even when
one consciously knows why such behavior occurs.* Many clients
devalue and disparage therapists' efforts to be helpful, and
that may cause therapists to feel rage and rejection (Meloy,
Haroun, & Schiller, 1990).

When clients are violent or intimidating, many therapists
understandably feel threatened and afraid, emotions that both
inhibit the desire to help and/or confront and arouse basic
defenses. Those defenses typically manifest in fight-or-flight
behavior, but some therapists may feel frozen, numb, or para-
lyzed in the face of physical threat.

Just as clients often harbor mistrust of words (and therefore
therapy), as a result of prior broken promises in life, so too may
therapists. Therapists who are deceived or misled by resistant
clients may experience an arousal of feelings that range from
anger to disgust, and that may recreate feelings from their own
earlier life experiences (Meloy et al., 1990). When therapists
work frequently with clients who lie or deceive, they may

develop cynical attitudes that are apparent to all clients and sabotage the therapy process. That becomes a self-fulfilling prophecy, as therapists anticipate being deceived and, not wanting to appear gullible, approach all clients as potential liars. Clients in turn oblige the expectation because they are predisposed not to believe in the possibility of an accepting, honest relationship. And so it goes. The end result of this cycle is therapeutic nihilism (Meloy et al., 1990), a therapist's cynical doubt that therapy can be effective with certain groups of people.

Some therapists doubt that anyone will honestly participate in a process of change. Often, therapists believe everyone will. Therapists may overrate the development of the treatment alliance and progress with clients who in reality are going nowhere (Meloy et al., 1990). Although it is difficult to be critical of anyone who is optimistic, the term *hopeless optimist* does suggest that optimism should be tempered with realism if for no other reason than the possible wasting of valuable resources on people who are not being helped.

Therapists often misunderstand clients by assuming they share experiences, feelings, and values (Meloy et al., 1990). This is an especially important problem when working with antisocial clients, who may deliberately lead the therapist into giving rosy assessments of his or her therapeutic progress. Such assessments may be advantageous to clients who are trying to achieve early release from treatment. Therapists need to be particularly alert to clients who display guilt and remorse when none exist. It is hard for many therapists to comprehend that some clients do not truly experience normal guilt.

It is probably impossible for therapists not to be either a little too pessimistic or optimistic at the beginning of treatment. We all have our own personalities and world views; we cannot be totally objective. Perhaps the most dangerous effect of the therapist's personality on the client is the unconscious encouragement of acting out, rebellion, or misbehavior. Some therapists unfortunately gain vicarious satisfaction from their clients' sexual encounters or flouting of authority. Clients who are already predisposed to inappropriate behavior are easily encouraged when therapists grin at tales of escapades or encourage accounts of binges or lost weekends. Therapists should seek consultation if their clients seem to get consistently worse rather than better in treatment while the therapy sessions seem to be friendly and productive.

In summary, not all client resistance comes strictly from within the client. The therapist's reactions to the client's behavior may exacerbate the problem. Some therapists are cynical toward clients, and their attitudes discourage treatment relationships; and sometimes the therapist may unconsciously desire the client to misbehave. That is iatrogenic (treatment-induced) resistance. The reactions of therapists to provocation and intimidation may impede treatment by blocking their desire to help or confront.

COUNSELING APPROACHES TO THE DIFFICULT CLIENT

Not everyone can agree on one therapy theory, and the disagreement is compounded when the client is difficult. Nevertheless, it is possible to categorize several different general approaches and discuss the pros and cons of each.

Emotive Approaches:

Most therapists are familiar with what are called "emotive approaches," therapy styles which are aimed at reflecting the client's feelings and cognitions to encourage exploration and self-examination and developing the relationship between therapist and client. Therapists, from person-centered therapists to psychoanalysts, may use active listening techniques to achieve these goals. Weiss (1990) described recent research on unconscious functioning from a psychodynamic perspective in which resistance is seen not merely as an unconscious act to block awareness of painful material but rather as an unconscious act to block interpersonal disclosure until the person feels safe. That research has profound implications for psychotherapy in underscoring the importance of accepting, non-judgmental relationships for therapeutic progress.

It is important when working with difficult clients to avoid focusing too quickly on the problem that triggered the referral. Many therapists are eager to begin problem solving and do not allow time for clients to explore their feelings about being in therapy and, if such be the case, about having been coerced into treatment. Given the understandable fear of many clients about being direct and open about their feelings, it becomes all the more important to build relationships and develop trust. As Weiss pointed out, the resistance may be unconscious, but the client may be well aware of the reluctance to participate (Weiss, 1990). In either case, when the therapist pushes too rapidly into the reason for referral, important opportunities to establish a cooperative relationship are lost.

Cognitive Therapy:

A second general category or approach is cognitive therapy. With difficult clients, cognitive therapists may elect to challenge clients' beliefs that inhibit participation in therapy and cooperation with the therapist. For example, some involuntary clients may resist participating in treatment because they believe they should get to do what they want to do when they want to do it or that they shouldn't have to do what they don't want to do. Rational-emotive therapists often attack such statements with logic and evidence. Such confrontation, however, may arouse defensiveness. Ellis (1985), in advocating for forceful persuasion, acknowledged that persuasion is called for when the client resists change but relationship building is essential when the client resists the therapist.

Lyddon (1990) classified cognitive therapies into two major types. One deals with surface change of irrational thoughts and beliefs; the other deals with deeper change of personal constructs and patterns of belief. Change of personal constructs is not easily amenable to argumentation and syllogistic reasoning; rather, it requires reflection and affective expression to facilitate cognitive restructuring. When clients have deep-seated characterological difficulties, it seems unlikely they will be able to examine their core difficulties without first developing some confidence and trust in a therapeutically. Again, this underscores the importance of relationship building.

Strategic or Paradoxical Approach:

A third general approach for working with difficult clients is the strategic or paradoxical approach. It is beyond the scope of this chapter to give a full explanation of any approach, however, the paradoxical approach is especially difficult to summarize.

When clients are defiant, paradoxical interventions can create cognitive binds that leave no opportunity for change. For example, when a client who does not trust the therapist is told that such mistrust is understandable, confusion results: the client hears a trustworthy statement from someone he or she did not expect to trust. The therapist might even direct the client to act cautiously based on the mistrust. A defiant client then becomes "compliant" by following the therapist's directive. Such paradoxical directives must be used cautiously, however. Unfortunately, it is tempting to use them as manipulative gimmicks rather than as carefully thought-out strategies for helping the person.

Other paradoxical strategies involve the use of exaggeration to reshape the client's perception. For example, a client who admits to not trusting the therapist might be asked if he or she mistrusts *everything* about the therapist. Few clients will admit they truly believe the therapist to be a spy for the FBI, and some lighthearted teasing about this may help establish that trust and mistrust are on a continuum. It then becomes easier to explore degrees of trust and mistrust and ways to improve the relationship. Of course, if clients do think the therapist is a spy from the FBI, it might be wise to consider a psychiatric consultation.

Another paradoxical strategy involves examination of positive intent behind negative behavior. Earlier, when discussing resistance, I contended that resistance must be seen as a necessary component of stability and integrity in the personality. People do what they do for reasons they think are appropriate or, at least, justified. For example, parents who are harsh with their children may feel that harshness to be justified in order to teach their children correct behavior. The parents' intent is positive, although the effects of the behavior may not be. Therapists who can identify positive intent and acknowledge understanding of it to the client may arouse less defensiveness from the client. That in turn may allow the client to explore the effectiveness of the behavior in achieving the desired goal. Often, when people feel personally criticized, they defend themselves by attacking their attacker.

Finally, paradoxical strategies acknowledge the great ambivalence that lies behind any significant change. A person with an alcohol problem, for example, has many reasons to quit drinking, including health, expense, job security, and family relationships. Still, there are also many reasons not to quit, such as loss of drinking companions and facing personal problems when sober and not anesthetized. A therapist who simply confronts the client with all the reasons to quit drinking will meet with great resistance because the reasons to continue drinking are still operative. Paradoxically, when the therapist can empathize with the client's ambivalence to change, the client is freer to fully explore both sides of the issue and take responsibility for the decision, whatever it may be.

STAGES OF ACCESSIBILITY WITH DIFFICULT CLIENTS

The fact that clients are not always ready for therapy needs to be recognized. As discussed earlier, when involuntary clients resist the very idea of therapy, the therapist must spend time trying to "sell" the client on the process. Menninger described all psychotherapy with this sales metaphor and contended that even voluntary clients must agree to terms with the therapist before therapy can proceed (Menninger, 1958).

Therapy proceeds in stages, especially in institutional contexts (Korn & McCorkle, 1959). In the first stage, there is a struggle for control, which may often be passive and covert. The therapist is often tempted to become either autocratic or permissive. Neither approach is effective. It is important to establish boundaries and expectations without becoming punitive toward the client.

In the next stage of therapy, the client may express overt rebellion by refusing to come to sessions or to participate in sessions. When this occurs, the therapist is well advised to let the natural consequences of nonparticipation take their course rather than becoming too personally invested in involving the client. For example, when a probationer does not come to therapy, the therapist may advise the probation officer and then let whatever happens happen. If the benefits of therapy have been explained, then clients can deal with their decisions without exhortations from therapists.

Often clients must get sick and tired of being sick and tired before they acknowledge the need for treatment. With alcoholism, therapists refer to this as hitting the bottom or gutter. It is often hard to watch clients do avoidable damage to themselves, but rescuing clients who don't want help is a form of co-dependency.

After clients have run into the wall enough times, they may finally return to the therapist and ask for help. A sincere request for help makes it much easier to establish mutually agreed-upon goals for treatment.

POINTS TO CONSIDER REGARDING TREATMENT

The following points may be helpful in guiding the progress of therapy:

1. Therapists must establish an environment in which communication can occur by examining factors that facilitate and inhibit communication. Clients will not talk if they feel threatened; most are more likely to talk if they sense that the therapist understands them.

2. The client's problem must be identified. What needs changing? What does the client think needs changing, if anything? What is blocking the change? Are there reasons why adapting would not be in the client's interest? Do the client's underlying character and values block normal relationships, or is the person capable of being influenced by feedback about the effect of his or her behavior on others?

3. When a client enters therapy involuntarily, therapists must understand and respond to impediments to change that arise as a result of the client's involuntary entrance into the counseling process. Does the client trust the therapist or does he or she feel uncertain about disclosing information to the therapist? Does the client doubt the value of counseling? Is the client angry at the therapist because the counseling mandate was involuntary?

4. The therapist must select an approach that appeals to the style of the particular client. How does the client learn? Through action-oriented techniques? Through insight? Through talk about feelings? By seeing someone else perform the new behavior?

5. Therapists must understand the points at which their clients may be receptive to new understanding. What stage of treatment has the client reached? When should clients be confronted and when should they be allowed to "stew in their own juices"?

6. Therapists must develop an awareness of self and of organization dynamics that hamper treatment. How can the therapist avoid inappropriate alliances with clients against other staff members? How can the therapist detect manipulation and respond therapeutically? Is the therapist responding appropriately to the client's transference and is the therapist fully aware of his or her own countertransference reaction?

7. Therapists must have a method to understand and approach clients' tactics of resistance. How do clients evade personal responsibility by attacking or confusing the therapist? What is the best approach the therapist can use to respond effectively to these tactics from a particular client? (Harris & Watkins, 1987)

CONCLUSION

Therapy with difficult clients can be challenging and gratifying as well as draining and frustrating. Therapists need to determine whether their formal training is sufficient for understanding the problem of the help-rejecting client. Fortunately, increasing attention in continuing education programs is directed to therapeutic techniques for working with special populations, such as drug offenders, batterers, public offenders, socioeconomically deprived clients, and others. Therapists have a professional obligation to continue beyond their academic training and think deeply about the practical problems people face in our world. Most therapists would have very few clients if they worked only with those who were articulate and "motivated." It is essential to develop skills to be effective with clients we consider difficult.

REFERENCES

Anderson, C., & Stewart, S. (1983). *Mastering resistance*. New York: Guilford Press.

Ansbacher, H. L. (1981). Prescott Lecky's concept of resistance and his personality. *Journal of Clinical Psychology, 37,* 791–795.

Dowd, E., & Seibel, C. (1990). A cognitive theory of resistance and reactance: Implications for treatment. *Journal of Mental Health Counseling, 12*(4), 458–469.

Ellis, A. (1985). *Overcoming resistance*. New York: Springer Publishing Company.

Harris, G., & Watkins, D. (1987). *Counseling the involuntary and resistant client*. Laurel, MD: American Correctional Association.

Korn, R., & McCorkle, L. (1959). *Criminology and penology*. New York: Rinehart and Winston.

Lyddon, W. (1990). First and second-order change: Implications for rationalist and constructivist cognitive therapies. *Journal of Counseling and Development, 69*(2), 122–127.

Meloy, R., Haroun, A., & Schiller, E. (1990). *Clinical guidelines for involuntary outpatient treatment*. Sarasota: Professional Resource Exchange.

Menninger, K. (1958). *Theory of psychoanalytic technique*. New York: Harper & Row.

Shertzer, B., & Stone, S. (1974). *Fundamentals of counseling*. Boston: Houghton Mifflin.

Weiss, J. (1990, March). Unconscious mental functioning. *Scientific American,* 103–109.

5

Brief Therapy with Difficult Clients

Lynn Loar, PhD, LCSW

Dr. Loar is Educational Coordinator of the San Francisco Child Abuse Council, San Francisco, CA.

KEY POINTS

- The brief, strategic approach to resolving problems lends itself well to clinical work with difficult clients: it focuses on teaching tangible behaviors, builds on strengths, avoids antagonizing and arguing with volatile clients, and normalizes behavior that might otherwise contribute to the isolation common among difficult clients.

- *Difficult clients* are persons so burdened by multiple problems and poor past experiences with helpers (medical or mental health providers, social service agents, educators) that they do not readily welcome treatment.

- Practical suggestions for working briefly with difficult clients include: building cooperation; defusing prior failed therapy; avoiding arguments; reframing; building on existing strengths; and encouraging clients to take up a hobby or pursue an interest to broaden their social contacts, interests, and potential support.

- The Mental Research Institute (MRI) model of brief strategic therapy has proven to be highly beneficial in the treatment of difficult clients. It emphasizes arriving at a clear, specific statement of the problem that reframes negative formulations positively and anticipates mastery of the problem.

INTRODUCTION

In an ideal world, any person with a significant problem would voluntarily seek the services of a mental health professional and say, "I have a problem that I am unable to resolve on my own, so I have come to ask your help." Such persons would be compliant with requests for information and suggestions about changes, and there would be ample time available for clinicians to work with them. However, with nonvoluntary clients, people with many problems, and other types of difficult clients, the situation is, unfortunately, very different. Therapists seeing clients who are participating in the process under duress must essentially declare, "You have a problem." Especially in cases of violence and abuse, clients would prefer to deny, minimize, or rationalize their problems. This start will likely be interpreted as blame and accusation, at least initially. Although therapists have considerable formal authority over court-ordered clients, especially involving consequences that can be threatened or imposed, this authoritative stance will likely be interpreted as an accusation and will elicit defensive reactions, withdrawal, or passive resistance rather than cooperation.

This chapter will provide the theoretical basis and several practical guidelines for working briefly with difficult clients. The main therapeutic challenge is to establish rapport and assist clients in making small but significant changes that will improve immediate functioning and possibly promote continued improvement.

DEFINITIONS AND PRINCIPLES

Therapy is defined as the process of assisting another (or others) in developing mastery and empathy, as well as in restoring growth and development. *Brief therapy* is an effective, time-limited approach that invokes clients' values, appreciates their strengths, and, in the best case scenario, is based on mutual respect. The objective for therapists employing a brief strategic approach is to recommend *small* changes that improve the presenting problem and, potentially, introduce more lasting improvement.

Difficult clients are persons sufficiently burdened by multiple problems and poor past experiences with helpers (medical or mental health providers, social service agents, educators) that they do not voluntarily seek assistance. Another party — a court, supervisor, spouse, or parent — compels them to undergo treatment. Voluntary clients often enter therapy because they feel depleted of energy and options, having tried everything else to no avail. Difficult clients, on the other hand, may feel more energetic and more able to manage on their own. They are more straightforward about their disinclination to undergo therapy. Therapists should understand that without a prior worthwhile experience with therapy, a person cannot know its possible benefits. Initial resistance should be viewed as a positive sign of strength and personal boundaries. Motivation will develop as clients experience the benefits of therapy. Thus, motivation is more properly viewed as an outcome measure of the usefulness of treatment.

The customary principles of *trust* and *confidentiality* apply more to voluntary clients. Difficult clients will not trust readily, nor is trust a reasonable expectation of them. Rather, therapists should aim to demonstrate their credibility and reliability, and should avoid triggering clients' mistrust. The use of mandatory reporting laws is one good example of this principle. Clarifying limits of confidentiality at the outset of treatment minimizes clients' surprise when a report of abuse or neglect must be made.

Unless a therapist fears for his or her physical safety, the report should be made in the presence of the client to avoid triggering mistrust, anger, and speculation. Making the report in a timely and responsible manner demonstrates the therapist's credibility, reliability, and forthrightness. The report should begin with a summary of the client's strengths and progress in treatment, followed by a description of the danger or abuse and the therapist's willingness to continue working with the client. In addition, the report should give the client the opportunity to speak with the authority. In doing so, the therapist models responsible behavior and the ability to deal with problematic situations.

In brief treatment with difficult clients, therapists must redefine their role. Therapists must demonstrate the usefulness of the sessions by respectful, active intervention. The artificiality of the relationship is a given, not limited by idealistic notions of trust and confidentiality. By being predictable and reliable, therapists honor boundaries and limits that establish a common ground within which progress can be made. Through constructive, practical suggestions, jointly created and consistent with the clients' world views and values, incremental change can begin during the first session. Setting a positive example from the start enables clients to experience the potential value of therapy and become increasingly motivated as the work continues.

THEORETICAL ORIENTATION

Regardless of a practitioner's theoretical persuasion, effective therapy has two essential ingredients: mastery and empathy. Sometimes called transference (in traditional psychoanalytic practice), corrective emotional experience (Alexander & French, 1946), or second-order change (Watzlawick, Weakland, & Fisch, 1974), such interventions result both in self-control or mastery of something previously thought to exceed a person's grasp and in a sense of relatedness or concern for others. A person who has self-control without interpersonal ties has the ability to prevent recurrence of inappropriate behaviors, but not the motivation for consistent and significant change. The converse of this is equally problematic. Acquiring an understanding of the deleterious effects of one's harmful behavior without also learning alternative responses would likely lead to despair, self-loathing, and relapse. Empathy provides the motivation to see the impact one has on others; mastery is the skill to implement the desired change.

Because preoccupation with a problem may reduce the energy available for growth, it is often useful for therapists to encourage advancement to "the next stage of life" (Haley, 1973). Forward-looking intervention is benign, requires no admission of failure by clients, allows problems and dysfunctional behaviors to be outgrown, and redirects attention to healthy maturation, of which the therapeutic change is one part. Particularly in work with children, who ideally progress rapidly from one developmental stage to the next and are usually eager to mature, such a developmental boost typically is welcomed by both the children and their family members. Presenting the problematic behaviors as vestiges of a younger age that are now ready to be outgrown alleviates feelings of shame and promotes normal growth and development. Dr. Milton Erickson suggests that clients and their families tend to seek the help of therapists when they are unable to meet the challenges of a new developmental stage and become stuck or symptomatic. "While focusing sharply on symptoms, Erickson's therapeutic strategy has as its larger goal the resolution of the problems of the family to get the life cycle moving again" (Haley, 1973).

BUILDING COOPERATION

It is essential to clarify at the outset that promoting cooperation in no way suggests condoning abusive or antisocial behavior; rather, it represents the most certain way to lead clients away from dysfunction. To be sure, a cooperative and pleasant interview will likely leave clients in better spirits than will a contentious one. Clients may be less prone to blame others for their problems or their need to undergo therapy. Also, if they are able to work cooperatively with therapists, they may become more resolved to attempt to manage their problems thoughtfully and may even feel more productive in general. At the very least, they will have experienced a more positive way of approaching difficult situations.

Initially, many clients are angry, defensive, or humiliated by having to meet with a therapist to address their handling of problems; legitimately, they may object to this type of intrusion into their private lives. It is crucial that counselors and clients form a partnership at the outset, lest limited energy and attention spans expire before the essential matters are addressed.

> A 6-year-old boy was interviewed at his school after a referral was made describing his poor hygiene, dirty clothes, and combative behavior with his peers. Midway through the interview, the boy looked intently at the top of the counselor's head and exclaimed, "You have gray hair; you must be very old." Meeting his parents later that day, the counselor began by stating enthusiastically that they had the most delightful child and repeated his remark. The parents were so embarrassed at their child's lack of tact that they were congenial and cooperative throughout the interview. The parents agreed that the child's appearance attracted a lot of negative attention from both peers and teachers, preventing others from enjoying this obviously bright and witty child. The interview concluded with the parents thanking the counselor for her interest in the child and with the mutual goodwill that comes with shared laughter.

DEFUSING PRIOR FAILED THERAPY

If clients have had prior experience with "the system," they may begin the first session with complaints and invective. Therapist should permit clients to state their prior objections, although not endlessly, for the following reasons:

- Clients will not listen to or focus on anything else until they have stated their complaints

- Complaints about past approaches should help therapists avoid potential pitfalls in the current therapy

- Allowing clients to state their objections will provide a picture of their outlook and indicate their level of emotional control

- Any tirade volunteered can be used to gauge the amount of responsibility taken by clients, the efficacy of efforts made previously, and especially the values of clients and their perspective of the problem

Without defending or discrediting the other professionals mentioned by the client, the therapist can say it is understandable if the client felt mistreated by what happened (using his or her wording) and can voice regret that things did not go better. The therapist can then express a desire to do better and be more considerate.

The client may gain incentive to listen and participate in therapy if asked to help by immediately pointing out when the counselor errs. This unites the therapist and the client in a common purpose, empowering the client by giving him or her an evaluative role.

AVOIDING ARGUMENTS

Although it is not too difficult to avoid obvious and overt arguing, disputes may occur in more subtle forms that are often unrecognized, especially when labeled otherwise — such as pointing out facts, clarifying realities, or reasoning. However, if a client does not readily respond to the opinion of his or her therapist, repeated presentation of this view — no matter how justified by reason or evidence — constitutes arguing. This jeopardizes rapport and hardens, rather than changes, the client's position.

Steps for avoiding arguments include: listening attentively, even to provocative and apparently misguided clients; agreeing with clients as much as possible, even if the agreement must be subtly qualified ("From what you say, it certainly sounds as if. . . ."); finding ways to praise or approve of anything clients say that sounds positive; and framing any comments, reservations, or advice in terms that are consonant with clients' own language and expressed views. Advice should be presented positively — neither resembling a put-down nor involving any loss of face.

> A recently divorced couple was referred for therapy because of alleged alcoholism and sexual inpropriety by the father. As it turned out, the parents were devout Mormons throughout their marriage. The mother and children remained active in their faith after the father left the home, but he withdrew from the church. He was not drinking excessively, only approximately two drinks per week, but this was indeed a taboo for the rest of the family. He was unwilling to yield this practice to placate his ex-wife. However, when the therapist talked to him about his children's need for stability and continuity, and their inability to handle so many changes so quickly, he agreed, for their sakes, not to drink when they visited him.

ADAPTING THE MENTAL RESEARCH INSTITUTE (MRI) MODEL

As pioneers in brief strategic therapy, the Mental Research Institute (MRI) team developed an approach to the solution of problems (Watzlawick, 1978; Watzlawick, Weakland, & Fisch, 1974). First, one develops a clear, specific statement of the problem that reframes negative formulations positively and anticipates mastery of the problem. Second, the unsuccessful efforts clients have made (called "attempted solutions" by the MRI team) should be examined to avoid repeating fruitless activities. Third, a clear, specific, practical solution should be developed so success will be recognized when reached. The intervention should be crafted in small, manageable steps that lead to the envisioned solution. Table 5.1 presents an adaptation of the MRI model for counseling difficult clients.

Table 5.1
ADAPTATION OF THE **MRI** MODEL
FOR **DIFFICULT CLIENTS**

- Discuss the solution first to avoid the denial and loss of face that accompany the admittance of wrongdoing. Many clients will refuse to find fault with their past behavior but will discuss constructively a plan for an improved future. This plan must be clear, specific, and sufficiently detailed to correct the problematic behavior. Once progress has been made, clients may more readily discuss the problem now outgrown with the benefit of hindsight.

- Add a developmental boost so clients, now "unstuck," are directed toward a healthy path of growth and development.

- Facilitate ties to the community so clients have a network of resources when therapy ends.

A counselor met with the parents of a 13-year-old boy after his school nurse found more than twenty bruises on his back and buttocks. The child had told her that he had stopped to play a video game on his way home from an errand, spent 75¢ without permission, and then lied about it, thereby infuriating his parents. During her initial meeting with the parents, the counselor learned that the mother, a waitress, came home from work each day and put all her change from tips in a jar. She suspected that her son stole quarters from this jar. The boy also lied about his homework and was failing math. The parents described the child as a thief and a liar and asked questions about "tough love" — the possibility of sending the child to jail for a weekend — and other severe measures to show the child the logical extreme of his misbehavior.

The counselor began by stating that she saw how much they cared about the child's future and how worried they were; they agreed. Her aim was to convey appreciation of their concern while also introducing the idea that they had a rather nice son with a video game habit and impulse control — typical of children his age. The counselor volunteered that if she were left alone in a room with a plate full of chocolates, she would probably steal one or two, eat them, and then lie about it if asked. She added that she paid taxes, worked 40 hours a week, and thought of herself more as chubby than as a thief or a liar. The parents laughed in recognition of a common human failing. She then asked the parents what they liked about their child, and, happily, they had much to say. They agreed that by focusing on the negatives they had almost forgotten the child's strengths.

Thus, the conversation shifted to a plan for the future that would focus on the child's strengths and lead him away from his problematic behaviors. The parents agreed that no physical force would be used in disciplining the boy and no loose change would be left around the house. The boy was paid $20 per month by the manager of the apartment complex for doing odd jobs. The parents, who had been cashing the check for him, decided instead to take the child to the bank to open his own account so he could deposit the checks. The parents agreed with the counselor's suggestion to call ahead and request that the person in charge of new accounts address the child as "Mister," put him on mailing lists, and promote earning interest by leaving money in the account.

The parents smiled at the thought of how pleased the child would be to be treated like an adult depositing his paycheck. Furthermore, they agreed that if they asked him to run an errand they would expect him to use his own money and then present his receipt to be reimbursed. Tipping was to be allowed for a job especially well done (since this was part of the family's language). Both the reimbursement and the child's weekly allowance were to be paid by check. As a result, the only cash around the house would be the child's money. The parents were enthusiastic about this new approach and also were aware that it would be easy to backslide. Thus, they readily agreed to a few more meetings to reinforce the progress made during the initial interview.

Benefits:

The MRI model is useful in counseling difficult clients for the following reasons:

- Brevity (difficult clients cannot tolerate long-term work, are wary of ongoing relationships, and possess too many problems to make more than a few sessions practical)

- Focus on behaviors that can be observed

- Respect for the values and strengths of clients and firm commitment not to argue with them

- Emphasis on small and tangible steps that both improve the problem of the moment and potentially introduce the beginning of profound and lasting change

By focusing first on the solution, instead of a definition of the problem, therapists can work with difficult clients without evoking their resistance or defensiveness about their past conduct; they can plan the immediate future in specific detail once the problem has been outgrown. Such respectful and collaborative work allows therapists to make suggestions, propose new approaches, and assist clients in building a network for future support.

CONSOLIDATING GAINS

A number of verbal techniques can be used to strengthen the gains made during therapy (Watzlawick, 1978; Weakland & Jordan, 1990). The positive reframing developed throughout the session can be thematically connected with the new, planned behavior. Rather than describing specifically what the new behavior should be (thereby infantilizing clients), therapists can offer an anecdote, analogy, or vignette as a prompt and permit clients to volunteer examples that they feel capture their situation (Haley, 1973). In addition, therapists can further strengthen clients' commitments to this prospective solution by replying, "Yes, but. . ." to their proposal. Deliberate, covert arguing not only gives clients an opportunity to work the bugs out of the new plans, but also fortifies their determination.

At this juncture, therapists should forewarn clients that minor setbacks and slips—normal parts of the learning process—*will* occur. Occasional stumbles are part and parcel of learning by trial and error. By recognizing that occasional backsliding is inevitable, clients can then be helped to develop nonpunitive ways to regroup rather than to impulsively deem the new approach a failure and return to familiar, problematic ways.

Because it is difficult to listen well when under stress, clients may not accurately retain the information contained in the session or be clear afterward about what they really must do differently in the future. Putting the new plans in writing for clients clarifies the steps to be taken, makes following through easier, and allows clients to document their efforts to any supervising system (the courts, probation, parole, etc.) when necessary. This need not be a cumbersome task, nor result in a formal document: simply use a sheet of carbon paper to make two copies of the steps a client agrees to take. Both the therapist and the client should sign and date the list; each should keep a copy. Typically, clients appreciate the clarity the agreement brings to the situation. Moreover, they can craft the agreement in their own language, with therapists providing little more than secretarial support (except when clients reach an impasse or propose something impractical). Clients are more likely to follow their own agreement than someone else's directive on how to lead their lives.

A follow-up letter can serve the same function as an agreement drafted during the session. Even in this format, clients should be given as much credit for the solution as possible. Therefore, the letter should describe and summarize their proposal. It can also contain referrals and information on services available in the community that clients might find helpful. Indeed, for diffident and perhaps tongue-tied clients, the letter can serve as a means of introduction to the new resource or provider of service.

> A family of six had lived in one room in a motel for several years. The parents had been together for 15 years but argued frequently. A referral was made to Child Protective Services when a liquor bottle thrown by the mother at the father accidentally hit one of the children on the forehead, creating a large bruise and lump. The parents said they would never deliberately hurt their children; the father added that they were not stupid people and knew better than to argue in the presence of their children. He said if they lived in a two-bedroom apartment, they would not have a problem; however, with all of them living in one room, there was no place to go. He stated energetically that their privacy was important; thus, they could not go outside to argue because the neighbors would know their business. As their solution, they proposed that they would no longer argue.

The counselor replied that however well-intended, this solution seemed unrealistic. She offered to provide some suggestions on obtaining financial assistance so they could move to larger quarters, although obtaining funding would take some time to accomplish. Therefore, she asked their indulgence with her next question: "Does this place have a laundry room?" After a shared chuckle, the parents agreed that they would argue in the laundry room and put a quarter in the dryer to muffle the sound for especially charged debates. The mother remarked that by the time they got all the way around to the other end of the building, they might not even feel like arguing. Although this is a positive statement by the mother, it is important not to agree too readily; agreement would reestablish the therapist's authoritative position and dampen the client's motivation to change. Therefore, the therapist remarked that if it was really important, they would, with effort, be able to resume the argument; if not, they could always save the quarter for the next time.

The agreement was signed by the parents, the school principal, and the counselor. The text of the agreement is as follows:

> The parents understand that their family was referred to Child Protective Services out of concern for the safety of their children. The agency recognizes the love and commitment of the parents for their children, as well as the considerable efforts the parents make with limited means to provide adequate food, clothing, shelter, and supervision for the children. The parents agree that, with the family living in a one-room apartment, any fighting between them constitutes a potential threat to the safety of the children. Therefore, in an effort to ensure the children's safety, the parents agree to: (a) contact the Catholic Social Services about housing subsidies so the family might move to a larger apartment, (b) conduct adult disputes in the laundry room, and (c) attend weekly family counseling sessions for 3 months, beginning by the end of the month (three referrals given).

BUILDING A NETWORK OF SUPPORT

Because difficult clients tend to be difficult people, they usually have few friends and sources of support. Moreover, they may have exhausted and burned bridges with more stable relatives, leaving them isolated and lacking the skills necessary to establish positive and supportive social ties with others or connections with programs in their community. In addition, because a client's involvement with his or her therapist is limited in duration and intimacy, a crucial part of any treatment plan should entail assisting the client to establish ties with others.

Often, the problems of difficult clients dominate their days and nights; few of them have hobbies, interests, or relationships free of the stress, antagonism, or high drama. Encouraging clients to take up a hobby or pursue an interest can yield benefits in a number of ways:

1. It may provide the necessary developmental boost to propel them beyond their problems and toward rewarding growth

2. It may develop social and applied skills in a normative (i.e., nonclinical) setting

3. It may help them form a more positive view of themselves

4. It may lead to friendships based on strength and a shared, productive interest

5. It may result in a lasting source of enrichment in an otherwise difficult life.

Therapists should prepare themselves to serve as "reality coaches" while their clients make these initial forays into the outside world. Difficult clients rarely are aware of how, and to what extent, they contribute to contentious exchanges. Therapists often will need to provide constructive feedback about how to approach others, become part of a group, and initiate a friendship while clients attempt to become more connected with others. This is a key ingredient to a successful outcome because it challenges the isolation so common among difficult clients. Therapy should not be terminated until clients have made at least one or two positive (and appropriate) attachments and have an awareness of the skills involved in forming such ties.

CONCLUSION

The brief strategic approach to resolving problems lends itself well to clinical work with difficult clients: it focuses on teaching tangible behaviors, builds on strengths, avoids antagonizing and arguing with volatile clients, and normalizes behavior that might otherwise contribute to the isolation common among difficult clients. The intention of this chapter is neither to suggest that the work is easy, nor to suggest that the clients will become pleasant and appreciative of the clinician's effort. Rather, the intent is to explore the challenges of working with especially troubled clients and to offer a few practical suggestions to make the work a bit easier.

REFERENCES

Alexander, F., & French, T. (1946). *Psychoanalytic therapy*. New York: Ronald Press.

Haley, J. (1973). *Uncommon therapy: The psychiatric techniques of Milton H. Erickson, M. D.* New York: W. W. Norton & Company.

Watzlawick, P. (1978). *The language of change: Elements of therapeutic communication*. New York: Basic Books.

Watzlawick, P., Weakland, J., & Fisch, R. (1974). *Change: Principles of problem formation and problem resolution*. New York: W. W. Norton & Company.

Weakland, J., & Jordan(-Loar), L. (1990). *Working briefly with reluctant clients: Child protective services as an example*. Family Therapy Case Studies, 5(2), 51–68.

FOR FURTHER READING

Loar, L., & Weakland, J. (1994). *Working with families in shelters: A practical guide for counselors and child care staff*. Alameda, CA: The Latham Foundation.

6

Research Findings on Short-Term Psychodynamic Therapy Techniques

Jeffrey L. Binder, PhD, ABPP

Dr. Binder is a member of the Core Faculty of the Georgia School of Professional Psychology, Atlanta, GA.

KEY POINTS

- In some clients, short-term psychodynamic therapies are capable of results once assumed to be achievable only with extended treatment.

- Although psychodynamic therapies are commonly associated with long-term treatment, short-term therapy has a long history, dating back to Freud's early treatments. This history is explored.

- Selection criteria for clients deemed suitable for short-term dynamic therapy are rather stringent and have included: capacity to discuss feelings, basic trust, motivation for self-knowledge, having a circumscribed problem,

and capacity to engage and disengage rapidly from treatment.

- Therapists should expand these criteria, emphasizing evidence for the client's characteristic capacity for interpersonal relating.

- Whereas classic psychoanalytic metapsychological theory has lacked a clear therapeutic focus, contemporary treatment models provide that focus. One such model, the *cyclical maladaptive pattern* (CMP) method, is discussed.

- Technical flexibility in therapy is essential. Several technical skills are presented, including the judicious use of interpretations.

INTRODUCTION

In the last few years, enough convincing empirical evidence has surfaced to demonstrate that with some clients, short-term psychodynamic therapies are indeed capable of results once assumed to be achievable only with extended treatment (Koss & Butcher, 1986). Although psychodynamic therapies are commonly associated with substantial length, short-term versions have a long history, dating back to Sigmund Freud's original treatments (Freud, 1895; Jones, 1955).

In fact, the payment and approval structures of many of the new managed health care services necessitate the use — or at least a trial — of short-term psychotherapy. It is the practitioner's responsibility to maintain high-quality care while operating under the severe constraints imposed by the evolving reimbursement systems. This chapter will familiarize the practicing mental health professional with research findings on one type of short-term strategy: psychodynamic therapy.

HISTORICAL BACKGROUND

The principles and procedures of all psychodynamic therapies are based on Freud's two most fundamental discoveries — *dynamic hypothesis* and *transference*. Dynamic hypothesis, the influence on conscious experience and behavior of unconscious mental processes (Freud, 1895, 1900), refers to the nature of psychological conflict. Freud's structural theory provides further specification (Freud, 1923). When a breakthrough into consciousness of unconscious content from the id is imminent, the ego automatically activates a danger signal that is subjectively experienced as anxiety. The danger stems from the superego's prohibitions against the unconscious material. The ego simultaneously activates defenses against this unacceptable content. A compromise is ultimately achieved between unconscious content and censuring forces, as well as the dictates of external reality. This compromise may manifest as personality characteristics or psychological symptoms (Freud, 1926).

Freud's second fundamental principle, transference, is the primary mode of expression in interpersonal relationships of intrapsychic conflict (Freud, 1895). Freud originally viewed this phenomenon as a resistance to therapeutic work because it involved reenacting childhood conflicts vis-à-vis the therapist as a substitute for remembering the original experiences. However, he eventually realized that it was also the primary means of identifying, examining, and modifying psychological conflict (Freud, 1909, 1912).

A widely adopted version that retains Freud's original viewpoint defines transference as the repetition of wishes, feelings, fantasies, attitudes, and defenses initially experienced toward parental figures from childhood and now inappropriately and unconsciously displaced onto current figures of emotional significance to the person (Greenson & Wexler, 1969).

Dynamic conflict and transference guided the development of the fundamental strategy of all psychodynamic therapies. For psychological conflict to be resolved, unconscious material must be allowed access to consciousness, where it can be mastered by the adult personality. This process requires removing the defenses against unconscious wishes, feelings, and cognitions. To remove defenses, the imagined dangers associated with unconscious contents first must be identified.

Interpretation is the major therapeutic intervention that facilitates the removal of defenses and clarifies unconscious material (Sandler, Dare, & Holder, 1992). The standard psychoanalytic strategy for interpreting intrapsychic conflict is first to interpret the defenses and their accompanying imagined dangers and then interpret unconscious wishes, feelings, and cognitions.

Psychological conflict is presumed to originate in childhood and, with time, persistently influences many areas of the person's life. The most immediate expression of conflict occurs in the therapeutic relationship as transference. The simultaneous identification of psychological conflict (expressed as behavior patterns and maladaptive attitudes in the transference), relationships outside therapy, and recollections from the past is called *insight* (Menninger & Holzman, 1973). The client's achievement of insight is assumed to be the catalyst for conflict resolution. The strategy for interpretively linking manifestations of conflict in the three areas of a client's life has been codified as the *triangle of insight* (Menninger, 1958; Menninger & Holzman, 1973) or the *triangle of person* (Malan, 1979) (Figure 6.1).

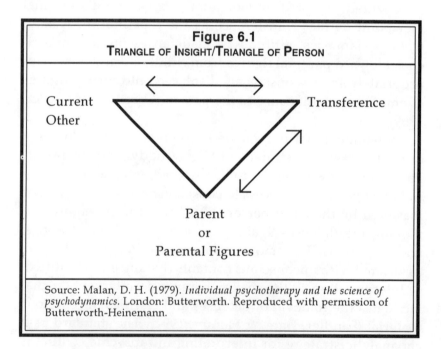

Figure 6.1
TRIANGLE OF INSIGHT/TRIANGLE OF PERSON

Current Other   Transference

Parent
or
Parental Figures

Source: Malan, D. H. (1979). *Individual psychotherapy and the science of psychodynamics*. London: Butterworth. Reproduced with permission of Butterworth-Heinemann.

Fundamental interrelated therapeutic strategies represented by sequentially interpreting defenses, anxiety, and impulses at the three corners of the triangle of insight have guided all psychodynamic therapies, regardless of modifications introduced in the specific implementation of these strategies.

Modifications to increase the efficiency of psychodynamic treatment were attempted during the first few decades of the

20th century. The aim of uncovering early conflictual child-hood memories and their associated affective "charge" was a primary factor in extending psychoanalysis (Freud, 1914; 1937).

Ferenczi and Rank (1925) and, two decades later, Alexander and French (1946) questioned the assumptions that therapeutic change required extensive reconstruction of childhood conflictual experiences and that depth and endurance of therapeutic results were proportionate to prolonged therapeutic exploration. These clinicians believed that all of the therapeutically important past was embodied in the current transference. Therefore, therapeutic change occurs when a client re-lives chronic conflictual patterns of behavior resulting from the transference and experiences a different outcome in his or her relationship with the counselor. Alexander and French (1946) termed this occurrence the "corrective emotional experience." To create such an experience, the counselor actively intervenes to promote high emotional engagement in the client and an expression of "core" conflicts in the immediacy of the transference. Furthermore, to avoid prolonged treatments in which clients become overly dependent on the therapy and counselor, these clinicians interrupted treatment, varied the frequency of sessions, and set termination dates. These innovative ideas served as an impetus for the development of contemporary short-term psychodynamic therapies.

THE FIRST GENERATION OF SHORT-TERM DYNAMIC THERAPIES

In the 1960s, several groups of psychodynamic clinicians — working independently until the 1970s — began to experiment with modifications of therapeutic technique in the context of short-term treatment. These investigators included the Tavistock group in England (Balint, Ornstein, & Balint, 1972; Malan, 1963, 1976), Peter Sifneos (1972, 1979) and James Mann (Mann, 1973; Mann & Goldman, 1982) in Boston, and Habib Davanloo (1979) in Montreal.

The short-term treatments developed by these clinicians

share five basic features. First, the explicit client selection criteria tend to be rather stringent. For example, suitable clients must be able quickly to describe a circumscribed area of conflict or problem, recall childhood memories clearly connected to the current problem, tolerate high emotional tension, have strong motivation for exploring internal experiences, and engage and disengage from the therapeutic relationship relatively quickly. Second, the counselor is very active in identifying a focused area of work that typically links the current problem with a specific hypothesized childhood conflict with parental figures. Third, the major therapeutic strategy is to link expressions in the transference of the focal conflict with evidence of the same conflict in the client's childhood recollections; this is called the *transference/parent link* (Malan, 1976). Fourth, the counselor actively uses confrontative questions and observations to deal with the client's resistance to emotional engagement in the work. Fifth, the counselor actively limits the length of treatment by carefully selecting clients, avoiding actions that foster client dependency, and, often, setting explicit end points for treatment.

With the exception of James Mann, who appears to have incorporated existential concepts into his treatment model, the first generation of short-term dynamic therapists adhered closely to traditional psychoanalytic principles. They adopted Freud's structural model of intrapsychic conflict as a framework for articulating a focus for therapeutic work. Within this problem focus, in their interpretive interventions, they emphasized one side of the triangle of insight—the link between transference and childhood memories.

This close adherence to traditional psychoanalytic concepts and principles tended to restrict the application of these short-term dynamic therapies. To develop transference/parent links early in therapy, the client must enter therapy capable of communicating childhood memories that rapidly coalesce into a coherent conflictual theme, which also is identifiable in current relationships and in the transference. This capability is more likely to be possessed by clients with relatively well-organized personality structures and/or good communication skills, regardless of the nature of their symptoms. As a consequence, many clients who might benefit from short-term therapy are excluded (e.g., persons with more severe personality disorders or those who, for whatever reasons, do not have ready access to relevant childhood memories).

The primary reliance on the therapeutic strategy of transference/parent interpretive links creates the potential for a serious contradiction in therapeutic aims. On the one hand, emphasis on the counselor's activity and attention to evidence of a focal conflict in the transference serves to heighten the client's emotional arousal and appreciation of how conflict is currently expressed. On the other hand, interpretive links to childhood recollections risk shifting the client's attention from current emotional experiences to relatively intellectualized discussions of distant formative experiences in childhood.

Another problem is created by defining the therapeutic focus in terms of Freud's highly abstract structural model. The focal problem is conceptualized in terms of unconscious wishes, defenses, and associated unpleasant affects. However, clients do not experience conflicts in these terms. People have internal experiences of relationships, with associated views of themselves and others, along with feelings, thoughts, attitudes, and fantasies. Accordingly, counselors talk with clients in these terms. Therefore, the counselor must make a tacit translation of his or her abstract conception of the client's conflict into language the client understands. Because there are no guidelines for making this translation, the typical result is a loss of clarity and specificity. Thus, Malan (1976) described the process by which a counselor defines a conflict focus as highly intuitive: it represents a gradual "crystallization" in the counselor's mind of an appropriate area of work. There are no explicit guidelines for teaching this process to counselors. Furthermore, there is a lack of reliability among counselors in formulating a problem focus for a given client. If each counselor must wait for a focus to crystallize in his or her mind, there is no way to encourage similarity in foci for counselors treating the same client.

THE SECOND GENERATION OF SHORT-TERM DYNAMIC THERAPIES

In the past few decades, new models of short-term treatment have appeared, which in varying degrees incorporate concepts and principles from interpersonal theory and cognitive psychology into a contemporary psychodynamic theoretical framework (Crits-Christoph & Barber, 1991; Horowitz, 1976; Luborsky, 1984; Strupp & Binder, 1984). The aim of such theoretical integrations is to maximize the use of concepts that are clearly explicable and closely tied to clinical experience. Teaching the models is therefore more effective, and the therapeutic strategies and tactics distinguishing each model are more amenable to empirical testing.

These new models of short-term treatment have resulted in advances in procedures for selecting clients who are likely to benefit from short-term dynamic therapy, in guidelines for clearly specifying a problem focus, and in the use of technical procedures for increasing the likelihood of a beneficial therapeutic outcome.

Client Selection:

Selection criteria for clients deemed suitable for short-term dynamic therapy have been rather stringent (Crits-Christoph & Barber, 1991; Davanloo, 1979; Malan, 1976; Sifneos, 1979). The original criteria were derived from dimensions of personality traditionally considered necessary for a client to benefit from psychoanalysis, and include such characteristics as the capacity to discuss feelings, basic trust, and motivation for self-knowledge. A prospective candidate for short-term therapy must meet additional criteria, including a circumscribed problem and the capacity to engage and disengage rapidly from treatment.

A problem with these criteria is the lack of evidence that counselors can use them in practice to predict a successful outcome with short-term dynamic therapy (Binder, Henry, & Strupp, 1987). Attempts to quantify various selection criteria (e.g., global adjustment, health-sickness, and expectancies about therapy) have yielded modest associations with outcome (Luborsky, Crits-Christoph, Mintz, & Auerbach, 1988). Lewis Wolberg (1980) foreshadowed these findings when, more than a decade ago, he advised that *everyone* should receive brief therapy, at the end of which a decision to continue could be made. An important implication in this recommendation is that in any given treatment, the quality of the therapeutic process (e.g., the therapeutic alliance) is a better predictor of outcome than pretreatment client variables (Luborsky et al., 1988).

Emphasizing pretreatment client variables as selection criteria assumes that the client will respond similarly to any therapist using a particular treatment model. However, it appears that treatment outcome is the result of an *interaction* between the client's characteristics, the counselor's style of relating, and the technical strategies employed (Luborsky et al., 1988; Piper, Azim, Joyce, McCallum, Nixon, & Segal, 1991). In support of this notion, recent empirical research has suggested that the client's measured characteristic "quality of object relating" is predictive of the type of therapeutic strategy that will prove successful. Clients with numerous problems in relating respond best to short-term dynamic therapy in which interventions emphasize help with current problems and maintain the client's experience of being supported by the counselor. Clients with a relatively good capacity for relating respond well to a prudent strategy of interpreting transference, including transference/parent links (Piper, Azim, Joyce, & McCallum, 1991).

When using short-term dynamic therapy, allow a great deal of latitude in the criteria used to select clients, emphasizing evidence for the client's characteristic capacity for interpersonal relating (Binder & Strupp, 1991). Also, employ selection criteria to guide therapeutic strategy rather than to include or exclude clients from this form of treatment.

Treatment Focus:

The reliance on classic psychoanalytic metapsychological theory does not provide clear-cut guidelines for formulating a therapeutic focus. The second generation short-term dynamic therapies are characterized by applications of clinical object relations theory, interpersonal theory, and concepts from cognitive psychology (Horowitz, 1988; Strupp & Binder, 1984; Weiss & Sampson, 1986). These contemporary treatment models view the personality as a hierarchical organization of relatively enduring internal transactions, with specific characteristics attributed to the self and to internal representations of significant others. Specific intentions, fantasies, attitudes, and feelings are associated with a given internal transaction model. Intrapsychic conflict is conceptualized in terms of opposing "wished for" and "dreaded" internal transactions (Horowitz, 1991). However, emphasis is placed on external expression in interpersonal relationships of internal transactions.

A good example of the principles and procedures guiding the formulation of a focus in these contemporary models is the *cyclical maladaptive pattern* (CMP) method associated with Time-Limited Dynamic Psychotherapy (Binder & Strupp, 1991; Strupp & Binder, 1984). Problems are conceptualized in a format that avoids abstract and vague formulations. A client's presenting problems are translated into interpersonal terms and organized into a format called the cyclical maladaptive pattern (Figure 6.2). The CMP is used as a heuristic, helping counselors to generate, recognize, and organize psychotherapeutically relevant information. It is not an absolute or final formulation of the problem; rather, it is used throughout the

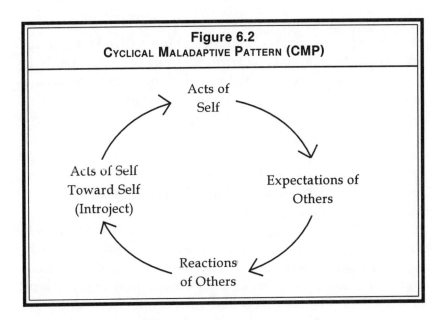

Figure 6.2
CYCLICAL MALADAPTIVE PATTERN (CMP)

course of treatment as a tool for keeping the counselor focused on a salient-conflict theme.

The CMP describes a central or salient pattern of interpersonal roles that includes the role in which the client unconsciously casts himself or herself; the complementary roles in which he or she casts others; and the maladaptive interaction sequences, self-defeating expectations, negative self-appraisals, and unpleasant affects that result. (When enacted with the counselor, this pattern is considered to be transference.) The CMP specifies four categories of information: (a) acts of self, (b) expectations of others' reactions, (c) acts of others towards self, and (d) acts of self toward self (introject).

Acts of self include both private and public actions, such as feelings and behavior, which vary in the degree to which they are accessible to awareness.

Expectations of others' reactions are imagined reactions of others to one's own actions. Such expectations may be conscious, preconscious, or unconscious.

Acts of others toward self are observed acts of others viewed as occurring in specific relation to the acts of self. Often, one unwittingly acts in ways that evoke feared, but anticipated, responses (the principle of complementarity). Under the influence of a maladaptive pattern, one also typically tends to misconstrue the interpersonal meanings of others' actions in a way that confirms one's wished for or feared expectations.

Acts of self towards self refers to how one treats oneself (e.g., self-controlling, self-punishing, or self-nurturing). These actions should be articulated in specific relation to the other elements of the format. How a person treats himself or herself tends to be a reflection of how he or she perceives treatment by others.

The cyclical maladaptive pattern ideally should encompass a pattern of interpersonal transactions that is both historically significant and a source of current difficulty. It is constructed, however, based upon information gathered from observations of the client's behavior elicited in the interview and from reports of current relationships. As information becomes available regarding relationships dating back to childhood, it provides a context in which ambiguous meanings of present events may be understood more easily. However, this historical information is not essential for formulating a cyclical maladaptive pattern.

Because formulation models like the CMP explicitly define the categories for organizing clinical information and require relatively low inference from clinical data, they are amenable to empirical quantification. Methods for reliably identifying a therapeutic focus have been developed for the "core conflict relationship theme" by Lester Luborsky and his research team (Luborsky & Crits-Christoph, 1990) and for the "plan diagnosis" by the Mount Zion research team (Silberschatz, Curtis, & Nathans, 1989). Plans currently are under way to operationalize the CMP. Future work by psychotherapy researchers on methods for precisely formulating dynamic foci may have further applications for the practitioner. It is crucial for dynamic therapists to take advantage of whatever tools become available to aid in identifying and tracking a meaningful therapeutic focus.

Technique:

The fundamental technical strategy of the first generation of short-term dynamic therapies relies on genetic transference interpretations or transference/parent links (Davanloo, 1979; Malan, 1976; Sifneos, 1979). Malan explicitly asserted that the frequency of transference/parent link interpretations was correlated positively with successful outcome.

The second-generation therapies place greater emphasis upon interpretation of here-and-now transference enactments, which are assumed to be effective in a wider range of clients and minimize the risk of transient intellectualized insights.

Interpretations of transference/parent links are used sparingly, and the rule of thumb is to use them *after* the client demonstrates appreciation of the current existence of a maladaptive interpersonal pattern (Luborsky, 1984; Strupp & Binder, 1984). Until recently, the therapeutic efficacy of interpretations, particularly of the transference type, has been accepted on the basis of clinical experience, which has an element of faith attached to it.

Recent advances in research methodology have resulted in various methods of empirically measuring and assessing the impact of psychodynamic techniques. Converging evidence indicates that interpretations of any kind are not predictive of successful outcome (Crits-Christoph, Cooper, & Luborsky, 1988; Henry, Strupp, Schacht, Binder, & Butler, 1992; McCullough et al., 1991; Piper, Debbane, Bienvenu, de Carufel, & Garant, 1986; Silberschatz, Fretter, & Curtis, 1986). These findings for short-term dynamic therapy are consistent with the more general finding that technical adherence to the prescribed interventions of a particular therapeutic model is not predictive of therapeutic outcome (Beckham, 1990; Beutler, 1991). One important reason for this is that using prescribed interventions is only one skill within the poorly understood array of skills that comprise therapeutic competence (Binder, Strupp, & Rock, 1992; Schaffer, 1982).

A technical skill shown to correlate with successful outcome is the counselor's consistent ability to make the content of interventions relevant to the agreed-upon therapeutic focus (Crits-Christoph et al., 1988; Silberschatz et al., 1986). Therefore, a precise initial formulation of the focus will facilitate attempts to offer consistently relevant interventions.

Another technical skill, or set of skills, involves maintaining a positive therapeutic alliance. Empirical evidence indicates that even a very subtle "negative process" can have a profoundly destructive impact upon treatment (Henry, Schacht, & Strupp, 1986; 1990). Binder and Strupp (1991) have warned that the pervasiveness of negative transference/countertransference processes and the difficulties they present to counselors have been underestimated. The adage "anything powerful enough to help can also harm" evidently is true for interpretations, particularly of the transference variety. The implication is clear: interpretations must be used judiciously and their impact monitored closely (Piper et al., 1991; Piper, Joyce, McCallum, & Azim, 1993).

CONCLUSION

Current formulations of short-term dynamic therapies indicate that:

- Greater latitude can be used in selecting clients

- It is essential to formulate and address consistently a precise and meaningful focus

- Technical flexibility is essential

- Interpretations should be used judiciously

Further research may demonstrate that skillfully delivered transference interpretations have a strong beneficial effect on the therapeutic process and its outcome. Such a finding would reinforce the notion that if interpretations are powerful "medicine," then they must be used with skill and care. In the meantime, convincing evidence demonstrates that short-term dynamic therapies produce significant benefits (Crits-Christoph, 1992; Crits-Christoph & Barber, 1991).

REFERENCES

Alexander, R., & French, T. M. (1946). *Psychoanalytic therapy*. New York: Ronald Press.

Balint, M.P., Ornstein, P., & Balint, E. (1972). *Focal psychotherapy: An example of applied psychoanalysis*. London: Tavistock Publications.

Beckham, E. E. (1990). Psychotherapy of depression research at a crossroads: Directions for the 1990s. *Clinical Psychology Review, 10*, 207–228.

Beutler, L. E. (1991). Have all won and must all have prizes? Revisiting Luborsky et al.'s verdict. *Journal of Consulting and Clinical Psychology, 59*, 226–232.

Binder, J. L., Henry, W. P., & Strupp, H. H. (1987). An appraisal of selection criteria for dynamic psychotherapies and implications for setting time limits. *Psychiatry, 50*, 154–166.

Binder, J. L., & Strupp, H. H. (1991). The Vanderbilt approach to time-limited dynamic psychotherapy. In P. Crits-Christoph & J. Barber (Eds.), *Handbook of short-term dynamic psychotherapy* (pp. 137–165). New York: Basic Books.

Binder, J. L., Strupp, H. H., & Rock, D. L. (1992). A proposal for improving the psychoanalytic theory of technique. In J. W. Barron, M. N. Eagle, & D. L. Wolitsky (Eds.), *Interface of psychoanalysis and psychology* (pp. 605–626). Washington, DC: American Psychological Association.

Crits-Christoph, P. (1992). The efficacy of brief dynamic psychotherapy: A meta-analysis. *American Journal of Psychiatry, 149*, 151–158.

Crits-Christoph, P., & Barber, J. (Eds.). (1991). *Handbook of short-term dynamic psychotherapy.* New York: Basic Books.

Crits-Christoph, P., Cooper, A., & Luborsky, L. (1988). The accuracy of therapists' interpretations and the outcome of dynamic psychotherapy. *Journal of Consulting and Clinical Psychology, 56,* 490–495.

Davanloo, H. (Ed.). (1979). *Short-term dynamic psychotherapy.* New York: Jason Aronson.

Ferenczi, S., & Rank, O. (1925). *The development of psychoanalysis.* New York: Nervous and Mental Disease Publishing Company.

Freud, S. (1895). Studies on hysteria. In *Standard edition, 2.* London: Hogarth Press.

Freud, S. (1900). The interpretations of dreams. In *Standard edition, 4–5.* London: Hogarth Press.

Freud, S. (1909). Notes upon a case of obsessional neurosis. In *Standard edition, 10.* London: Hogarth Press.

Freud, S. (1912). The dynamics of transference. In *Standard edition, 12.* London: Hogarth Press.

Freud, S. (1914). Remembering, repeating, and working through (Further recommendations on the technique of psychoanalysis, II). In *Standard edition, 12.* London: Hogarth Press.

Freud, S. (1923). The ego and the id. In *Standard edition, 19.* London: Hogarth Press.

Freud, S. (1926). Inhibitions, symptoms, and anxiety. In *Standard edition, 20.* London: Hogarth Press.

Freud, S. (1937). Construction in analysis. In *Standard edition, 23.* London: Hogarth Press.

Greenson, R. R., & Wexler, M. (1969). The nontransference relationship in the psychoanalytic situation. *International Journal of Psychoanalysis, 50,* 27–38.

Henry, W. P., Schacht, T. E., & Strupp, H. H. (1986). Structural analysis of social behavior: Application to a study of interpersonal process in differential psychotherapeutic outcome. *Journal of Consulting and Clinical Psychology, 54,* 27–31.

Henry, W. P., Schacht, T. E., & Strupp, H. H. (1990). Patient and therapist introject: Interpersonal process and differential psychotherapy outcome. *Journal of Consulting and Clinical Psychology, 58,* 768–774.

Henry, W. P., Strupp, H. H., Schacht, T. E., Binder, J. L., & Butler, S. F. (1992). *The effects of training in time-limited dynamic psychotherapy: Changes in therapeutic outcome.* Unpublished manuscript, Vanderbilt University, Nashville.

Horowitz, M. J. (1976). *Stress response syndromes.* New York: Jason Aronson.

Horowitz, M. J. (1988). *Introduction of psychodynamics.* New York: Basic Books.

Horowitz, M. J. (1991). Introduction. In M. J. Horowitz (Ed.), *Person schemas and maladaptive interpersonal patterns* (pp. 1–10). Chicago: University of Chicago Press.

Jones, E. (1955). *The life and work of Sigmund Freud. (Vol. 2).* New York: Basic Books.

Koss, M. P., & Butcher, J. N. (1986). Research on brief psychotherapy. In S. L. Garfield & A. E. Bergin (Eds.), *Handbook of psychotherapy and behavior change.* (3rd ed.). (pp. 627–670). New York: John Wiley & Sons.

Luborsky, L. (1984). *Principles of psychoanalytic psychotherapy: A manual for supportive/expressive treatment.* New York: Basic Books.

Luborsky, L., & Crits-Christoph, P. (1990). *Understanding transference.* New York: Basic Books.

Luborsky, L., Crits-Christoph, P., Mintz, J., & Auerbach, A. (1988). *Who will benefit from psychotherapy: Predicting therapeutic outcome.* New York: Basic Books.

Malan, D. H. (1963). *A study of brief psychotherapy.* New York: Plenum Press.

Malan, D. H. (1976). *The frontier of brief psychotherapy*. New York: Plenum Press.

Malan, D. H. (1979). *Individual psychotherapy and the science of psychodynamics*. London: Butterworth.

Mann, J. (1973). *Time-limited psychotherapy*. Cambridge, MA: Harvard University Press.

Mann, J., & Goldman, R. (1982). *A casebook in time-limited psychotherapy*. New York: McGraw-Hill.

McCullough, L., et al. (1991). The relationship of patient-therapist interaction to outcome in brief psychotherapy. *Psychotherapy, 28,* 525–533.

Menninger, K. (1958). *Theory of psychoanalytic technique*. New York: Basic Books.

Menninger, K., & Holzman, P. S. (1973). *The theory of psychoanalytic technique*. (2nd ed.). New York: Basic Books.

Piper, W. E., Azim, F. A., Joyce, S. A., McCallum, M., Nixon, G., & Segal, P. S. (1991). Quality of object relations vs. interpersonal functioning as predictors of alliance and outcome. *Journal of Nervous and Mental Disease, 179,* 432–438.

Piper, W. E., Azim, F. A., Joyce, S. A., & McCallum, M. (1991). Transference interpretations, therapeutic alliance, and outcome in short-term individual psychotherapy. *Archives of General Psychiatry, 48,* 948–953.

Piper, W. E., Debbane, E. G., Bienvenu, J., de Carufel, F., & Garant, J. (1986). Relationships between the object focus of therapist interpretations and outcome in short-term individual psychotherapy. *British Journal of Medical Psychology, 59,* 1–11.

Piper, W. E., Joyce, A. S., McCallum, M., & Azim, F. A. (1993). *Concentration and correspondence of transference interpretations in short-term psychotherapy*. Unpublished manuscript, University of Alberta, Edmonton.

Sandler, J., Dare, C., & Holder, A. (1992). *The patient and the analyst: The basis of the psychoanalytic process. (2nd ed.)*. Madison, CT: International University Press.

Schaffer, N. D. (1982). Multidimensional measures of therapist behavior as predictors of outcome. *Psychological Bulletin, 92,* 670–681.

Sifneos, P. (1972). *Short-term psychotherapy and emotional crisis.* Cambridge, MA: Harvard University Press.

Sifneos, P. (1979). *Short-term dynamic psychotherapy: Evaluation and technique.* New York: Plenum Press.

Silberschatz, G., Curtis, J. T., & Nathans, S. (1989). Using the patient's plan to assess progress in psychotherapy. *Psychotherapy, 26,* 40–46.

Silberschatz, G., Fretter, P. B., & Curtis, J. T. (1986). How do interpretations influence the process of psychotherapy? *Journal of Consulting and Clinical Psychology, 54,* 646–652.

Strupp, H. H., & Binder, J. L. (1984). *Psychotherapy in a new key: A guide to time-limited dynamic psychotherapy.* New York: Basic Books.

Weiss, J., & Sampson, H. (1986). *The psychoanalytic process: Theory, clinical observations, and empirical research.* New York: Guilford Press.

Wolberg, L. (1980). *Handbook of short-term psychotherapy.* New York: Grune & Stratton.

7

Current Practice and Procedures of Group Psychotherapy

Martin G. Allen, MD

Dr. Allen is in private practice and is Clinical Professor of Psychiatry, Department of Psychiatry, Georgetown University School of Medicine, Washington, D.C.

KEY POINTS

- Group therapy may appear to be a modern phenomenon; however its origins date back to ancient history. This history is briefly examined.

- Group therapy is effective. It has proven useful in both short- and long-term therapy.

- Group therapy is appropriate for people who have the ability to relate to others; it is particularly helpful for those who have character disorders, problems of sexual or social relatedness, forms of hysterical personality, and depression.

- Some groups of people, such as adolescents, the elderly, and alcoholics, are best treated in homogeneous groups. Other adults are probably best treated in groups that are heterogeneous in age, gender, personal background, and psychopathology.

- Combining group and individual therapy is often helpful. Although it presents certain challenges, combined therapy gives patients the opportunity to work through highly individualized issues first and then bring them back into the group.

- Various issues pertaining to group therapy are discussed: the use of medication with group psychotherapy patients, regression, and therapeutic approaches.

HISTORICAL BACKGROUND

Group therapy is often thought of as a relatively modern phenomenon, one that has been popularized by such current modes of treatment as encounter sessions and 12-step programs. In fact, today's groups have their origins in ancient history.

Ancient Greece:

Aristotle held as his basic premise that humans are social animals. The Greek dramatists used the interaction between individuals and groups to present the tragic drama. Often, this included the presence of a chorus, who observed and commented on the drama and personalities.

Eighteenth and Nineteenth Centuries:

Mesmer, the famous hypnotist, held group hypnotic sessions in the early 1700s. The nineteenth-century French sociologist Gustave Le Bon, who studied the psychology of crowds, believed the conduct of a group to be markedly different from that of the individuals who compose it. Le Bon emphasized two points. First, the group is capable of a higher level of altruistic sacrifice, giving, and compassion than any one individual in the group. Second, a group is also capable of cruel, aggressive ferocity beyond the nature of any one member.

Early Twentieth Century:

The early 1900s was a period of great interest in group therapy (Allen, 1990b; Ettin, 1988; Mullan & Rosenbaum, 1978). The American sociologist Charles Cooley studied the primary "face-to-face" group, which he believed was referable to the basic primary group, the family. Also at that time Joseph Pratt, a Boston internist, undertook what is generally considered today to be the first attempt at group psychotherapy. In 1905, after he organized tuberculosis patients into groups in a classroom-like setting, Pratt reported increasing self-confidence and self-esteem. Alfred Adler first used group methods in Europe, and Jacob Moreno, the famous psychodramatist, worked with groups in the period between 1910 and 1914.

The World War I–World War II Period:

The interwar period saw further use of group therapy (Allen 1990b; Ettin, 1989; Mullan & Rosenbaum, 1978). Edward Lazell established lecture classes for patients at St. Elizabeth's Hospital in Washington, D.C., and several years later, L. Cody Marsh, a minister who later became a psychiatrist, also described his group methods of psychotherapy. In 1921, Freud (although not a practitioner of group therapy) published his seminal work on group psychology (Freud, 1955). Freud, expanding on the initial work of Le Bon, studied the qualities of leadership and the contribution of the individual's ego ideal to leadership. The binding force of the group, Freud believed, was very much related to the leader and the identification of group members with the leader. Freud also traced group behavior back to the family. In 1935, Wender reported group therapy with borderline patients using psychoanalytic concepts; Harry Stack Sullivan began his work with groups of inpatients at St. Elizabeth's Hospital; and Kurt Lewin undertook his investigations into group process, the impact of the leader upon the structure and function of a group, and the climate of the group in its relationship to productivity. Lewin stated that it is usually easier to change individuals in a group than to change any one of them separately. This generalization, derived from studies of group function, is a basic tenet of group psychotherapy.

Post–World War II:

Some psychoanalysts, notably Trigant Burrow, Lewis

Wender, and Alexander Wolf, became interested in "group psychoanalysis" and started working with individuals in a group setting. Techniques also evolved as work on group methods continued both in the United States and in England. In 1946, the National Education Association assigned research observers to discussion groups for the purpose of reporting the interactions and behavioral sequences of each meeting. Soon participants found that the interactional observations were helping them understand their own behavior and the development of groups. One year later, the National Education Association organized workshops in Bethel, Maine, to study group process and group behavior, the individual's role in the group, and how personal and professional skills might be acquired through group sessions. At the same time, W. R. Bion was developing theories of group dynamics and group therapy at the Tavistock Hospital in England. Bion's "Basic Assumption" groups — which he defined as those of pairing, dependency, and fight/flight — have helped group therapists understand group patterns that detract from the "work" (task) of group psychotherapy. This Tavistock model of group interaction focuses on leadership, the individual's relation to the leader, and to authority in general. The emphasis is on the group as a whole, rather than on individuals in the group (Rioch, 1970).

The Past 25 Years:

During the 1960s, as encounter, sensitivity, and marathon groups were developing and being popularized, many clients were working in more standard forms of group therapy, where they dealt with conflicts, interpersonal relations, and transference distortions. Group therapy is now used with those who are taking medications as well as those who are not, and it may be combined with individual therapy under certain conditions. Group therapy is also widely useful for both inpatients and outpatients.

As with other therapeutic approaches in counseling, an

eclectic approach has evolved over the years. Group therapy is used increasingly for specific populations (children, adolescents, and the elderly) and for patients with specific problems (eating disorders, substance abuse disorders, or victims of violence). Also, as briefer therapies become more important in meeting reimbursement guidelines of payers such as health maintenance organizations (HMOs), the use of time-limited group therapy is increasing (Allen, 1990a).

THE EFFICACY OF GROUP PSYCHOTHERAPY

Group psychotherapy works. Many outcome studies have demonstrated both short-term and long-term changes in clients (Bloch & Crouch, 1985; Corsini & Rosenberg, 1955; Kelman, 1963; Mann, 1966; Opalic, 1989; Pattison, 1967; Yalom, 1985; Yalom et al., 1967), and those of us who regularly work with group therapy see its benefits for clients with both acute and long-term problems.

Kelman (1963) outlined how group therapy affects the induction of therapeutic change with clients through the processes of compliance, identification, and/or internalization. Analyzing the roles of therapist, patient, and group in the induction of therapeutic change, he discussed the concept of corrective emotional experience and its relevance to therapeutic change, both in individual and group therapy. Of course, the basic importance of commitment, motivation to continue in therapy, and engagement in the therapeutic work is essential for meaningful change to occur.

Yalom (1985) identified several factors necessary to effect therapeutic change in group therapy. They include installation of hope, universality, imparting of information, altruism, the corrective recapitulation of the primary family group, development of socializing techniques, imitative behavior, interpersonal learning, group cohesiveness, catharsis, and existential factors. Of these, Yalom found group cohesiveness to be the most important factor in bringing about therapeutic change. As with all forms of therapy, some combination of intellectual and experiential insight should occur and lead to both internal and external growth, development, and symptom relief.

ADMINISTRATION AND PROCEDURE

Much has been written about factors such as the length of group therapy, the location, the membership composition, and the periods of preparation. Authors have advocated a wide range of procedures. I will summarize my procedure and administration, recognizing that conducting group therapy has no one "right" method. Many experienced and thoughtful group therapists practice in a variety of ways.

In group therapy—as with all forms of therapy—a basic trust and therapeutic alliance in the context of ongoing therapeutic work is essential. It involves the development and maintenance of a safe "holding" environment in which participants can be free to express thoughts, feelings, and fantasies. The group therapist must function not only to facilitate interaction among the group members but also to foster a sense of basic trust in an atmosphere of therapeutic work. As such, the group therapist may sometimes function as a referee, transference object, facilitator of interpersonal interaction, and interpreter of verbal or nonverbal behavior; at other times, he or she serves as a supportive, understanding listener. The group therapist usually is responsible for deciding who may enter the group and for dealing with issues of termination and with members who are disruptive to the group.

I prepare patients for group therapy in a variety of ways. I ask them if they have previously participated in any experiential or therapy groups and what that experience was like. I also inquire as to their experience in other groups such as vocational, educational, friendship, and social groups. I pay particular attention to behavior in groups compared with behavior in dyadic or intimate situations. Many patients find that their emotions, feelings of competitiveness, and reactions to authority intensify in group situations. Others comment that they feel comfortable in one-on-one situations but are often anxious, uncomfortable, silent, or overwhelmed in group situations. If a patient reveals that he or she feels uncomfortable with the opposite sex, I often mention that mixed group therapy affords the opportunity to understand how and why relating differs between the sexes and to see what areas of human experience are shared and what areas have differences. By mentioning group therapy in the initial consultation, the patient starts thinking about that treatment method.

I specifically select patients for group (or combined) therapy when I hear of problems in relating to other people, in feeling socially isolated, in verbalizing emotions and feelings (especially to others), in assertiveness and self-esteem, and of feeling different, inferior, or intimidated by others. Patients who have a poor observing ego are also appropriate. They all can gain from hearing others' revelations about themselves or expressing feelings to which they can relate. These patients also may have valuable observations and insights toward others; when they contribute to the group, it can be pointed out that their observation was helpful, perceptive, and might apply to themselves as well, seeing in others what we are unable to see in ourselves and expressing for others what we are unable to express for ourselves.

When patients are resistant or anxious about revealing themselves in a group, I say, "I'll be there with you," or "I realize this might be difficult for you, but I think ultimately it will be helpful." By mentioning group therapy early in the therapeutic process, it is not so surprising when the subject is raised suddenly later during therapy. Group therapy can be mentioned several times, so the patient can get used to the idea without feeling rejected or forced into a group. Perhaps the most important factor in dealing with resistance or anxiety about group therapy is the attitude of the therapist recommending it. If the therapist is comfortable and believes in group therapy in general and for the patient in particular (and is not recommending group therapy out of convenience or anger at the patient), that attitude will be conveyed to the patient. Also, if group therapy is presented as a natural evolution of development and progress in therapy itself, the patient can perceive group therapy as a sign of advancement and progress.

I do not have a fixed period of time for preparing patients. Some are referred for group therapy, whereas others refer themselves, having had a beneficial experience in the past. The latter are often able to join a group after one or two initial evaluation sessions. Other patients may enter treatment in a crisis situation, such as divorce, and they may not be ready or able to join a group for some time. In such cases, I often mention the possibility of group therapy "in the future" if it seems possible and appropriate. Some therapists have spoken about the importance of a lengthy evaluation and developing a treatment relationship prior to entering group therapy to ensure a strong patient-therapist alliance, whereas others have advocated the group itself as the focus of treatment. These opposing views are based on whether membership in the group stems from a relationship to the group therapist or an emotional attachment to the group as a whole.

When discussing group therapy with prospective clients, I emphasize the importance of being present and expressing thoughts and feelings as openly as possible. I ask each prospective member to make a commitment to the group for at least 5 months, to underline the seriousness of the commitment, to give the patient a chance to meet the group members and get involved in the group, and to minimize the potential disruptiveness of a "revolving door" situation in which membership changes frequently.

My group therapy sessions last 1–1½ hours; most groups have a duration of 1–2 hours. I bill patients at the end of the month and ask to be paid before the 15th of the following month. I charge for all sessions in which the group meets, even if a patient is absent from the group, because I am providing ("selling") a total ongoing therapeutic process. Also, every participant is expected to attend the group and has a membership "place" in the group. If a patient is late or absent for any reason, that behavior needs to be questioned (preferably in the group) as an expression of resistance or acting out. In addition, I announce my vacations well in advance, in case patients would like to plan their vacations for the same time.

Once a year, I conduct an extended session with the group to increase openness, intimacy, and cohesiveness and to decrease rigid defenses (Allen, 1990c). The extended session, in the context of ongoing group psychotherapy, often results in breakthroughs and insights that may not have been achieved otherwise or may have taken much longer to achieve. Some therapists schedule several extended sessions in a year.

Absences, side effects of medications, fees, and the like are discussed in the group setting, if possible. In fact, everything should be brought into group therapy. In keeping with that philosophy, I do not forbid discussions or contact between group members outside of group sessions, because such a restriction is unnatural, cannot be enforced, and deprives the therapy of potentially useful material. The basic recommendation remains: All thoughts, feelings, fantasies, and behaviors should be discussed in the therapy group, including any instances of contact outside group meetings.

Some group therapists insist on charging the same fee to all patients; however, I recognize that a patient may be subject to special circumstances (e.g., he or she has lost a job, is a student without income, or has been terminated by his or her insurance company), in which case he or she may pay a reduced fee. A difference in rates among patients may promote feelings of jealousy or rivalry, with a variety of accompanying fantasies; these can and should be discussed and explored in the group setting.

SELECTING PATIENTS FOR A GROUP

Criteria for group therapy are based on an ability to relate to others (Grunebaum & Kates, 1977). That specifically implies an ability to relate to and react to others and a reasonable degree of appropriate affect and interpersonal awareness.

Some groups, such as adolescents, the elderly, and alcoholics, are best treated in homogeneous groups. Adults are probably best treated in groups that are heterogeneous in age, gender, personal background, and psychopathology.

Conditions for which group therapy is particularly appropriate include character disorders, problems of sexual or social relatedness, forms of hysterical personality (especially conflicts "acted out" in the group setting), and depression, if the person is verbal.

Patients who generally are less suitable or not suitable for group therapy include those who are unable to relate to others because of a strong affectual block, as with catatonia; the grossly agitated or psychotic who are hallucinating or delusional; retarded people who are depressed, nonverbal, and manifest psychomotor retardation; patients actively abusing alcohol or hallucinogenic drugs, which impairs their ability to attend regularly and relate to others; persons with organic mental disease who are disoriented; and persons of inadequate intelligence. In addition, sociopathic patients are usually poor risks for interactional group therapy: often they are destructive in the group and unable to receive and process feedback from other patients.

CASE STUDY I

A woman in her 20s was referred for group psychotherapy by her individual therapist after forming a highly sexualized, delusional transference. The client felt that her therapist was seducing her each time he blinked his eyes, crossed his legs, or shifted position in his chair. She had frequent romantic and sexual fantasies. She bought a dog, named it after her therapist, and slept with it each night. Although the therapist attempted to bring reality into the situation and reduce the transference, it was not diminished in its intensity or erotic quality. A referral to group therapy was made in the hope of diluting the transference. The client did enter group therapy, but the delusional, erotic transference persisted. Therefore, individual therapy was terminated, and the client was able to work in group therapy without developing the intense, sexualized transference toward the group therapist or any group member.

CASE STUDY II

A man was continually provocative, angry, and insulting to cover internal depression and pain. He had recurrent depression with strong borderline personality features manifested by paranoid thoughts, lability, and great anger. He avoided intimacy and pain by provoking and insulting everyone, both at work and in personal relationships. He had managed to alienate and reject everyone around him. As a result, the therapist had great ambivalence about his joining the group and wondered whether he would be destructive to the therapeutic process. When he joined the group, he was unable to insult and alienate "all the people all of the time." Consequently, one or two people in the group consistently were able to empathize with him, feel his underlying pain, and tell him that they understood how he was feeling. Gradually, he was able to trust both the therapist and the group, listen to others more attentively, and realize the effect he was having on others.

COMBINING GROUP AND INDIVIDUAL THERAPY

Group and individual psychotherapy can be combined in a variety of ways (Bloch & Crouch, 1985; Ormont, 1981; Rutan & Alson, 1982; Yalom, 1985). One option, individual therapy with one therapist and group therapy with another, demands communication (and trust) between the individual and therapist. Such treatment is especially useful for patients who have massive separation anxiety and for whom therapeutic contact with at least one therapist is supportively essential. Although such therapy can promote splitting, such a defensive "primitive" mechanism may be observed, pointed out, and understood in the living situation. It can be very useful for a patient to express anger at one therapist, who may represent a parent, and receive support, love, and comfort from the other. Combined therapy also gives patients the opportunity to work through highly individual issues first and then bring them into the group. Some patients begin with individual therapy and are able to gradually add (or substitute) group therapy for individual sessions as they move from the dyadic relationship of individual therapy to the more complex matrix of interpersonal relationships symbolic of entering the world beyond the mother-child dyad. With combined therapy, patients often learn from one another in a group, identify with others' issues, and grow and learn as they see others doing the same. They can then bring issues from the group into individual sessions, and conversely, bring issues from individual sessions into group therapy, where they can receive varied feedback.

In addition, patients who are in a "crisis," as occurs following divorce, job loss, or trauma, often need additional time in therapy. They are more likely to benefit from a group that meets only once a week, rather than one that meets two or three times a week. In any case, a patient may have more conflicted, secretive, "shame-filled" issues that they feel more able to work on individually, rather than expressing them in a group. Still, some patients have more intense transferential conflicts in the individual therapy situation and may feel more able to broach highly charged, conflicted issues in the group setting, where they feel support from other group members.

Sometimes when combined therapy is used with some but not all patients in a group, feelings of jealousy and rivalry may ensue. Such emotions, which are based on the reality of the differences, can often be used in fruitful exploration of differences in original family relationships. Issues such as whether a patient feels favored or rejected, understood or not understood, are affectually charged ones that should be explored and worked through in combined therapy. In addition, "difficult" patients who are often highly resistive and are silent or angry can often profit from combined therapy. They may have reached an impasse in individual therapy, so the therapist can receive "help" in understanding, observing, and working with them in the group. In particular, patients who are not psychologically minded and have little observing ego are often able to profit from combined therapy. Even though they may be perceived as boring or frustrating in individual therapy, with the living experience of group therapy and the observations and feedback from group members, they may develop more of an observing ego as they learn from both the therapist and other participants to observe, understand, and work through personal conflicts.

Another issue that comes up in combined therapy is confidentiality and the importance of having every subject open to discussion in both individual and group therapy. With patients in combined therapy, it is essential that they understand that every issue needs to be addressed in both therapies. When the group and individual therapists are not the same person, patients need to understand that regular and open communication between both therapists will take place. Sometimes patients will be reluctant to bring up information individually if they know it will be discussed in the group, and they may ask me not to reveal such information to the group. Although I will not agree to their request specifically, I do say I will wait for the time when they are able to bring it up in group and I will "look forward" to that time. Therefore, while not agreeing to withhold personal or guilt-laden information from the group for an indefinite time, I will support, encourage, and emphasize the importance and necessity of all issues being brought into the group on the patient's initiative. In fact, no conflicts, behaviors, fantasies, or experiences should be withheld from the group, if openness, mutual trust, and group cohesiveness are to be maintained and expanded.

In addition, patients are often very different in individual and group therapy, and both the therapist and client may be quite surprised by that difference, which needs to be acknowledged, observed, understood, and worked through. Eventually it may be traced to the contrast between how a person feels in the one-to-one dyadic mother-child relationship versus the larger family group, or how one behaves in the small intimate family when compared with actions in the external world. As the therapeutic process continues, some integration between such discrepancies may take place. Combined therapy enables the therapist to experience and observe a client interacting with others — not just hear reports about such interactions.

In combined therapy, an individual therapist may have a blind spot and not be observing or aware of certain verbal or nonverbal behaviors. In the group setting, with the observation and feedback of many members, such difficulties or countertransference blocks are much less likely. Also, resistances and denials that might be avoided or rationalized in individual therapy may often be more openly confronted and realized in the group setting. Then they can be brought back into the individual sessions for further therapeutic work.

Combining individual and group therapy with a different therapist in each setting is sometimes helpful. For example, if a patient has developed a psychotic transference, group therapy with a different therapist may help resolve that situation. For a fragile, borderline patient or a dependent patient with a great deal of separation anxiety, having a separate group therapist (who takes vacations at a different time) is helpful in maintaining continuity of care. Conversely, if a patient has become too dependent or too symbiotically fused with a therapist, adding group therapy (especially with a different therapist) may help to separate gradually from the first therapist. Also, if a therapist has significant unresolvable countertransference issues or is feeling especially hostile toward, frustrated with, or sexually attracted to a patient, adding group therapy (especially with a different group therapist) can help the overall therapeutic work. Even after consultation or supervision, a sense of bewilderment, confusion, or lack of understanding or empathy with a patient (thereby affecting the overall therapeutic alliance) may be dealt with by adding group therapy with another therapist.

Group and individual therapy with the same therapist is especially appropriate for patients who are very anxious in groups but who have gradually developed a sense of trust and alliance with their therapist. For such patients, entering group therapy with the trusted therapist gives some sense of reassurance. Also, with some borderline patients, splitting may be so disruptive that the same therapist might be indicated for both group and individual therapy. However, the patient may split among the group members, thereby presenting the group with the pathologic activity. Individual therapy sessions in addition to group therapy may also be appropriate for patients with special crises in their lives — job loss, divorce, or exacerbations in their emotional states, such as emerging suicidal thoughts in the setting of depression.

PSYCHOANALYTIC GROUP PSYCHOTHERAPY

Years ago, psychoanalysts who started practicing group psychotherapy would often focus on one client for a prolonged period of time, with the analyst or group making interpretations. Such "psychoanalysis in groups" is less common today (Locke, 1961; Wolf & Schwartz, 1962; Wong, 1983). Currently, a psychoanalytic approach to group therapy is one in which attention is paid to fantasies, dreams, internal conflicts, and other aspects of conscious and unconscious mental activity (Ezriel, 1952, 1980; Wong, 1983). Psychoanalytic group therapy assumes that a structural change will take place over time, with the resolution of infantile conflicts and the working through of highly cathectic issues. It is a less supportive, more intensive working-through, growth, therapeutic process.

In psychoanalytic group therapy, the patients are most often verbal, are more "healthy," and have good access to their experiencing and observing egos. Such patients bring into the group — for all to observe and experience — the internal objects, representations, fantasies, drives, and drive derivatives in an ever-changing mosaic. A complex interactional matrix of multiple transferences and projections of both real and fantasied objects from both childhood and later life develops. All are interwoven in a rich, multicolored, multidimensional tapestry.

In group therapy, multiple transferences and projections are more likely, and instead of being a problem or deficit to therapy and insight, they can be viewed as enriching, facilitating enhancements to the therapeutic process. Mechanisms such as splitting, projective identification, and denial are more likely to be recognized by the individual and by other group members (Wong, 1983).

The group therapist provides a relatively safe environment, both psychologically and physically containing, to facilitate interaction and expression, to provide a blank screen for transference development, and to recognize that more intense and more relevant transferences may develop toward other group members. In addition, observations and interpretations toward both individuals (about interpersonal interactions) and the group as a whole can be made either by the leader or by other group members. Such interpretations and observations are hopefully made when their timing and nature is therapeutically useful in achieving insight and mutative change. The overall goal is to be conscious of one's needs and desires (especially narcissistic and exhibitionistic needs that are more likely with the group as an audience) and to focus on the group "task" of therapy (Rioch, 1970). Psychoanalytic group therapy provides symptom relief, personal growth, psychological insight, mutative change, structural change, and awareness of unconscious conflicts and their childhood origins.

OTHER GROUP THERAPY APPROACHES

Like individual therapy, other group therapy approaches can be classified as interpersonal, existential, supportive, cognitive, or confrontive (Kelman, 1963; Mullan & Rosenbaum,

1978; Rothke, 1986; Yalom, 1980, 1985; Whitaker, 1987). In any case, the therapeutic goals may need to be modified from the more ambitious, extensive, long-term goals of psychoanalytic group therapy. Such goals may focus more on the beginnings of interpersonal sharing, mutual support, or symptom relief. In addition, some groups might focus on support for abstinence from alcohol, whereas others work on understanding and support for patients who have been sexually abused. In all cases, the degree to which a group can develop cohesiveness, trust, mutually shared values, and understanding determines how completely the therapeutic goals can be achieved. Group therapy may be extremely useful in a supportive or symptom-reducing manner without necessarily enhancing personal growth and structural change. But if there is great disparity, distrust, and separateness in a group—and as a result the different needs and goals are not met—it will lead to fragmentation and dissolution of the therapeutic experience.

USE OF MEDICATIONS WITH GROUP PSYCHOTHERAPY PATIENTS

As with all patients, medications may be specifically indicated for physiologic, cognitive, or affective signs and symptoms. When this occurs, the group therapist has a clear responsibility to refer the patient to an expert in the field.

Salvendy and Joffe (1991) have presented a comprehensive discussion of this subject with excellent clinical examples. The patient or other group members may view the use of pharmacology in a positive or negative way. Also, as we know, side effects may complicate treatment with medications. In such cases, side effects need to be discussed beforehand and whenever they occur. In group therapy, it is important to raise these subjects in the group, not separate from the overall group process. Other patients in the group may have experienced side effects and may have been helped (or not helped) by medication. In any case, the use of medications can be a point of sharing between clients that is often beneficial. The patient will feel less alone and less anxious in dealing with a medication and its side effects when fellow patients can compare and discuss their experiences with the same medication.

CASE STUDY III

A very bright female graduate student was depressed and borderline, with bulimia, self-destructive relationships with both men and women, and compulsive stealing. She had been hospitalized and received medication during the hospitalization, but she adamantly refused medication subsequently, even though she had periods of near-psychosis and suicidal thoughts. Over the course of several years, she connected well with her therapy group — expressed feelings about herself, a symbiotic relationship with her mother, and abandonment by her father — and established an increasing sense of trust and attachment to members of the group. However, she still refused medication during crises, even when recommended by her therapist. During one session, other group members were discussing the subject of medications. She turned to the therapist and said, "Tell me that I don't need medications, that they would not be helpful." The therapist responded by saying he could not tell her that, because he did not believe it. After hearing how medications had helped other clients in the group, she reluctantly agreed to a trial of antidepressants. Within 2 weeks, she reported feeling better. In the following weeks, she related how her whole life was changing, that she was increasingly optimistic, and that daily suicidal thoughts had disappeared. Clearly, several factors helped change her mind about medications: her sense of trust in the therapist and the group; seeing improvement in other group members when medications were added; and acknowledging unresolved painful memories, symptoms, and feelings.

REGRESSION IN GROUP THERAPY

The potential for regression in group therapy always needs to be evaluated in terms of its tendency to facilitate ego strength and therapeutic change or, conversely, ego fragmentation and clinical deterioration. Such an evaluation needs to be performed both before and during any form of therapy, including group therapy.

Frequently, we find that a patient's potential for regression is different in group therapy than in individual therapy. In individual therapy, patients may fragment and regress when transference develops (transference "psychosis") in the closeness of the dyadic relationship. In such cases, patients feel especially anxious and find the intimacy too threatening or fragmenting. This may be attributed to a special erotic attachment or perhaps a history of significant physical, sexual, or emotional abuse. For such patients, the therapy group can provide a haven—a sanctuary in which they find more support, understanding, and reality validation.

Conversely, some patients are more likely to regress in group therapy when the group represents the unconscious, the primitive libidinal state, the primitive maternal object, or even the intrauterine existence. Others may regress and fragment because of the presence of one particular group member to whom they have an especially strong (often transference-based) reaction that they are unable to work through. For these patients, individual therapy often provides a haven where they feel nurtured, supported, and more intact.

In either case, combined therapy should be considered a way of providing both a "haven" and an opportunity to deal with the intensity of a regressive experience. For some patients, the intensity and fragmentation proves too great; consequently, a reformulation of the therapeutic plan must be instituted.

Obviously, an assessment of the regressive potential is related to evaluation of diagnosis and ego boundaries. In general, patients who have hysterical or borderline characteristics and who are more likely to be both emotional and active in the group process are also more likely to fragment and regress in that setting. Conversely, obsessional character types, who are usually more intellectualized and controlled, may benefit.

SUMMARY

Patients should be selected for groups based on the composition of the group and the patient's suitability for profiting from a group therapy experience. Therapist styles may differ, as they do in individual therapy, but providing an atmosphere in which a patient may profit from the feedback and interpretations of both the therapist and group members is most often a growth-enhancing experience. Group therapy may be combined with individual therapy. Combined group and individual therapy may enhance the clinical improvement and therapeutic experience for the patient. In recent years, time-limited groups have been developed for specific populations (college students, divorced persons, patients with posttraumatic disorders) or for specific administrative requirements such as those presented by HMOs. In addition, specific populations such as children, adolescents, the elderly, substance abusers, and same-sex groups may enhance the group experiences of members who can focus on specific problems or experiences.

REFERENCES

Allen, M. G. (Ed.). (1990a). Group psychotherapy. *Psychiatric Annals, 20.*

Allen, M. G. (1990b). Group psychotherapy — past, present and future. *Psychiatric Annals, 20,* 358–361.

Allen, M. G. (1990c). Using extended sessions in ongoing group therapy. *Psychiatric Annals, 20,* 368–371.

Bloch, S., & Crouch, E. (1985). *Therapeutic factors in group psychotherapy.* New York: Oxford University Press.

Corsini, R. J., & Rosenberg, B. (1955). Mechanisms of group psychotherapy processes and dynamics. *Journal of Abnormal and Social Psychology, 51,* 406–411.

Ettin, J. (1989). "Come on Jack, tell us about yourself": The growth spurt of group psychotherapy. *International Journal of Group Psychotherapy, 39,* 35–57.

Ettin, M. (1988). "By the crowd they have been broken, by the crowd they shall be healed": The advent of group psychotherapy. *International Journal of Group Psychotherapy, 38,* 139–167.

Ezriel, H. (1952). Notes on psychoanalytic group therapy. *Psychiatry, 15,* 119–126.

Ezriel, H. (1980). A psychoanalytic approach to group treatment. In S. Scheidlinger (Ed.), *Psychoanalytic group dynamics* (pp.109-146). New York: New York University Press.

Freud, S. (1955). Group psychology and the analysis of the ego. In *Standard edition of the complete works of Sigmund Freud, Vol. 18* (pp. 67-143). London: Hogarth Press.

Grunebaum, H., & Kates, W. (1977). Whom to refer for group psychotherapy. *American Journal of Psychiatry, 134,* 130–133.

Kelman, H. C. (1963). The role of the group in the induction of therapeutic change. *International Journal of Group Psychotherapy, 13,* 399–432.

Locke, N. (1961). *Group psychoanalysis: Theory and technique.* New York: New York University Press.

Mann, J. (1966). Evaluation of group therapy. In J. L. Moreno (Ed.), *International handbook of group psychotherapy* (pp.129-148). New York: Philosophical Library.

Mullan, H., & Rosenbaum, M. (1978). *Group psychotherapy, theory and practice* (2nd ed.). New York: The Free Press.

Opalic, P. (1989). Existential and psychopathological evaluation of group psychotherapy of neurotic and psychotic patients. *International Journal of Group Psychotherapy, 39,* 389–422.

Ormont, L. (1981). Principles and practice of conjoint psychoanalytic treatment. *American Journal of Psychiatry, 138*, 69–78.

Pattison, E. M. (1967). Evaluation studies of group psychotherapy. *International Journal of Psychiatry, 4*, 333–358.

Rioch, M. (1970). The work of Wilfred Bion on groups. *Psychiatry, 33*, 56–66.

Rothke, S. (1986). The role of interpersonal feedback in group psychotherapy. *International Journal of Group Psychotherapy, 36*, 225–239.

Rutan, J. S., & Alson, A. (1982). Group therapy, individual therapy, or both. *International Journal of Group Psychotherapy, 32*, 267–282.

Salvendy, J., & Joffe, R. (1991). Antidepressants in group psychotherapy. *International Journal of Group Psychotherapy, 41*, 465–480.

Whitaker, D. S. (1987). Some connections between a group analytic and a group focal conflict perspective. *International Journal of Group Psychotherapy, 37*, 201–217.

Wolf, A., & Schwartz, E. (1962). *Psychoanalysis in groups.* New York: Grune & Stratton.

Wong, N. (1983). Fundamental psychoanalytic concepts: Past and present understanding of their applicability to group psychotherapy. *International Journal of Group Psychotherapy, 33*, 171–191.

Yalom, I. D. (1980). *Existential psychotherapy.* New York: Basic Books.

Yalom, I. D. (1985). *The theory and practice of group psychotherapy.* New York: Basic Books.

Yalom, I. D., et al. (1967). Prediction of improvements in group therapy. *Archives of General Psychiatry, 17*, 159–168.

8

Avoiding Conflict in Group Therapy: Ethical and Legal Issues in Group Training and Practice

Jim Gumaer, EdD, and Alan Forrest, EdD

Drs. Gumaer and Forrest are Professors of Counselor Education at Radford University, Radford, VA, and licensed professional counselors in private practice.

KEY POINTS

- Training standards and ethical guidelines for group therapists are generally inconsistent and vague, as are group therapy training practices.

- Group therapy increases the likelihood of ethical dilemmas due to intensified intrapsychic, intragroup, and intergroup interactions.

- A model focusing on initiation issues, ongoing counseling issues, dangerousness and legal liability, and group termination issues can help group therapists avoid ethical and legal conflicts.

- Group therapists must conduct a vigorous screening process and continue to address issues such as voluntary versus involuntary participation, withdrawal, and confidentiality throughout the duration of the group.

- It is imperative for group therapists to be knowledgeable regarding statutes and local agency procedures for determining when a breach of confidentiality is warranted so as to avoid liability.

- Group therapists should inform patients of a group's time frame and thoroughly document treatment, as it is not always possible to recognize potential ethical problems and the risk of malpractice is not always apparent.

INTRODUCTION

Although emphasis on consumer protection and ethical counseling practice in the helping professions has increased throughout the past decade, little attention has been devoted to ethics
in group therapy or the legal implications of unethical group
therapy practice. A computer search of the counseling and
therapy literature revealed fewer than twenty published sources related to these topics. The paucity of literature is revealing
and raises a serious question: Why is so little information on
this topic available? In a survey of seven states, Herlihy,
Healy, Cook, and Hudson (1987) found that 191 ethical complaints had been filed since licensing was enacted by each
state. None of the complaints could be attributed directly to
the practice of group therapy. One significant conclusion cited
by the authors was that licensing board members were concerned with the ethical practices of licensees.

In order for counselors to practice ethically, we believe
three steps must be taken by mental health professionals: (a)
obtain knowledge of the ethical codes for their respective
professions, (b) pursue critical thinking regarding ethical situations in groups and arrive at thoughtful decisions based on
professional standards of practice, and (c) demonstrate group
ethics through supervised clinical competency.

ETHICAL AND LEGAL ISSUES IN TRAINING

Corey and Corey (1992) recommended familiarity with the
following sources: *Professional Standards for the Training of
Group Workers* (Association for Specialists in Group Work
[ASGW], 1990); *Guidelines for the Training of Group Psychotherapists* (American Group Psychotherapy Association, 1978);
Ethical Standards (American Association of Counseling and
Development, 1988); *Ethical Principles of Psychologists* (American Psychological Association [APA], 1989); *Ethical Guidelines
for Group Counselors* (ASGW, 1989); and "Some Perspectives on

the Legal Liability of Group Counseling in Private Practice" (Paradise & Kirby, 1990).

However, knowledge alone does not lead to ethical practice. Pope, Tobachnick, and Keith-Spiegel (1987) found widely disparate views among APA members concerning what behaviors they believed to be unethical. Similarly, Robinson and Gross (1989) found that having taken a course in ethics did not improve a counselor's ability to recognize whether situations involved a violation of professional standards. These authors also reported that group therapists did not make more ethical decisions with increased training. A course in ethics merely suggested appropriate ethical behavior (Robinson & Gross, 1989). Other studies (Gumaer & Duncan, 1982; Gumaer & Scott, 1986) substantiated that no significant differences exist among the levels of education obtained and the ability to identify ethical or unethical behavior. Therefore, it appears that knowledge of professional standards by itself is necessary, although not sufficient, to produce ethical behavior by therapists in group practice.

After obtaining a rudimentary knowledge of ethical practice, group therapists must be able to apply this knowledge to hypothetical case situations involving ethical and unethical behavior. A study using clinical vignettes that required ethical decision making by counselors was conducted by Tymchuk and colleagues (1982). The results indicated that therapists were not consistent with one another in the ethical decision-making process. Similar situations could be constructed to professional guidelines that are specifically designed to examine thoughtfully ethical and legal issues in the facilitation of group therapy (Corey, Corey, & Callanan, 1993; Gumaer & Scott, 1985) or in consultation with experts (Gumaer, 1982).

Carroll (1985), Shapiro and Shapiro (1985), and Conyne, Dye, Gill, Leddick, Morran, and Ward (1985) all agreed that inadequate training of group therapists is a significant critical issue in group therapy. Yalom (1985) noted that without continual vigilance to training, group therapy could become a second-rate treatment modality. There is no substitute for training competent, ethical counselors for supervised clinical group therapy. To be competent, therapists must be able to demonstrate their knowledge and thinking in practice. In other words, they must behave ethically with clients while supervised in a group therapy practicum and internship before practicing alone. To do otherwise is to allow ill-trained therapists to practice on an unsuspecting and uneducated public.

Functioning within a professional knowledge base of expected ethical behavior provides a solid starting point. More important, this will lead to informed, thoughtful judgments for ethical decision making and behavior. To achieve these latter two postures, counselors require supervised experience in leading groups before completing programs of study and continued supervision for several years after beginning practice. Unfortunately, in counselor training programs, a great disparity exists in course requirements and offerings, especially as they relate to ethics and legal issues in relation to group therapy.

DEFINING GROUP COUNSELING/THERAPY AND TRAINING STANDARDS

Growth-centered group counseling has been defined as helping clients maximize personal resources to cope more effectively with their daily lives; problem-centered group counseling has been defined as helping clients mediate personal conflicts that will impede healthy development of the individual if left unresolved (Gumaer, 1984). The ASGW (1990) made similar differentiations by defining group counseling as seeking "to help group participants to resolve the usual, yet often difficult, problems of living through interpersonal support and problem-solving. . . . Non-severe career, education, personal, social, and developmental concerns are frequently addressed" (pp. 9–10). Group psychotherapy is then defined as seeking "to help individual group members to remediate their in-depth psychological problems" (p. 10).

Although the distinctions between the two types of group therapies suggest extensive differences in minimum standards of training, the only differences observed are in recommended knowledge competency, where the ASGW suggested for group counseling ". . .at least one course beyond the generalist is necessary" (p. 12). For group therapy, "Course work should be taken in the areas of group psychotherapy, abnormal psychology, psychopathology, and diagnostic assessment. . . ." (pp. 12-13). The ASGW standards do not differentiate minimum skills training through supervised practice for the two types of groups. For both types, the standard states a minimum of 10 hours of observation and participation in a group (20 hours is recommended) and a minimum of 45 clock hours leading or co-leading a group supervised by a qualified therapist (60 hours is recommended).

On a different level, the American Group Psychotherapy Association (AGPA) has a training program that provides a certificate on successful completion. The minimum program requirements are 90 hours of didactic instruction in group therapy, 60 hours in leading groups, 25 hours of qualified supervision while leading groups, and 60 hours of participating as a group member (Corey, 1990).

The American Psychological Association (APA, 1981) has also provided a set of ethical principles and standards of clinical practice to assist counselors in their ethical decision making. Although this document contains ten ethical principles that address areas such as a therapist's responsibility to maintain high standards of practice, client confidentiality, professional relationships, assessment techniques, and even the care and use of animals in research, there are no specifically mentioned guidelines that examine the ethical principles of a counselor engaged in group therapy. In a more recent report (APA, 1992), there is no mention of guidelines for counselors in the practice of group psychotherapy. Also, in a national survey of members of the APA that identified ethically troubling incidents, none addressed the ethical dilemmas encountered in group therapy (Pope & Vetter, 1992).

Perhaps it is believed that training in the ethics of group therapy for counselors is obtained through clinical experience as well as an understanding and use of general standards of psychological practice as established by the APA. Ethical decision making and training are reportedly provided in 94% of graduate-level training programs; however, the content and structure of such training differ significantly (Tymchuk et al., 1982). Gregory and McConnell (1986) believe that general ethical principles are covered in most graduate psychology training programs, but group ethical guidelines receive no direct study or review.

However, in an effort to assure the welfare of group participants, the APA (1971) formulated a set of guidelines to help counselors conduct growth or encounter groups. The guidelines explicate specific measures to be followed by group counselors: (a) entry into a group should be voluntary, (b) confidentiality should be discussed, and (c) professional and appropriate ethical obligations should be observed.

Clearly, disagreements about vague definitions and training standards increase the opportunity for conflict among professionals regarding who is competent to provide group therapy. Likewise, the various professional associations (APA, ASGW, American Counseling Association [ACA], National Association for Social Workers [NASW], and American Association for Marriage and Family Therapy [AAMFT]) that have developed and adopted different training standards and ethical guidelines for group leaders exacerbate the confusion.

ADDRESSING DIFFICULT ETHICAL AND LEGAL ISSUES

Kottler (1982) observed that there are unique issues associated with group work that may place group therapists in positions in which ethical dilemmas are more likely to occur. First, group dynamics are likely to increase the level of emotional intensity of interactions, thereby resulting in a greater likelihood of verbal abuse among clients. It is obvious that group therapists have reduced control over the behavior of individual clients within the group and the group itself. In addition, there exists an increased potential for the development of client and therapist dependencies. Second, with increased intensity, both positive changes and possible harm to clients are apt to be accelerated in groups and, therefore, are more difficult to monitor and control. Furthermore, it is more difficult to ensure confidentiality in a group.

DePauw (1986) presented a time line to address some of these difficult ethical issues in individual counseling. We believe this time line provides an excellent model for group therapists to use in helping them avoid conflict with ethical and legal issues. The adapted model includes four areas: initiation issues, ongoing counseling issues, dangerousness and legal liability, and group termination issues.

Initiation Issues:

Most group therapists recruit group clients through simple written announcements, from court-ordered or colleagues' referrals, or from their own individual therapy practices. In these instances, there is often little specific information provided to prospective group clients regarding the nature of their therapy in the group environment. Also, in organizing the group, little attention is focused on screening and selecting group members.

One of the primary responsibilities of the group therapist involves the protection of the general welfare of all clients who are members of the therapy group. This is an area that must not be compromised and begins with announcing the group, screening clients, and informed consent.

In announcing a group, Corey and Corey (1992) suggested that announcements be as specific as possible to avoid unrealistic expectations and to present an accurate picture of the group experience. Therapists should at least include statements addressing the purpose of the group, time limits and duration for the group, their own qualifications, and fee structures. These statements provide the basis for initial screening and informed consent.

When organizing a group for a successful therapeutic experience, one of the leader's most important functions is screening participants. Screening involves selecting members who will be as compatible as possible in terms of individual therapeutic goals, group purpose, socioemotional and personality characteristics, gender, and cultural influences. We recommend individual interviews before beginning the group to provide initial personal contact between the therapist and client and to determine the readiness levels of potential members. For high-risk clients (such as those suffering from psychosis), group therapy may not be initially appropriate. These clients may require extended individual treatment before being placed in a small, problem-centered group therapy environment. In addition, placing high-risk clients with low-risk clients increases the anxiety and psychological risks of the low-risk clients. If harmful to group members, such behavior on the part of therapists could be perceived as malpractice. The group screening interview also provides the therapists with the opportunity to offer additional information to prospective clients so they can make informed choices regarding group participation.

Informed consent is defined as obtaining a client's consent to become involved in the counseling process (Stricker, 1982) and disclosing to the client the procedures used and potential risks and benefits of such approaches (Corey, Corey, & Callanan, 1993). It involves informing clients of their rights and responsibilities as participants. It is our contention that most group counselors do not adequately address and process these issues with prospective group participants. Most clients recruited to participate in a group counseling experience some anticipatory anxiety. As group counselors, if we can provide clients with a clear and concise description of group procedures, possible experiences, and potential effects, much of the anxiety and discomfort will be reduced. More specific information may be required when increased risks are present. There are potentially more risks involved in group work as compared with individual counseling; therefore, discussing any possible negative effects is important.

Prior to participation in a group, it is essential for group therapists to discuss fully with each client that differences occasionally will occur in the group process between individual therapy goals and identified group goals. Thus, if specific issues of a particular client are, or become, incompatible with the goals of the group, this must be discussed with the group leader. If the concern cannot be resolved sufficiently, the client may have to be withdrawn from the group. It is suggested that these issues be discussed with clients prior to their participation in the group so an informed decision about joining the group can be made.

We recommend consulting *Ethical Guidelines for Group Counselors* (ASGW, 1989), which states that group members be informed regarding the following: a statement of goals and purposes of the group; entrance procedures, time limitations and termination procedures; rights and responsibilities of the group therapist and group members; specific counseling strategies and techniques to be used; and personal psychological risks involved in the group. Upon completion of the screening interview, it may be prudent to have clients acknowledge this information by signing a written contract agreeing to the terms of group participation. This documentation would insure group members' consent and voluntary participation.

Ongoing Counseling Issues:

Several key issues must be addressed by group therapists throughout the duration of the group. These ongoing issues include, but are not limited to, voluntary versus involuntary participation, withdrawal, and confidentiality.

Group counselors should consider the differences between

voluntary and involuntary participation in a group counseling experience. *Voluntary participation* is defined as group members who decide to participate of their own volition or on the basis of group counseling information received from a variety of possible sources (Trotzer, 1989). A client who volunteers to participate in group counseling is likely to be highly motivated and derive some value from it. Group counselors enlisting participants who have willingly made a commitment will have greater group success because such clients have acknowledged a desire for help and taken the responsibility for placing themselves in this type of counseling modality.

Involuntary participation is defined as group members who are unwilling to participate in the group counseling process but are required to do so. Adolescents, substance abusers, and prisoners are examples of involuntary participants. Group counselors must determine whether an involuntary group participant will work toward positive change and not disrupt the group by being a difficult member. The ethical issue here consists of "forcing" a person "for his or her own benefit" to participate when he or she is clearly opposed to the intervention. This is frequently the case with clients who are in denial that a specific problem exists. There are some authors (Mahler, 1969) who subscribe to the position that involuntary participation in group therapy can have positive benefits for group members. We believe that this issue requires careful evaluation, because although there may be benefits, harmful effects remain possible.

An additional issue is the participation of clients in group counseling who are not emotionally prepared for the experience. For some counselors, individual counseling is a prerequisite for participating in a therapeutic group. Individual counseling serves to help clients identify problems and establish specific personal treatment goals. To place clients arbitrarily into a group without considering their psychological differences may be harmful to both the clients and the effective functioning of the group. These concerns must be appraised by counselors prior to clients' placement into a group.

After careful evaluation, if a group member becomes disruptive or abusive to himself, herself, or others, the group leader has an ethical — and possibly legal — responsibility to remove this person from the group. In addition, if a client wishes to withdraw voluntarily from the group at any time, we believe the group leader should honor the request. However, before the withdrawal occurs, the leader should also seek to understand the client's reasons for group withdrawal and, if appropriate, process these reasons within the group context. The therapist should hold an exit interview and receive permission to explain the client's withdrawal to continuing participants if appropriate. Even though we recommend working to keep the group intact once it has begun, we recognize the existence of unique situations that require withdrawal of participants. These situations should always be documented carefully in treatment notes.

Confidentiality is the most frequent ethical dilemma reported by the membership of the APA (Pope & Vetter, 1992). The purpose of confidentiality is to safeguard clients' privacy. It is paramount for group counselors to do all that is within their influence to ensure the confidentiality of each group member. Therefore, we believe it is the responsibility of all group counselors to state openly and explicitly their positions on client confidentiality.

Group counselors have an ethical, moral, and legal responsibility not to reveal information without clients' knowledge and consent unless, of course, they become a danger to themselves or others. Although group counselors are bound by the regulations of confidentiality, they are unable to ensure that any of the members in the group will respect confidentiality. This is difficult, because trust is an underlying tenet to the effective functioning of any group and such trust evolves only when group members believe that what they say will not be disclosed outside the group.

It is essential for confidentiality to be discussed with each client during the initial interview, reviewed upon beginning the first session of the group, and emphasized regularly thereafter. Group leaders also need to inform group clients about the potential consequences of an intentional breach of confidentiality. Once confidentiality guidelines have been established and become group norms, the possibility of breached confidentiality decreases. As with individual therapy, group therapists need to specify the limits of confidentiality during the pregroup interview. These limits include a client's condition that presents a clear danger to themselves or others, consultation with professional colleagues as necessary, and court mandates to review records.

Records include any notes or data that are used in the evaluation, treatment planning, and documented communication regarding treatment of clients with other professionals. At any time, a group therapist may ethically consult with a competent professional regarding the treatment of a group member — *provided informed consent has been obtained*. Also, a release of information from counseling records may be obtained only when granted in writing from the client. It is essential for group therapists to become familiar with state laws regarding the limits of confidentiality.

Dangerousness and Legal Liability:

Paradise and Kirby (1990) identified confidentiality and the duty to protect as group therapy issues that could lead to liability. They warned that because group therapists generally do not provide sufficient commentary regarding the limits of confidentiality and group members' duty to maintain confidentiality, possible civil action could result from a client harmed through improper disclosure. They further indicated that group counselors could be held liable for acts of group members and that a violation of confidentiality could be viewed as a breach of contract. Because group therapists cannot guarantee confidentiality regarding client self-disclosures, it is crucial for all participants to be advised before group participation of this limitation and comprehend the potential problems it could pose throughout the course of group therapy.

For example, let us examine the danger of a group member's disclosing that he or she has acquired immunodeficiency syndrome (AIDS). Some group therapists might decide to exclude the client immediately from further group therapy or discontinue any further treatment altogether while attempting to refer the client to an "appropriate" treatment site. If allowed to continue to participate in group therapy, this client would be extremely vulnerable to group members' negative reactions to the disclosure. It is even possible the disclosure could be "leaked" by the therapist or group members outside the group, creating discriminatory behavior by others that could cost the client employment, marriage, or community status. Indeed, group counselors have a duty to protect group members from themselves and others.

The ASGW (1989) stated that when a group member's condition indicates a clear and imminent danger to the member, others, or physical property, group counselors should take reasonable action and/or "inform responsible authorities." However, the words "reasonable" and "responsible" are open to interpretation; although group therapists may be behaving ethically according to professional guidelines, they may be behaving illegally.

Legal protection of confidentiality varies from state to state (Lynch, 1993). For example, to the best of our knowledge, Maryland does not allow for breach of confidentiality, even when the lives of others are threatened (Knapp & Vandecreek, 1982). On the other hand, California requires therapists "to warn" and "to protect" identifiable potential victims of clients (*Tarasoff v Board of Regents of the University of California*, 1976). In the *Tarasoff* case, the court made it clear that therapists had a duty to protect intended victims when clients could be identified as dangerous. However, in some cases, the court also found that warning a threatened person might be too radical a course of action to constitute "reasonable care," whereas in other cases, warning potential victims might not provide sufficient action (Gross, Lamb, & Weinberger, 1987). Group therapists must be knowledgeable regarding state statutes and local agency procedures for determining when a breach of confidentiality is warranted.

Furthermore, a group therapist has an ethical and legal responsibility to breach confidentiality with suicidal clients when sufficient evidence indicates that they are dangerous to themselves. Liability for suicide is frequently sought for breach of duty and causation on the part of the therapist. Breach of duty occurs when therapists are found to be negligent in treating clients in ways that conform to the standard of care. Swenson (1987) identified two ways to interpret the duty to care in suicide liability: failure to prevent suicide, and responsibility for causing suicide.

Liability for failure to prevent suicide has been successfully upheld in court. Where a duty to prevent suicide exists, the most frequent instance is in a custodial relationship; e.g., when a client is hospitalized or ordered by court into residential treatment. When a client is under custodial treatment, more restrictive measures of care are required. The duty of care is breached if suicide could have been reasonably anticipated and procedures were not implemented to prevent it (*Dinnerstein v United States*, 1973; *Meier v Ross General Hospital*, 1968).

Therapists are deemed responsible for causing suicide when it has been determined that they were negligent in treatment. Behaviors that may be considered negligent are: breach of confidentiality, inappropriate early release from therapy due to insurance restrictions or payment difficulties, directives or techniques that exacerbate the stressed or depressed condition, nurturing an unhealthy dependence and then terminating therapy, sexual relationships with clients, overprescription of medications to severely depressed patients, and an inability to diagnose or predict suicidal behavior.

All group therapists are responsible for careful evaluation and screening of potential group members. This evaluation should include a socioemotional history, including past suicide attempts, present suicidal ideation, or abusive behavior with loved ones. Group members who suffer from a personality disorder, substance abuse, depression, a sleep disorder, or profound losses are at risk for suicide.

As indicated with dangerous clients, group counselors have a duty to protect their membership from unreasonable psychological risks by providing reasonable standards of care in the group. As mentioned previously, the dynamics of group therapy often intensify intrapsychic, intragroup, and intergroup interactions. When the intensity of therapy increases, so does the potential for psychological benefits and harm. Group therapists are responsible for managing and weaving these dynamics to enhance group members' therapeutic benefits.

In screening participants and throughout the duration of the group, group therapists must explore the psychological risks of therapeutic involvement in the group. Group members are expected to participate in therapeutic techniques that reduce defensiveness and intensify exposure of the psyche. These risks are necessary for psychological and life changes, yet group members may not fully understand the perils of such participation.

Corey and Corey (1992) discussed the potential harm to group members through scapegoating, group pressure to participate and to change, breaches of confidence, inappropriate reassurance, and unsuitable hostile confrontation. In addition, Lakin (1991) identified four group therapy forces that could be managed by group therapists in a positive or negative way: cohesiveness (the power of belonging); consensual validation and group standards for reality testing; emotional expressiveness; and pressures from sanctioned disclosures. He further suggested that failure to comply with group norms can lead to indoctrination that may be considered unethical.

Group Termination Issues:

Evaluation of group participants begins with screening, continues throughout the life of the group, and is completed only when clients terminate treatment. We subscribe to the concept that group termination begins with the inception of the group. This concept implies that, if a predetermined time frame has been established for the duration of the group, members are informed periodically as to the number of sessions remaining. If the group is open and ongoing, it becomes the therapist's responsibility to evaluate constantly client's progress to enhance a timely exit from the group and to promote continuous growth toward independence. On occasion, group members may exit when the group is no longer productive for them or they are disruptive. Should these events occur, therapists have an ethical obligation to discuss alternative therapies and to refer clients to competent counselors.

All group experiences should be formally evaluated by competent group members at the time of group termination. Evaluation of the group's and individual clients' progress is necessary to ensure effective group therapy practice.

SUMMARY

In our opinion, training standards and ethical guidelines for group therapists are inconsistent and vague, as are group therapy training practices. This creates uninformed practices that lead to group therapists' placing themselves in ethical and legal jeopardy. In closing, we offer the following helpful hints to minimize the ethical and legal risks associated with group therapy:

- Become familiar with state statutes related to group therapy and the professional codes of ethics of the respective professional association

- Evaluate and screen all participants prior to group therapy

- Develop a diagnostic profile and keep specific treatment notes for each client

- Keep updated records

- Document that informed consent issues were covered during screening

- Make specific treatment plans for individuals within the context of the group's therapeutic goals

- Avoid all dual relationships with group members, especially sexual encounters

- If confidentiality must be violated, discuss it with the client and obtain a written release

- If the client refuses to sign a release, document the refusal

- Consult with respected colleagues or clinical supervisors when confronted with difficult situations

- Participate annually in continuing education activity

- Purchase adequate professional liability insurance

Being able to recognize potential ethical problem areas in various counseling situations is imperative, because the risk of malpractice is not always apparent. To be sure, no one is exempt from the pain associated with legal proceedings, and any therapist practicing group counseling should be prepared to manage them effectively.

REFERENCES

American Association of Counseling and Development. (1988). *Ethical standards*. Alexandria, VA: Author.

American Group Psychotherapy Association. (1978). *Guidelines for the training of group psychotherapists*. New York: Author.

American Psychological Association. (1971). *Guidelines for psychologists conducting growth groups*. Washington, DC: Author.

American Psychological Association. (1981). *Ethical principles of psychologists*. Washington, DC: Author.

American Psychological Association. (1989). *Ethical principles of psychologists*. Washington, DC: Author.

American Psychological Association. (1992). *Ethical principles of psychologists and code of conduct*. Washington, DC: Author.

Association for Specialists in Group Work (1980). *Ethical guidelines for group leaders*. Falls Church, VA: Author.

Association for Specialists in Group Work. (1990). Professional standards for the training of group workers. *Together, 20*(1), 9–14.

Carroll, M. R. (1985). Critical issues in group work in education: Now and 2001. *Journal for Specialists in Group Work, 10*(2), 98–102.

Conyne, R. K., Dye, A., Gill, S. J., Leddick, G. R., Morran, D. K., & Ward, D. E. (1985). A retrospective of critical issues. *Journal for Specialists in Group Work, 10*(2), 112–115.

Corey, G. (1990). Theory and practice of group counseling (3rd ed.). Pacific Grove, CA: Brooks/Cole.

Corey, M., & Corey, G. (1992). *Groups process and practice* (4th ed.). Pacific Grove, CA: Brooks/Cole.

Corey, G., Corey, M., & Callanan, P. (1993). *Issues and ethics in the helping professions* (4th ed.). Pacific Grove, CA: Brooks/Cole.

DePauw, M. E. (1986). Avoiding ethical violations: A timeline perspective for individual counseling. *Journal of Counseling and Development, 64*(5), 303–310.

Dinnerstein v. U.S. 486 F.2d. 34 (Conn. 1973).

Gregory, J. C., & McConnell, S. G. (1986). Ethical issues with psychotherapy in group contexts. *Psychotherapy in Private Practice, 4*(1), 51–62.

Gross, R. H., Lamb, D. H., & Weinberger, L. E. (1987). Assessing dangerousness and responding appropriately. *Journal of Clinical Psychiatry, 48,* 9–12.

Gumaer, J. (1982). Ethics and the experts: Insight into critical incidents. *Journal for Specialists in Group Work, 7*(3), 154–161.

Gumaer, J. (1984). *Counseling and therapy for children.* New York: Free Press.

Gumaer, J., & Duncan, J. (1982). Group workers' perceptions of their philosophical ethical beliefs and actual ethical practices. *Journal for Specialists in Group Work, 7*(4), 231–237.

Gumaer, J., & Scott, L. (1985). Training group leaders in ethical decision making. *Journal for Specialists in Group Work, 10*(4), 198–204.

Gumaer, J., & Scott, L. (1986). Group workers' perception of ethical and unethical behavior of group leaders. *Journal for Specialists in Group Work, 11*(3), 139–150.

Herlihy, B., Healy, M., Cook, E., & Hudson, P. (1987). Ethical practices of licensed professional counselors: A survey of state licensing boards. *Counselor Education and Supervision, 27*(1), 69–76.

Knapp, S., & Vandecreek, L. (1982). Tarasoff: Five years later. *Professional Psychology, 13,* 511–516.

Kottler, J. (1982). Ethics comes of age: Introduction to the special issue. *Journal for Specialists in Group Work, 7*(3), 138–139.

Lakin, M. (1991). Some ethical issues in feminist-oriented therapeutic groups for women. *International Journal of Group Psychotherapy, 41*(2), 199–215.

Lynch, S. K. (1993). AIDS: Balancing confidentiality and the duty to protect. *Journal of College Student Development, 34,* 148–152.

Mahler, C. A. (1969). *Group counseling in the schools.* Boston: Houghton-Mifflin.

Meier v. Ross General Hospital, 69 Cal. 2d. 420, 71 Cal. Rptr. 903,445 P.2d 519 (1968).

Paradise, L. V., & Kirby, P. C. (1990). Some perspectives on the legal liability of group counseling in private practice. *Journal for Specialists in Group Work, 15*(2), 114–118.

Pope, K. S., Tobachnick, B. G., & Keith-Spiegel, P. (1987). Ethics of practice: The beliefs and behaviors of psychologists as therapists. *American Psychologist, 42*(11), 993–1006.

Pope, K. S., & Vetter, V. A. (1992). Ethical dilemmas encountered by members of the American Psychological Association: A national survey. *American Psychologist, 47*(3), 397–411.

Robinson, S. E., & Gross, D. R. (1989). Applied ethics and the mental health counselor. *Journal of Mental Health Counseling, 11*(3), 289–299.

Shapiro, J. L., & Shapiro, S. B. (1985). Group work to 2001: HAL or haven (from isolation)? *Journal For Specialists In Group Work, 10*(2), 83–87.

Stricker, G. (1982). Ethical issues in psychotherapy research. In M. Rosenbaum (Ed.), *Ethics and values in psychotherapy: A guidebook* (pp. 403–424). New York: Free Press.

Swenson, E. (1987). Legal liability for a patient's suicide. *Journal of Psychiatry and Law, 14,* 409–434.

Tarasoff v. Board of Regents of the University of California, 131 Cal. Rptr. 14.551 P.2d 334 (1976).

Trotzer, J. P. (1989). *The counselor and the group* (2nd ed.). Muncie, IN: Accelerated Development, Inc.

Tymchuk, A. J., Drapkin, R., Major-Kingsley, S., Ackerman, A. B., Coffman, E. W., & Baum, M. S. (1982). Ethical decision making and psychologists' attitudes toward training in ethics. *Professional Psychology, 13*(3), 412–421.

Yalom, I. D. (1985). *The theory and practice of group psychotherapy* (3rd ed.). New York: Basic Books.

FOR FURTHER READING

American Association for Marriage and Family Therapy. (1988). *AAMFT code of ethical principles for marriage and family therapists*. Washington, DC: Author.

American Mental Health Counselors Association. (1980). *Code of ethics for certified clinical mental health counselors*. Alexandria, VA: Author.

Association for Specialists in Group Work. (1989). *Ethical guidelines for group counselors*. Alexandria, VA: Author.

Conyne, R. K., Wilson, F. R., Kline, W. B., Morran, D. K., & Ward, D. E. (1993). Training group workers: Implications for the new ASGW training standards for training and practice. *Journal for Specialists in Group Work, 18*(1), 11–23.

Gumaer, J., & Martin, D. (1990). Group ethics: A multimodal model for training knowledge and skill competencies. *Journal for Specialists in Group Work, 15*(2), 94–103.

Taylor, R. E., & Gazda, G. M. (1991). Concurrent individual and group therapy: The ethical issues. *Journal of Group Psychotherapy, Psychodrama, and Sociometry, 44*(2), 51–59.

9

Marriage and Family Therapy: Theories and Applications

Stanley C. Feist, PhD

Dr. Feist is Emeritus Professor of Psychology, The State University of New York College of Technology, Farmingdale, NY.

KEY POINTS

- Marriage and family therapy is a rapidly growing, multidisciplinary field, drawing members from the fields of social work, psychology, psychiatry, nursing, pastoral care, and mental health counseling. Historical influences on the field are examined.

- Marriage and family therapy can be explained by using the framework of "circular" thinking, which emphasizes that a situation may have been generated by a complex series of causes rather than a single cause. That is, a family functions as a system of behaviors in which any one action influences the behavior of others.

- A healthy, functioning family system accepts feedback, is flexible, and is open to change. A poorly functioning family system preserves family homeostasis at all costs; it uses feedback to maintain an unhealthy stability and resists change.

- Certain techniques outlined in this chapter are part of almost every family treatment process. They lead to therapeutic goals, which maintain the family's sense of self and of operational competence while challenging maladaptive behaviors.

- Several theories and applications are discussed, including communications family therapy and Bowenian Multigenerational Theory.

INTRODUCTION

Marriage and family therapy is a rapidly growing discipline. Membership in the American Association for Marriage and Family Therapy (AAMFT), founded in 1942, has increased 500% in the past 10 years (Piercy et al., 1986). This demonstrates the increasing popularity of a treatment modality that was virtually unknown 40 years ago.

From the very beginning, marriage and family therapy has been a multidisciplinary field, drawing members from the ranks of social work, psychology, psychiatry, nursing, pastoral care, and mental health counseling. Their varying perspectives have given strength to the field. At the same time, the diversity of professional publications has made it difficult to coordinate the collected knowledge.

Social workers must be credited with early recognition of the importance of treating the family. In addition, Alfred Adler and his student, Rudolph Dreikurs, did early work on child guidance and family treatment in the 1920s (Nichols, 1984). They worked in a team, psychiatrist-psychologist-social worker, with a focus on the child's family environment. Marriage counseling centers began to emerge in the early 1930s in several major U. S. cities; however, they generally saw only one member of the couple (Thomas, 1992).

Whereas the early psychoanalysts used a medical model of linear causation of emotional disorder, Harry S. Sullivan, working with schizophrenic clients, emphasized the importance of the hospital "family" — the nurses, attendants, and aides — as a substitute family. Freida Fromm-Reichmann (1948) also realized the importance of the family in the development of disorders, but neither of them carried their idea through to involve the family of origin in actual treatment.

In 1931, J. Moreno (1945) provided one of the earliest approaches to group therapy with psychodrama, in which participants acted out family problems. A little later, John Bowlby (1949) used family meetings as a factor in therapy but only as an auxiliary part of the treatment at the Tavistock Clinic in London, England.

The Palo Alto groups can justifiably claim to be a major factor in the development of family treatment. Gregory Bateson's Project for the Study of Schizophrenia began in 1953 at Palo Alto and involved Jay Haley and John Weakland. The following year, Don Jackson and William Fry joined them. The Bateson group published *Towards a Theory of Schizophrenia* (Bateson, Jackson, Haley, & Weakland, 1956), which included preliminary thoughts on the "double bind" theory, and later a more conclusive work on metacommunciations in the family of a schizophrenic (Bateson, Jackson, Haley, & Weakland, 1963).

In 1959, Don Jackson founded the Mental Research Institute and was primarily interested in treating families with problems. Jackson worked at various times with Virginia Satir, John Weakland, Paul Watzlawick, and Jay Haley. Jackson (1954) published a paper entitled "The Question of Family Homeostasis," in which he first describes the move toward balance or homeostasis when a family feels threatened. Later, Jackson and Weakland (1959) further demonstrated how clients' symptoms maintained equilibrium, even if maladaptive, in their families.

Among others who also worked with a schizophrenic child at about the same time was Murray Bowen, who arrived at the conclusion that both parents of the child needed to be included in the therapy to detriangulate, or clarify, the emotional relationships within the family (Bowen, 1961, 1978). This led to the development of a didactic therapy intended to clarify and define relationships between the parents and to help each family member take a responsible stand for his or her convictions. Bowen struggled to remain impartial and separate from the undifferentiated ego mass of the family. He forced the family members to solve their own problems, thereby becoming more stable and dependable.

The Child Guidance movement was also influential in the development of family therapy (Ginsberg, 1955). Child Guidance was originally supposed to prevent the occurrence of serious problems in children. It was soon evident that the child, although armed with proper knowledge, was still helpless before the powerful emotional forces in the family. The next step for many therapists was to include the mother in the session. It then became apparent that the mother's behavior toward the child was influenced by the relationship between the mother and the father, and the circle of influence enlarged.

Nathan Ackerman (1958) applied psychoanalytic thinking to family therapy. He began using the prevailing child guidance model in which the therapist treated the child while a social worker dealt with the mother. In the 1940s, he began to see both the child and the mother and then went on to include everyone in the household in the treatment sessions. Psychoanalytic trained, Ackerman was always aware of the individual's inner needs and emotions (Hoffman, 1981). His *Psychodynamics of Family Life* (1958) is considered by some to be the establishing document of family therapy.

Currently Jay Haley and Cloe Madanes teach and apply their version of communications theory — *strategic family therapy*. Haley (1963) describes how he uses Milton Erickson's directive therapy by assigning a task designed to unbalance the family system so that it may be restructured in a more efficacious manner. Paradoxical prescriptions are part of this treatment.

Another contemporary therapist is Salvador Minuchin. His structural therapy (Minuchin, 1974) is designed to reestablish the emotional boundaries that determine the closeness or distance between family members. Minuchin looks at the enmeshment or disengagement present in dysfunctional families and works to restructure dysfunctional boundaries.

Several therapists from Italy have contributed a great deal to the field of marriage and family therapy. Among them are Maurizio Andolfi (1980), who studied with Minuchin and who uses strategic and structural concepts along with paradoxical interventions in an attempt to reorganize family interaction.

Mara Selvini-Palazzoli (1978) of the Milan group reportedly commented, "Family systems is a way of thinking, not a garage for repairing families." Palazzoli, along with Luigi Boscolo, Gianfranco Ceccin, and Guiliana Prata, developed a unique approach to working with families.

Others have significantly contributed to marital and family therapy. They include: Ivan Boszormenyi-Nagy and Krasner (1986); Duhl, Kantor, and Duhl (1973); Lynn Hoffman (1981); Peggy Penn (1985); Virginia Satir (1983); Lyman Wynne (1988); and Carl Whitaker (who introduced a provocative "psycho-therapy of the absurd" in 1975). Space does not permit me to explore the theories of these and the other numerous outstanding family therapists who should be mentioned here.

THE CONCEPTUAL DEVELOPMENT OF FAMILY THERAPY

Linear versus Systems Thinking:

Most traditional psychotherapies are based on the medical model of linear causation of disorders. If you have a sore throat, the problem is caused by a bacterial infection of the mucus membranes of your throat. In the emotional analogue, if a person is immoral and unethical (in other words, a socio-path), the problem probably stems from improper accultura-tion, lack of superego development, or some specific cause, depending on one's theoretical viewpoint. The linear view is grounded in the concept of a particular cause or causes for a specific disorder (Nichols, 1984). Emotional and behavioral problems are seen as caused by some prior event, learning, or disease. This is linear thinking.

If a person has a problem, the problem must originate inside him or her or stem from his or her particular way of perceiving situations. It has always been evident to individual therapists that family influences were important in shaping personali-ties. However, it was considered that the person's internalized view of childhood events was the more dominant influence. Often the client was separated from his or her natural environ-ment and treated in isolation from the family in order to rearrange his or her inner patterns. Sometimes interpersonal contact with the family would be absolutely forbidden. Al-though linear treatment may alleviate or reduce the symptomatic behavior in the individual, the family was expected to readjust, with the symptoms exhibited in another manner by another family member.

Systems or Circular Thinking:

The concept of circular causality may offer a more meaningful explanation of many disorders (Thomas, 1992). Circularity examines the interactions among all the participants in a situation and may consider the internal system of an involved individual as well. Causality is circular in systems thinking. When one family member does or says something, that action is a stimulus for another family member to respond. The response stimulates additional interaction between the same or other family members that continues in a circular manner (Hubert & Hubert, 1986). Because the family therapist believes that the current daily influences of the family are the significant factor, the family must be seen in therapy as a group to rearrange these external forces in the here-and-now.

Basic to all family theory is the concept of the family as a homeostatic system. The troubled person in the family, often called the "identified patient" (IP), bears the symptoms for family dysfunction. The symptoms are viewed as a functional way to maintain homeostasis. Intervention in the system will require an adjustment for the family if it is to retain the homeostatic balance. The task of the therapist is to intervene in such a way that a new balance can be achieved that does not include the maladaptive symptoms. Inappropriate intervention allows restabilization without change; the symptoms continue. The systems approach views the symptoms as functional, but maladaptive.

Family therapy was modeled after group therapy and based on concepts of group dynamics, specifically the understanding that groups are more than the mere sum of the personalities involved. Processes emerge that are the product of the interactions of the cluster of personalities. Group therapists realized that the best results were often obtained by considering both group dynamics and the inner dynamics of the individual. Most family therapists continue to use some group therapy methods as means of promoting interactions among the family members.

The concept that the psychopathology in the family had a function provided another step in the development of family therapy. Freud, in his *Psychopathology of Everyday Life* (1901/1960), takes note of the purpose served by psychopathology in the individual. Further, studies of schizophrenic families demonstrated that the deviant behavior of a child often triggered a negative feedback loop that helped maintain family togetherness. Thus, the deviant behavior was maladaptive for the child's individual functioning, but provided an adaptation for the family structure. This explains why another family member would develop symptomatic behavior when the behavior of the first IP began to be less symptomatic. For this reason, the IP and the family as a unit are likely to exhibit behavior that tends to be rigid and inflexible. They fear losing whatever function they do have (Jackson & Weakland, 1959). Jackson coined the term "family homeostasis" (1954) for a family's reluctance to change. In other families, which Freud called "runaways," an ascent in deviant behavior creates an increase in stress, thus sparking the need for change to occur.

We see here some of the essentials for thinking about family functioning as a system of behaviors in which any one action influences the behaviors of others. A circularity of interaction exists in any group situation, and intervention at any one point can change the whole system. This is the basis of systems theory as applied to therapy.

The two basic views of a system are as a cybernetic or closed mechanistic system, or as an open system. The closed system uses self-regulating feedback loops, as in home climate control: a thermostat causes the heating or cooling system to turn on or off because of a simple change in temperature. In the normal course of events, nothing else can operate that system. This is a goal-seeking system, with maintenance of a constant temperature as the goal. The analogy, however, is somewhat of an oversimplification; there is oil and/or electricity as an energy input from outside of the system and human adjustment to keep everything in proper function.

The general or open systems theory seems to offer a more useful explanation when examining human family behavior. People are not like machines; they are interactive and creative. They are affected by and actively influence their environment, with an active interchange of materials, energies, or information with the environment. The system behaves as a whole; change in any one part alters the whole system. This theory offers a completely new way to view and to alter what is usually considered to be maladaptive behavior. Once the therapist can discover the special purpose of the symptoms, it becomes possible to replace the maladaptive family behaviors with other behaviors that are more functional.

A healthy, functioning system accepts feedback, is flexible, and is open to change. A poorly functioning family system is involved in preserving family homeostasis at all costs; it uses feedback to maintain an unhealthy stability and resists change. This concept of system functioning can be applied to one person as well as to a family or any larger organized whole. It may not be necessary to give up the traditional ideas of psychoanalytic insights for the individual, yet one must be extremely careful not to slip into the linear mode when the circularity of the family is not readily evident. This is especially important when one has been trained initially in some aspect of psychodynamic theory.

No matter what the specific theoretical preference of the therapist may be, symptoms in any one member are seen as functional to the family systems organization, restoring stability by expressing and deflecting family tension. Papp (1976) outlined the following basic systemic postulates:

- The family is viewed as a whole, greater than the sum of its parts or members.

- Each member's behavior can only be understood within the context of the family unit.

- Change in any one member of the system will affect all other members of the system.

- The family regulates itself through feedback loops (cybernetic circuits), which provide balance (homeostasis) to the system.

- No one event linearly causes another to occur. Rather, behaviors are parts of larger circular patterns that recur over time to balance the family and permit it to move through various developmental stages.

The circular approach does not perceive symptoms as disease but rather as a maladaptive attempt on the part of the organism to maintain a comfortable state of function. For example, alcoholism probably began as an attempt to relieve stress and pain but somehow got out of hand; neurotic behavior is considered to have been designed to adapt to an emotionally charged situation but became exaggerated and developed into impaired functioning.

Usually the family goes to therapy because one family member is showing symptoms of a disorder. Instead of viewing this person as the patient, we see the whole family as the patient needing treatment. The person with symptoms is merely the one who has been chosen to act out the disorder of a malfunctioning family system. The maladaptive states we see in a person simply reflect the intensity of the problem in the larger family system. Systems thinking may eventually give us some clues into other situations in which adaptive symptoms became the focus for a totally different problem.

NEED FOR THEORY

Early practitioners of family therapy were theorists only in the sense that they developed theories after the fact to rationalize their methodology. However, theories are necessary if the efficacy of the methodology is to be tested.

Therapists are frequently impatient with theory; they want to learn the techniques and get on with the treatment. However, techniques are the specifics and the details; they can be learned by rote but then offer only a very limited repertoire of therapeutic behaviors. Using techniques without some master plan often leaves the therapist in a confused state when the clients do not respond to the technique as planned. Theory is something better than technique, although one must also carry a large "bag of tricks." Theory offers an understanding of the master plan of family behavior, as well as an overall methodology for treatment. Having mastered the theory, the therapist is less likely to get stuck in the morass of family emotion.

Certain techniques are part of almost every family treatment process. They lead to therapeutic goals, which maintain the family's sense of self and of operational competence while challenging the maladaptive behaviors. Some of these are described by Hoffman (1981):

- *Joining:* accommodating members of the family to win their confidence and acceptance

- *Maintenance:* highlighting the positive behaviors, ideas, and the strengths of family members

- *Tracking:* following both content and process of family members' contribution to sessions, using their metaphors, and asking for expansion of their ideas

- *Mimesis* (nonverbal component of joining): responding to the affect, pace, mood, and posture of the family

- *Challenging:* confronting the family myths and their varied behavioral versions

- *Reframing* (the basic intervention of all therapies): putting the problem in terms of the client's voluntary behavior rather than framing the client as a helpless victim

- *Boundaries* (both theoretical and concrete, one reflecting the other): observing an evolutionary process of negotiating boundaries and positions in the healthy family

- *Enactment*: stimulating family interaction to observe and change transactions and structure

- *Unbalancing*: restructuring by upsetting the established boundaries that the family desires to maintain

- *Interpersonal intensity*: therapist's using of self

- *Linear perspective*: exploring the theoretical and unreal of each person in the family as a unique, independent being

- *Interactional or circularity perspective*: observing how each family member influences the behavior of all other family members *ad infinitum* (the feedback loops)

COMMUNICATIONS FAMILY THERAPY

In the early days of family therapy, a few basic theories formed the groundwork for much that followed. Communications family therapy is among them. This theory stemmed from the work of Gregory Bateson, an anthropologist who did research on schizophrenic communications. His interest, along with that of J. Haley and Don Jackson, was scientific rather than therapeutic. Bateson's observations led him to believe that interchange of messages between people defined their relationships, and these relationships were stabilized by homeostatic processes in the family. Bateson, Jackson, Haley, and Weakland generated the double-bind theory of schizophrenia by deductive reasoning; only afterwards did they see families to test the theory (Nichols, 1984).

The communications people are systems purist; they concentrate on the input and the output of the system. Families are seen as error-controlled, goal-directed systems. Family interactions are analyzed using cybernetics, general systems theory, and game theory. Although communications theories describe families as open systems, they treat them as closed systems in their clinical work.

The therapy is concentrated on the nuclear family, with little or no input from the extended family or the community. Clinical attention is to the here-and-now in an ahistorical approach. When parents communicate clearly in a focused, well-structured, flexible manner, their children are regarded by teachers and peers as competent both academically and socially. Behavior disorders or symptoms are seen as communicated messages, statements made by the system in an attempt to maintain the family homeostasis. Pathological families are enmeshed in very strong homeostatic patterns of communication that are seen as dysfunctional from the outlook of the larger society. They are inflexible and very strongly resist change; change is experienced as threatening rather than as an opportunity for growth. Lyman Wynne's (1977) concept of communication deviance shows a correlation between negative, derogatory, disparaging, and critical remarks and pathology in the family.

The goal of communications family therapy is to identify the symptom as the dysfunctional message that needs to be changed, then interrupt the positive feedback loop that perpetuates that message (Watzlawick, Beavin, & Jackson, 1967). The therapist is an outsider who supplies what the relationship cannot—a change in rules.

This is similar to the linear approach of Albert Ellis's rational emotive therapy, a cognitive approach to psychotherapy. The major difference is that Ellis works with individuals rather than families. The therapist can point out the offending messages or can manipulate the family in order to effect change. The first method depends on the cooperation and good will of the family; the second does not. It is an attempt to beat the family at their own game, willing or not. The general method follows from the "black box" concept of communications technology. You need not know exactly what is contained inside of your computer; you need know only what to put into it and what output to expect.

One technique of communications therapy has the family members speak only in the "I" language — not for any other member — and to speak directly to, not about, each other. Body language, posture, facial expression, gestures, and physical proximity are very important aspects of communication and are carefully noted by the therapist. All behavior is communicative; therefore, people are constantly and consistently communicating, even when no words are spoken.

Therapy consists, in part, of reframing, so that the symptoms are not perceived as involuntary. The self-fulfilling prophesies or hidden expectations are revealed to the family and then cognitively altered. The therapist rephrases and redefines the family's activities in a positive way, allowing family members to communicate more openly with one another and move more closely together. This is primarily an intellectual and scholarly approach, rather than founded upon empiricism.

The practice of communications therapy and theory, one of the first and most influential schools of family therapy, is no longer a separate school of family therapy: its concepts have been absorbed by the entire field. Three major models of communication theory have emerged. Haley developed a model that emphasized communication and power, Jackson developed a model emphasizing communication and cognition, and Satir developed a model emphasizing communication and feeling. Paul Watzlawick, John Weakland, Theodore Lidz, and Lyman Wynne, among other renowned therapists and theorists, had their beginnings in communication therapy and theory. All communications theories emphasize how people relate to each other.

BOWENIAN MULTIGENERATIONAL THEORY

Murray Bowen was trained as a psychiatrist and as a traditional psychoanalyst at the Menninger Clinic. While doing individual therapy with schizophrenic clients, he noted the extreme emotional "stuck-togetherness" between the mother and child. He proposed that in human beings, two conflicting forces coexist—one moving toward individuation and autonomy, the other toward togetherness or fusion. He viewed the symbiosis or fusion as the intense emotional process upon which schizophrenia was later superimposed. After he had the mother stay in the hospital with the client and treat both, it soon became evident that the fathers were equally entangled through active support of the symbiosis or through submissive departure and isolation. A triangle had formed where there had been a primary dyad of mother and father. The triangulation may stabilize the family but may also prevent useful resolution of dyadic conflict (Bowen, 1966).

Bowen came to believe that the whole family had to be treated as a unit to bring about the desired change in the identified patient. Bowen's emphasis was on individuals becoming differentiated, individuating, and becoming unstuck. Bowen suggested that emotional illness is multigenerational; that is, it has its origin somewhere in a previous generation in which the family members had difficulty separating from the family core. The feeling of stress is maladaptationally reduced by "triangling in" — by involving a child (the next generation) in a symbiotic relationship. This is called "fusion" and results in an undifferentiated ego mass, more recently called "nuclear family emotional system." Then the child is stuck. This emotional stuck-togetherness amplifies until the disturbance reaches a point of serious maladaptation for living—an emotional disorder. The generational boundaries become blurred and indistinct. It becomes the task of therapy to reform these generational boundaries, to detriangulate the client so that the fusion is dissolved and differentiation can occur. The classic triangle is the close mother and child and a passive, withdrawn father. If the father tries to get close to his child, the mother becomes upset, afraid she will become left out and isolated.

Six interlocking concepts form the basis for Bowen's theory: (a) emotional triangle, (b) differentiation of self, (c) nuclear family emotional system, (d) family projection process, (e) multigenerational projection system, and (f) influence of sibling position.

Emotional triangles:

Emotional triangles are the smallest stable relationships in families. Relationships made up of two significant persons are unstable; when tension arises, a third person or thing is triangulated. When two lovers experience tension, one turns to a friend, a parent, a therapist, alcohol, etc. Marital conflict sometimes provides a "solution" to the dilemma. Conflictual marriages are extremely intense emotional relationships in which a period of extreme closeness is followed by a strongly separating argument that allows each to feel justified in maintaining distance until the next cycle.

Differentiation of Self:

Differentiation of self is both intrapsychic and interpersonal. Intrapsychic differentiation allows the separation of thoughts from feelings, whereas interpersonal differentiation allows individuation from significant others in the family system. Individuation is the opposite of fusion. The person who accomplishes differentiation is capable of thinking and feeling, of strong emotions and spontaneity, of rational restraint from acting on impulse.

Nuclear Family Emotional System:

Nuclear family emotional system deals with the forces in families that operate multigenerationally in recurrent cycles and were previously called undifferentiated family ego mass or emotional stuck-togetherness. Lack of differentiation from parents results in a child who is emotionally cut off from them. In turn, this leads to fusion in marriage for the child. The poorer the differentiation of the person prior to marriage, the greater the fusion with a spouse after marriage. This condition is unstable and may manifest itself as reactive emotional distance from spouse, physical or emotional dysfunction in one spouse, overt marital conflict, and/or projection of the problem onto a child.

The use of emotional cutoff reflects, solves, and creates a problem. It reflects the presence of an emotional fusion problem, solves the problem by creating distance and reducing anxiety, and creates a problem in that it isolates and alienates people who could benefit from each other if they were only able to relate better (Nichols, 1984).

Fusion is an interesting paradox that provides both a source of and a relief from anxiety. The more intense the emotional needs of people in a relationship, the more they look to the relationship to fulfill those needs and relieve the anxiety. However, the emotional pressures of the intense relationship forces them into compromised, uncomfortable positions — an impossible paradox.

Family Projection Process:

The family projection process describes how the fusion of the parents is transmitted to the children. The mother believes that she sees certain insecurity in a child and behaves toward that child as if that insecurity were real. The child accepts and is molded by the mother's belief and behavior, and begins to behave as the mother does. The emotional fusion — the lack of differentiation between parent and child — may be manifest as a warm, dependent bond, or an angry, conflictual struggle. The child's functioning is stunted either way.

Multigenerational Projection System:

The multigenerational transmission process describes how the family emotional process is handed down from one generation to the other. Clifford Sager (1976), who discusses the multigenerational approach, contends that dysfunctional behaviors or patterns are passed from one generation to the next in some nonverbal manner. Problems transmitted across the generations can be helped by open discussion and subsequent recognition of the situation.

Influence of Sibling Position:

Bowen (1978) concurred with Toman (1961) on the importance of birth order position. Although Toman's conclusions are not empirical, they have attracted much interest. The hypothesis states that a child's birth order position in the family fosters the development of specific personality characteristics in that child. Bowen proposes that the family projection system may interfere with this process if a child has been triangulated between the parents. In this case, the typical characteristics may not occur. Knowledge of the general characteristics and an awareness of the family dynamics is beneficial in predicting a child's role in the family emotional process; this information is helpful in understanding and predicting multigenerational transmission of family patterns.

BOWENIAN THERAPY TECHNIQUES

Bowenian family therapy is designed to identify the patterns that originated in the past yet have a strong detrimental hold on the clients in the present. He uses genograms to understand family relationships (Bowen, 1980); finds the fusions, the triangles, and the undifferentiated ego mass; then detriangulates to allow the family members to differentiate and foster emotionally supportive relationships that allow sufficient freedom for each family member to become a unique individual. All this is done using an analytic approach.

The therapist must be on guard to avoid becoming emotionally triangulated by a couple in accordance with the basic assumption that emotional tension between two people results in their trying to trap a third person in the emotional issues between them. The therapist needs to set the proper tone for the sessions — lively enough to be meaningful, calm and cool enough to remain objective. The therapist, using provocative questions and comments to regulate the amount and intensity of interaction, forces the couple to interact directly. Balance between thinking and feeling needs to be maintained through the therapist's control of the situation.

The interaction must not be allowed to become destructive and attacking. This can sometimes be achieved by having each party talk to the therapist rather than to each other. In this way, couples who have not listened and heard one another for years may now be given the opportunity to listen and understand their partners. Change requires talking plus willingness to listen. Sometimes a point can be made by using the indirect technique of telling about another couple with a similar problem and their difficulties in dealing with that problem.

Bowen believed that every family therapist must detriangulate from his or her family of origin and be free internally of all crippling entanglements of past and present before taking full responsibility for clients. Bowen did this for himself in a clever and enterprising manner. He wrote letters to each of his family members, telling what gossip and rumors specific to others had spread to him. Then he told them when he would be coming home for a visit. He showed up as promised and had to deal with a very upset group of people. After things died down, many family relationships were better than they had been before. Bowen felt free and his family had benefited as well. In the same way that a classical psychoanalyst must undergo a personal analysis in order to understand and stay clear from destructive countertransference, the Bowenian family therapist must differentiate from the family of origin so as not to be triangulated. This is the family correlate of countertransference (Nichols, 1984).

The therapist helps family members deal with each other with a calm rationality, teaching each to state his or her own feelings by using the "I" language, thus differentiating from the family mass. After sufficient progress toward differentiation in the nuclear family has been accomplished, both are encouraged to explore, and eventually differentiate from, their own families of origin. Genograms (Bowen, 1980) are used to explore and understand family relationships. The emphasis on extended social and family groups goes beyond the nuclear family.

CONCLUSION

Marriage and family therapy is fast becoming the treatment of choice for many clients and many therapists. Many clients probably find it easier to confront a relationship problem, which they may believe is the sole province of their partner, rather than admit to a personal deficiency. Therapists find marriage and family therapy to be a dynamic, exciting, and efficacious way to work.

This chapter has been only a brief introduction to the intricacies of the marriage and family mode of treatment. Further reading includes: the psychoanalytic family therapy of Nathan Ackerman, strategic therapy of Jay Haley, structural therapy of Salvador Minuchin, behavioral family therapy of Gerald Patterson, Carl Whitaker's experiential therapy, and the many other variations of each conceived by so many creative, competent professionals. The field as a whole "is full of challenge, full of surprises, and highly rewarding" (Bloch & Simon, 1982).

REFERENCES

Ackerman, N. W. (1958). *The psychodynamics of family life: Diagnosis and treatment of family relationships*. New York: Basic Books.

Andolfi, M. (1980). Prescribing the family's own dysfunctional rules as a therapeutic strategy. *Journal of Marriage & Family Therapy, 6,* 9-41.

Bateson, G., Jackson, D. D., Haley, J., & Weakland, J. (1956). Toward a theory of schizophrenia. *Behavioral Science, 1,* 270-283.

Bateson, G., Jackson, D. D., Haley, J., & Weakland, J. (1963). A note on the double-bind. *Family Process, 2*, 251-264.

Bloch, D. & Simon, R. (Eds.). (1982). *The strength of family therapy: Selected papers of Nathan Ackerman.* New York: Brunner/Mazel.

Boszormenyi-Nagy, I. & Krasner, B. R. (1986). *Between give and take: A clinical guide to contextual therapy.* New York: Brunner/Mazel.

Bowen, M. (1961). Family psychotherapy. *American Journal of Orthopsychiatry, 31*, 40-60.

Bowen, M. (1966). The use of family in clinical practice. *Comprehensive Psychiatry, 7*, 345-374.

Bowen, M. (1978). *Family therapy in clinical practice.* New York: Jason Aronson.

Bowen, M. (1980). Preface. In E. A. Carter & M. McGoldrick (Eds.), *The family life cycle: A framework for family therapy.* New York: Gardner Press.

Bowlby, J. (1949). The study and reduction of group tension in the family. *Human Relations, 2*, 123-128.

Duhl, F. J., Kantor, D., & Duhl, B. S. (1973). Learning, space and action in family therapy: A primer of sculpture. In D. A. Bloch (Ed.), *Techniques of family therapy.* New York: Grune & Stratton.

Freud, S. (1960). *The psychopathology of everyday life: The standard edition of the complete psychological works of Sigmund Freud.* (Edited and translated by J. Strachey). London: Hogarth Press. (Original work published in 1901).

Fromm-Reichman, F. (1948). Notes on the development of treatment of schizophrenics by psychoanalytic psychotherapy. *Psychiatry, II*, 263-274.

Ginsberg, S. W. (1955). The mental health movement and its theoretical assumptions. In R. Kotinsky & H. Witmer (Eds.), *Community programs for mental health.* Cambridge, MA: Harvard University Press.

Haley, J. (1963). *Uncommon therapy.* New York: Norton.

Hoffman, L. (1981). *Foundations of family therapy.* New York: Basic Books.

Hubert, D. J. & Hubert, C. E. (1986). Sabotaging siblings: An overlooked aspect of family therapy with drug dependent adolescents. *Journal of Psychoactive Drugs, 18*(1), 31-41.

Jackson, D. D. (1954). Suicide. *Scientific American, 191*, 88-96.

Jackson, D. D. & Weakland, J. H. (1959). Schizophrenic symptoms and family interaction. *Archives of General Psychiatry*, 618-621.

Minuchin, S. (1974). *Families and family therapy.* Cambridge, MA: Harvard University Press.

Moreno, J. L. (1945). *Psychodrama.* New York: Beacon House.

Nichols, N. (1984). *Family therapy concepts and methods.* New York: Gardner Press.

Papp, P. (1976). Family choreography. In Guerin (Ed.), *Family therapy: Theory and practice.* New York: Gardner Press.

Penn, P. (1985). Feet forward: Future questions, future maps. *Family Process, 24*(30), 299-310.

Piercy, F. P., et al. (1986). *Family therapy sourcebook.* New York: Guilford Press.

Sager, C. (1976). *Marriage contracts and couple therapy.* New York: Brunner/Mazel.

Satir, V. (1983). *Conjoint family therapy,* 3rd ed. Palo Alto: Science and Behavior Books.

Selvini-Palazzoli, M., et al. (1978). *Paradox and counterparadox.* New York: Jason Aronson.

Thomas, M. B. (1992). *An introduction to marital and family therapy.* New York: Macmillan.

Toman, W. (1961). *Family constellation.* New York: Springer Publishing Co.

Watzlawick, P.A., Beavin, J. H., & Jackson, D. D. (1967). *Pragmatics of human communication.* New York: W. W. Norton.

Whitaker, C. (1975). Psychotherapy of the absurd: With a special emphasis on the psychotherapy of aggression. *Family Process, 14,* 1-16.

Wynne, L. (1977). Schizophrenics and their families: Research on parental communication. In J. M. Tanner (Ed.), *Developments in psychiatric research.* London: Hoddler & Stroughton.

Wynne, L. (1988). An epigenetic model of family processes. In C. J. Falicov (Ed.), *Family transitions: Continuity and change over the life cycle* (pp. 81-106). New York: Guilford Press.

10

A Problem-Centered Approach to Interviewing in Family Therapy

Donald R. Catherall, PhD

Dr. Catherall is Executive Director, The Phoenix Institute, Chicago, IL.

KEY POINTS

- The primary goal of the problem-centered approach to interviewing is to identify and resolve the presenting problem. The family is helped to identify maladaptive problem-solving patterns and acquire more effective problem-solving mechanisms.

- The five levels of the intervention structure are: identifying the problem; developing solutions; implementing solutions; resolving interpersonal conflicts; and resolving intrapersonal conflicts.

- In problem-centered family therapy, the therapist must establish an alliance with each individual and also with the family system as a whole.

- To identify the problem, the therapist must ascertain how each family member views the conflicts.

- When developing solutions, the therapist must help the family members reach an agreement regarding which methods are appropriate for addressing their dilemma.

- During the implementation of the solution, the therapist must help direct both in-session and extra-session behavior in order to recognize whether the solution is successful and to determine why it may be failing.

Source: Catherall, D. R. (1989). Interviewing in family therapy: The problem-centered approach. In J. C. Hanson (Ed.), The family therapy collections (pp. 49–69). Rockville, MD: Aspen Publishers, Inc. Copy right (c) 1989 J. C. Hansen. Reprinted by permission of J. C. Hansen.

INTRODUCTION

Generations of therapists have struggled with the complexities of maintaining a therapeutic focus in the treatment of individual clients. They have been faced with a number of decisions, involving issues such as the degree to which they will structure the interview, how active and directive they will be, how they will define the therapeutic contract, and how they will build and maintain a therapeutic alliance. The field of family therapy further complicates these decisions by introducing a new dimension to the interview: the presence of other family members.

Family therapists quickly discovered that many techniques that work in individual therapy are contraindicated with families. The nondirective style of client-centered and psychoanalytic therapies is simply not possible with most families when they enter treatment. Such families are usually in a state of crisis, are often chaotic, and need the therapist to structure the interviews so they may discuss the immediate problem in a coherent manner. During the early phases of treatment, family therapists usually are required to be active; passive therapists can easily lose control of interviews when families are in crisis.

Families generally enter treatment to deal with specific problems (Pinsof, 1983a) rather than to increase self-understanding, personal growth, or self-actualization. In family therapy, the therapeutic contract almost always can be defined in terms of resolving a specific problem. Virtually all forms of family therapy begin with discussing the family's presenting problem, which offers a logical focus for the interview. Family therapy approaches begin to differ as the presenting problems are discussed and the therapist moves toward intervention strategies. Different methods of discussing the presenting problem constitute different intervention strategies, just as deciding who must be present constitutes choosing an intervention strategy.

Family therapists view the therapeutic alliance differently from individual therapists (Pinsof & Catherall, 1986). With a family, the therapist must establish an alliance not only with individuals but with the entire system, and must consider the effect of an alliance with any family member on the alliance with the other members. Family members may have conflicting goals for therapy, which places the therapist in a difficult position. Family members often are divided into various coalitions and are quite sensitive to whose side the therapist takes (Sluzki, 1978). The therapist must somehow maintain an alliance with the whole system and with the individual members, despite the conflicts and differences.

The advent of systems theory changed not only the interpersonal context of therapy (i.e., who is present) but the overall manner in which symptoms and problems are understood. Many family therapists have been exposed to the theories and methods of individual approaches and can conceptualize the presenting problem from both intrapersonal and systemic perspectives. However, this abundance of theoretical viewpoints can lead to considerable confusion in choosing intervention strategies. Many therapists adopt one perspective and stand by it in all situations, which is not always adaptive. A better approach is to have a theoretical framework that integrates intrapersonal and systemic perspectives. Such a framework should suggest when to employ which perspective in selecting interventions.

The problem-centered approach (Pinsof, 1983a) organizes multiple theoretical perspectives into a structure of clearly prioritized intervention strategies. It offers a framework that structures the content of the interviews and defines the therapist's role in helping families resolve their problems. This approach also attends to the development and maintenance of the therapeutic alliance (Pinsof & Catherall, 1986). The presenting problem is accepted as the central organizing feature of the therapy, and its solution is the focus of the interviews.

THE PROBLEM-CENTERED MODEL

The problem-centered approach to family treatment was pioneered by Epstein and colleagues (1978, 1981) at McMaster University, where it became known as the McMaster model. Later, it was refined, elaborated, and extended beyond family therapy by Pinsof (1983a) at the Family Institute of Chicago; this researcher initially drew on Kaplan's work on sexual disorders (1974, 1979). In particular, this researcher adopted her method of organizing theoretical models and associated interventions in a hierarchical fashion. She broadened the McMaster model into a comprehensive framework for integrating family, couple, and individual therapies. Because this chapter focuses on family therapy, readers interested in a broader examination of the conceptual framework of the model should refer to Pinsof (1983a) on integrative problem-centered therapy.

The goal of treatment in the problem-centered model is the resolution of the presenting problem (or any new problem the family targets), "the ultimate reference point to which all therapist interventions must be related" (Pinsof, 1983a). The therapeutic task helps the family acquire more effective problem-solving mechanisms to deal with the presenting problem and similar problems in the future. The therapist must identify maladaptive problem-solving patterns in the family and teach the family to recognize and modify them. The therapist approaches the family system with the assumption that a constellation of factors maintain the system's inability to resolve the problem and that the therapist must identify and modify this "problem maintenance structure" (Feldman & Pinsof, 1982).

The problem maintenance structure is approached in a straightforward manner. It assumes that family members are psychologically healthy, want to cooperate, and can use direct assistance. More extensive and indirect assistance is used only if the patient system proves unable to make effective use of direct minimal assistance. The problem maintenance structure is then hypothesized to be more complex and less superficial.

INTERVENTION STRUCTURE

The interventions are ordered in a hierarchical structure that stems from the presenting problem and a consensually derived adaptive solution. Once the solution is agreed upon, the family is directed to implement the solution strategy. The therapist then assists the family and offers expertise concerning the solution strategies. The therapist's role often is educational and focuses on issues such as lack of information, resources, or competence in employing behavioral techniques. Interventions are directed toward improving the patient system's ability to employ the adaptive solution.

If the family cannot implement the solution with appropriate help from the therapist, the therapist must explore the problem-solving block by developing and testing hypotheses about its nature. The hypotheses are organized hierarchically and explored methodically along the block determinant continuum, which organizes hypotheses from simple explanations of a relatively immediate origin to more complex explanations of a more remote origin.

The therapist first develops and tests hypotheses that assume the block is at the level of systemic or interpersonal functioning. The therapist's role becomes less educational as he or she actively explores the interpersonal nature of the system, looking at issues such as power distribution, communication of affect, quality of structural boundaries, and assignment of roles. Interventions in this range of the block determinant continuum are directed toward surfacing suppressed emotions, resolving interpersonal conflicts, identifying and reducing catastrophic fears, and weakening inappropriately rigid boundaries or strengthening weak boundaries.

When efforts to resolve systemic block determinants fail, the therapist should explore hypotheses related to individual psychopathology. This is the most remote end of the block determinant continuum. The therapist's role here is more psychodynamic in nature, exploring the intrapsychic origins of the problem-solving block; interventions are directed toward helping the individual separate historical issues from the current situation, confront irrational fears and expectations, and build ego strength. Successful work at this intrapersonal level is always followed, or accompanied, by further work at the interpersonal (systemic) level. Individuals are encouraged to act on their insights to change their behavior in their ongoing intimate relationships.

The intervention structure does not correspond to the usual chronological stages of treatment, such as beginning, middle, and termination. The problem-solving blocks are pursued from immediate to remote determinants, but then the focus moves back to interpersonal and behavioral blocks. The focus can move around on the block determinant continuum, not only in resolving one blocked behavior but in pursuing new blocks and new problems. Thus, the problem, which is the reference point of the treatment, may change as treatment progresses. The intervention structure can be expressed in terms of identifying the problem, developing solutions, implementing solutions, resolving interpersonal blocks, and resolving intrapersonal blocks. The focus of the therapy moves through these categories and may span more than one at any given point in the process.

THE INTERVENTION STRUCTURE IN ACTION

Identifying the Problem:

The process of identifying the problem is best accomplished with all relevant family members present. This provides the therapist with the most direct access to the significant interpersonal components of the problem maintenance structure. Hence, the initial telephone contact should be lengthy enough to establish who belongs to the system. Everyone who resides in the household should be requested to come to the initial session. Others who are strongly involved with the family should also come (e.g., extended family who live nearby). This rule applies if the problem involves a symptomatic member or a generational conflict; if the presenting problem is a marital conflict, the first session is usually conducted only with the couple.

The first goal of the initial session is to establish a beginning alliance with all family members. The second goal is to establish the nature of the presenting problem. These goals often are accomplished simultaneously as the alliance is facilitated by the manner in which the therapist investigates the problem. The alliance develops in a therapeutic atmosphere in which each member (regardless of age) is understood to have his or her own opinions and feelings.

> Each member is asked to give his or her opinion on the nature of the problem, how he or she feels about the problem and the sequelae of the problem, and what he or she has done to try to solve the problem. Each aspect of this triad is explored in depth, particularly the attempted solutions. The therapist must know the specifics of how each solution was implemented and why it failed. Frequently, an appropriate solution was attempted but was not supported by all the members, not pursued long enough, or not used consistently. This process is conducted in an atmosphere of nonjudgmental data collection: the therapist is empathic with each individual's perspective but offers no opinion until all members have presented their views. The therapist's task at this point is to clarify, empathize, and understand.

Case Dialogue:

> *Therapist*: I would like to hear from each of you about how you see the problem. Would you like to begin, Mr. A? What do you see as the problem you are here to work on?
>
> *Mr. A*: Well, the problem is our son, Jack. He's always mouthing off to his mother and won't do anything she tells him. The two of them are always arguing.
>
> *Therapist*: And what have you done to try and solve this problem?
>
> *Mr. A*: I tell Jack I will give him a whipping when I get home if his mother says he's mouthing off to her. And we have grounded him and taken away the use of the car.

Therapist: What about the whippings? Have you given him a whipping?

Mr. A: Several times.

Therapist: Have these things changed Jack's behavior in any way?

Mr. A: Nope; he's still arguing with her all the time.

Therapist: I see. Mrs. A, what about you? What do you see as the problem?

Mrs. A: As my husband said, Jack just won't do anything I tell him. He's disrespectful and he does as he pleases. If I try to appeal to him, all I get is smart-mouth answers.

Therapist: So, how are you feeling about this problem?

Mrs. A: I'm fed up. At first, I wanted Jack to be happy with what I asked him to do. Now I don't care; I just want cooperation.

Therapist: All right, Mrs. A. Let me speak to Jack. Jack, what do you feel is the problem? Your parents both say you are disobedient and have a smart mouth. But I want to know how you see it.

Jack: I'm not disobedient. Ask them. I haven't gone out once since they grounded me. And other people don't think I'm a smart aleck. It's just my mom. She's always on my case about something. She never lets up. She's always asking questions about my friends and what I do with them. I do what she asks when it's reasonable.

Therapist: Jack, how do you feel about this constant bickering between you and your mom?

Jack: I hate it. I feel like I'm at war and there's nobody else on my side.

Therapist: Does your dad ever take your side?

Jack: No. Sometimes he just tries to stay out of it; other times he comes down on me and says I have to do whatever Mom says. But he never says she's wrong.

Therapist: What have you done to try and get along better with your mom?

Jack: I just try to be reasonable with her, but it doesn't work. She doesn't listen to me when I explain something. I know I get sarcastic sometimes, but it's because she's not listening to me.

Therapist: All right, Jack, thank you. Mrs. A, Jack says that he's not disrespectful or disobedient in general. He feels that the problem is mostly between you and him. What do you think about that?

Mrs. A: It's true that I'm the one he's always mouthing off at, but then I'm the one who has to deal with him the most.

Therapist: All right then. It sounds like we agree that the problem occurs primarily between Jack and Mrs. A, who feels Jack is disrespectful and won't cooperate with her. And Jack feels that Mom doesn't listen to him and asks unreasonable things of him. And everyone agrees that Jack and Mom are arguing too much.

Developing Solutions:

The goal of the therapy in this phase is to reach an agreement with the patient system regarding the appropriate solution to the problem. The adaptive solution considers the available resources and calls upon the family to perform behaviors that would logically help resolve the presenting problem. Previous failures to employ the same solution strategy are not considered adequate reason to ignore the strategy. Instead, the therapist works with the family to establish agreement that the adaptive solution can resolve the presenting problem if employed effectively.

The nature of the adaptive solution is not terribly profound nor difficult to understand. Rather, the solution is usually obvious and based on common sense; it is often something that family members have already tried. The use of relatively sophisticated, complex, and imaginative psychological theories is not necessary in developing the adaptive solution; these theories come into play if the family cannot employ the adaptive solution.

Usually, the therapist should begin working on identifying potential adaptive solutions by the end of the second session or the beginning of the third session.

Case Dialogue:

Therapist: Now that we agree that the problem is that Jack and Mrs. A are arguing too much, I would like to clarify what we are working toward. Mrs. A needs Jack to speak to her more respectfully and be more cooperative. Jack needs Mrs. A to listen to him more carefully and not make unreasonable requests. If these things happen, the arguing should diminish. Let's discuss how these things can be brought about. Mrs. A, how will you know if Jack is being more respectful?

Mrs. A: He should not swear at me or say things like "That's stupid" when I ask him to do something. And he should not be sarcastic! He should stay in the room when I am talking to him and not turn his back.

Therapist: I want to make sure that you understand what it is you do that your mother feels is disrespectful.

Jack: Yeah, I understand.

Therapist: All right, let's talk about cooperation. I think the problem here is when Jack feels his mom's request is unreasonable. Mrs. A, how would you like Jack to tell you if he thinks your request is unreasonable?

Mrs. A: I certainly don't want him to say it's stupid!

Therapist: What would you prefer he say?

Mrs. A: Just that he thinks it's unreasonable.

Therapist: Can you do that, Jack?

Jack: Sure, I do it all the time but she doesn't listen.

Therapist: Do you explain why you think it's unreasonable?

Jack: Yeah.

Therapist: All right then. Mrs. A, is there a way that you can demonstrate to Jack that you listened to his explanation and understand it?

Mrs. A.: I don't know. What if I still feel my request is reasonable?

Therapist: I have an idea. How about if you use a technique called "checking it out"? Jack, if you feel your mother is not understanding your explanation, you can check it out by asking her to explain your position back to you. Then, if she doesn't understand it entirely, you can explain further. Would you be willing to do this, Mrs. A?

Mrs. A: You mean if he asks, I should tell him why he thinks my request is unreasonable?

Therapist: That's right. It's a way of demonstrating that you are listening and that you understand.

Mrs. A: Well, I can do that, but what if I still feel that my request is reasonable?

Therapist: In that case, Jack should go ahead and do whatever you are requesting. You may not like that, Jack, but your mother should still be in charge. However, I would add that in the next session we will then discuss all the requests Jack felt were unreasonable. If Jack can convince you that certain requests are unreasonable, then new rules can be negotiated. Do you understand what that means, Jack? Once your mother has demonstrated that she has listened, you must abide by her decision and save your arguments for the next session in here.

Jack: Sounds like "Jack loses" to me.

Therapist: Not necessarily. This can help stop the bickering. You do "lose" at the time of the hassle if your mother insists on your doing what she asks, but you will have an opportunity to influence the family rules so that it doesn't happen again. But until a rule changes, you must do as your mother requests. That means your mother gets the cooperation she wants and you get to make sure that she really listens to your side.

Jack: Yeah, okay. I'll try it.

Implementing Solutions:

When an adaptive solution has been established, the focus of the therapy shifts to its implementation. The therapist's role changes: He or she is no longer simply clarifying, understanding, and exploring options, but coaching in-session behavior and directing extra-session behavior. The therapist actively monitors the family's efforts at employing the adaptive solution.

The therapist is mandated to assume an oversight role by the family's agreement about the adaptive solution. The therapeutic mandate is therefore dependent on genuine agreement about the adaptive solution. If the family has not really accepted the adaptive solution, the therapist's mandate is unclear, and the family may resist interventions because of apparent lack of relevance.

The stage of solution implementation becomes the central platform for the hierarchical structure of theoretical perspectives and associated interventions. All further interventions are accomplished in order to return to implementing the adaptive solution.

If the family is unable to implement the adaptive solution, the therapist looks for maladaptive patterns in their problem-solving behavior. Once maladaptive patterns are identified, they are brought to the family's attention. The family is then directed to avoid the maladaptive pattern and to learn new adaptive patterns of problem solving. Maladaptive patterns simply may be the result of inadequate information or understanding of behavioral change techniques, or they may be the manifestation of maladaptive formations in the family's structure of roles, boundaries, and distribution of power. Interventions may be educational (or psychoeducational), behavioral, or structural.

Educational or psychoeducational interventions might be used to help a family understand and deal better with a disabled member, such as a child with a learning disability or an adult with schizophrenia (Anderson, Hogarty, & Reiss, 1980). Behavioral interventions might be used to help a family deal with an acting-out child (Kaye, 1984) or to help a couple overcome sexual dysfunctions (Kaplan, 1974). Structural interventions might be used to help a family with ineffective power distribution across generations (Minuchin, 1974). The choice of which interventions to use depends on the therapist's assessment of the nature of the maladaptive problem-solving pattern and the family's failure to obtain adequate benefit from earlier interventions.

At this point in the therapy, the therapist begins to form hypotheses concerning the problem maintenance structure. The therapist explores these hypotheses in a hierarchical fashion, ruling out simple and superficial explanations before pursuing more complex explanations. The primary focus of these initial hypotheses falls on determining the interpersonal function of the problem or symptom. The therapist investigates the immediate block determinant first and then moves along the continuum toward more remote determinants if the maladaptive patterns persist.

Case Dialogue:

Therapist: Good afternoon. It's been a week since we've seen each other. How has it gone? Were there any opportunities for Jack and Mrs. A to discuss Mrs. A's requests?

Mrs. A: Well, I think it's been mixed. Jack was better about not calling me names but he still argued when I asked him to put away the lawn mower, garden tools, hose, and sprinkler. He said it wasn't his job, and when he finally did it, he just dumped the stuff on the floor of the garage.

Therapist: I see, so he did the job but not in a very satisfactory way. What did you do when you found that he had dumped the stuff on the floor of the garage?

Mrs. A: I yelled at him and he yelled at me. He still didn't get everything put away properly; my husband had to do it when he got home.

Therapist: Sounds like we have to define cooperation a little better. Jack, did you feel that your mom listened to you during this interaction?

Jack: All I said was that it wasn't my job. I didn't have to ask if she understood; she knows whose job the yard work is. It's Dad's job.

Therapist: How did you feel about having to do your dad's job?

Jack: I didn't like it; it made me mad.

Therapist: Mad at whom?

Jack: At Mom.

Therapist: All right, this makes me think we need to clarify a couple of points. One is that cooperation means doing the job to your mom's satisfaction. Do you accept that, Jack?

Jack: Yeah, okay.

Therapist: Another is that there needs to be a way for Jack to express his resentment. Mrs. A, is it okay with you if Jack is angry, as long as he still gets the job done?

Mrs. A: I understand his feeling angry, but I won't tolerate what he does with it sometimes.

Therapist: What does he do with it?

Mrs. A: You know — getting hostile, disrespectful, calling me names.

Jack: She yelled at me first. You'd start yelling too if she was yelling at you.

Therapist: You're saying she provoked it. Why did you yell, Mrs. A?

Mrs. A: I guess I was frustrated when I discovered he had just dumped the stuff. I thought we had worked it out. You're going to say I shouldn't yell at him either.

Therapist: Well, I don't think it excuses Jack's behavior. But, yes, these escalations require two parties. I would like you both to make an effort to control your tempers and discuss things rationally. Mr. A, where were you when your wife and Jack had the argument about the gardening tools?

Mr. A: I was at the office. I usually work on Saturdays. I found out about it when I got home that evening.

Therapist: Jack said that the yard work was your responsibility. Is that right?

Mr. A: Pretty much. I enjoy working in the garden and have assumed responsibility for all the outdoor work.

Therapist: So did you leave the tools out in the first place?

Mr. A: Well, I had them out, but it's not like I left them out. I often leave the hose and sprinklers set up and just move them around.

Therapist: Did Mrs. A say anything to you about putting it away?

Mr. A: I don't think so.

Mrs. A: Yes I did. I asked you to put the lawn mower away early in the week because it didn't belong on the patio. You said you'd do it later.

Therapist: So you asked your husband to do it first, but he didn't do it. Then you and Jack got into a hassle over it. How did you feel when Mr. A didn't do it?

Mrs. A: Oh, I know how busy he is. He often forgets little things. I have learned to live with that.

Therapist: And it doesn't make you angry when your husband forgets to do these little things?

Mrs. A: Well, it used to make me mad, but, like I said, I've learned to live with it.

Therapist: What kinds of things do you get angry at your husband for now?

Mrs. A: Well, nothing really. I wish he was around more but. . . . Sometimes it irritates me that he puts me off so much; he's always got other things that take priority. He's a very busy man.

Therapist: It seems that you have learned to put up with disappointment from your husband, but you won't tolerate it from your son.

Mrs. A: My husband never speaks to me in the tone that my son does!

Therapist: Do you ever speak to your husband in the tone that you use with your son when you are irritated?

Mrs. A: No, my husband never gets me that angry.

Resolving Interpersonal Blocks:

If direct efforts to implement the adaptive solution are not effective, then the therapist should explore unresolved difficulties between family members. Blocks at the interpersonal level can stem from conflicts between members or from systemic rules concerning certain behaviors, thoughts, or feelings. The therapist maintains the mandate while shifting the focus ("defocusing") to these blocks by indicating how the interpersonal dimension is an aspect of the adaptive solution. The underlying premise is that system members must be able to work together effectively to implement the adaptive solution. If they are impeded by unresolved conflicts or prohibited from certain behaviors, thoughts, or feelings, then they are not working together effectively. Working together implies more than simply not interfering with each other; it includes the provision of emotional support.

When the therapist makes the transition to working on interpersonal blocks, there is a change in the communicative process. In general, family members are encouraged to speak directly to each other rather than about each other to the therapist. During this phase, the therapist helps the family communicate by asking clarifying questions and acting as a type of referee. The therapist may need to block excessive expressions of hostility or call a halt to nonproductive lines of discourse. The therapist must carefully track the topic and help the family stay on the subject rather than bring in unrelated grievances or unnoticed topic shifts. The therapist's goal is to help the family learn to communicate more effectively; he or she makes the family aware of its maladaptive communication patterns and trains family members to recognize them as they occur.

The therapist can make the transition to the interpersonal level by exploring the quality of "emotional access" across the various relationships. Emotional access can be seen in the expression of both positive and negative feelings (and associated thoughts and behaviors), and includes both affective responsiveness and affective involvement (Epstein & Bishop, 1981). If a relationship is restricted to only one or the other of these feelings, or if the relationship tolerates only a narrow range of feelings, then it is likely that a deficiency in the emotional access exists. If it is the marital/parental relationship that is suffering, it usually follows that there are problems in the child-rearing patterns.

Constrictions in emotional access often are accompanied by catastrophic expectations. Certain thoughts and feelings are not expressed because of fears of what could happen if they were to be expressed. Family members may avoid disagreeing, becoming angry or sad, or being affectionate because they fear the consequences of these actions. It is important to uncover these fears and determine whether they are realistic. Irrational fears can be defused in this way, and validated fears can give the therapist a more precise understanding of the nature of the system and the block(s).

Case Dialogue:

Therapist: You say that you never speak to your husband in the angry tone that you sometimes use with Jack. Tell me something. What do you think would happen if you were to get that angry with Mr. A?

Mrs. A: Why, I really don't know.

Therapist: Give me your best guess.

Mrs. A: Well, I suppose if I were to get really very angry, he might just leave.

Therapist: Do you think that you hold back on your anger at Mr. A because inside you fear that he would leave you?

Mrs. A: I don't know. Perhaps.

Mr. A: What has all this got to do with her problem with Jack?

Therapist: I'm thinking that your wife may displace some of her anger at you onto Jack because she is too fearful of getting angry at you directly.

Mr. A: Displace what anger at me?

Therapist: I'm not sure. That's a good question.

Jack: She's angry at you because you're never around. You never want to do anything with us.

Therapist: Jack, you said your dad never wants to do anything with "us." Are you angry at him for never being around?

Jack: Yes. Well, no, not exactly. I'm more perpetually disappointed.

Therapist: Maybe creating problems with your mother serves the purpose of getting your dad involved. Mrs. A, what about what Jack is saying? Are you dissatisfied with how much your husband is around and involved with the family?

Mrs. A: I've always wanted him to be with us more. It used to make me angry, but I've come to expect it.

Resolving Intrapersonal Blocks:

If problem-solving blocks do not seem to be determined primarily by current interpersonal factors, the therapist should entertain hypotheses about the intrapsychic dynamics of individual members of the patient system. When the therapist defocuses to blocks at the intrapersonal level, his or her role shifts: the therapist becomes less directive and active, often increasing the use of interpretation and focusing more on the therapist-client relationship. These changes can be experienced by some clients as an abandonment or as blaming. The shift in the therapist's role, along with the associated shift in the expectations of the client(s), should be processed as they occur. In some instances, the therapist may choose to see system members individually or refer them for long-term work with other therapists. The therapist should make a referral rather than do the individual work personally if he or she feels that excessive involvement with one member will threaten the alliance with the whole system or with other members.

Blocks at the intrapersonal level include unresolved conflicts from earlier relationships and personality defects that interfere with present functioning. Work on these issues should be accomplished in conjoint sessions whenever possible, because the significant other(s) can share in the insights and provide support to the individual who is temporarily the focus of the therapy. Some intrapersonal work may need to be done in individual sessions because of excessive attacking and scapegoating in the conjoint sessions. However, the goal of the intrapersonal work is always to facilitate resolution of the interpersonal issues being worked on in the conjoint sessions.

Defocusing away from the interpersonal to the intrapersonal level again causes a change in the communicative process. The individual is encouraged to become reflective and to report on inner experience. Moreover, the individual is accepted as the best authority on his or her experience, and other family members are not allowed to attack that person's feelings. It can be a time when blaming decreases and understanding increases as individuals are able to "own" their issues.

The transition from interpersonal to intrapersonal occurs in a variety of ways. Perhaps most often, a member will spontaneously bring up historical issues and acknowledge a possible connection with the current interpersonal problem. Pinsof's remote block determinant operation (1983b) is a technique for defocusing from the current interpersonal context to the historical. The therapist works with an individual to heighten his or her awareness of his or her affective reaction to the problematic situation under discussion and asks the individual to think back to the first time he or she ever felt the way he or she is now feeling. An important aspect of this operation is that the therapist establishes a clear distinction between the current interpersonal discussion and the sudden request to think back beyond the current relationship.

Working at the interface between the intrapersonal and interpersonal levels often results in family members developing a better awareness of how their current feelings are influenced by transferences. This component of the work emphasizes the individual's responsibility for changing his or her current behavior after the development of insight. But change is also sought among the other family members, who should understand the individual better and be able to respond to him or her in a more adaptive way. Thus, all family members retain responsibility for change.

Case Dialogue:

Therapist: Mr. A, were you aware that your family wanted you around more?

Mr. A: I've always known that my wife wanted me home more. I have a very demanding career. It doesn't give me a lot of free time.

Therapist: From what Jack was saying, it sounds like you aren't very available even when you are home.

Mr. A: I'm pretty tense when I come home. I need time alone to wind down. I always have. That's why I like working in the garden.

Therapist: What happens when you do spend time with the family? Do you enjoy it?

Mr. A: It's okay. We have a nice life.

Therapist: Do you come from a family that spent a lot of time together?

Mr. A: No more than average. My father was gone a lot. He was generally upset about something when he was around.

Therapist: What do you mean?

Mr. A: My father was very critical. I liked not having him around because he was always down on either me or my mother. And they fought a lot. It was not much fun to be around.

Therapist: Did you fight with him?

Mr. A: No, I didn't stand a chance against him.

Therapist: So what did you do?

Mr. A: I just stayed out of his way as much as possible. I left home at 17 and never went back, except for short visits.

Therapist: Are you doing the same thing now?

Mr. A: What do you mean?

Therapist: Are you staying away from the home to avoid conflict?

Mr. A: It's certainly no fun to be around when the two of them are going at it.

Therapist: Perhaps you avoid closeness with your wife because you don't want to get into a situation where you can be easily hurt by her criticism — as you were by your father's.

Mr. A: I don't know about that.

Mrs. A.: When we have a disagreement, you always tell me I'm being too critical.

Therapist: It seems that your wife is afraid to express her anger at you for fear you'll leave, and you're afraid to get close to her for fear she'll hurt you with her criticism. But the less you are around, the more angry she gets, and then turns it on Jack. And the more Mrs. A fights with Jack, the less you want to be around because the result is a conflictual home like the one you escaped. You're caught in a vicious circle.

Mrs. A.: How do we get out of it?

Therapist: Well, you have to learn to express your displeasures directly to your husband — despite his fear of criticism. And, Mr. A, you have to take a chance and get more involved with your family. And Jack has to learn to be more cooperative and express his displeasures in an acceptable fashion. This coming week, I would like to focus again on Jack and Mrs. A learning to interact more respectfully. But I would also like to have Mr. A more available to Mrs. A. Now, how can we go about arranging that?

THE THERAPEUTIC ALLIANCE

Bordin (1979) recommended viewing the therapeutic alliance in terms of the tasks, bonds, and goals of the therapy. To foster a positive alliance, the therapist and client must be in agreement about the goals, the therapeutic tasks must be accepted by the client as relevant, and a bond between the therapist and the client must be present. Although Bordin's model was developed for an individual therapy paradigm, the same conditions apply in family therapy; but they become more complicated due to the potential for multiple alliances. Family therapists have an alliance with each individual as well as with the entire system. Thus, alliance with one individual may threaten the alliance with another (Pinsof & Catherall, 1986). Usually, families are struggling actively with problems and place a greater demand on the therapist to do something than do many individual clients. The intensity of the demand and the fertile ground for countertransference reactions make family therapists especially vulnerable to bringing their own issues into the therapy; they need structure to guide their interventions (Catherall & Pinsof, 1987).

The problem-centered model is designed to maintain the best possible therapeutic alliance throughout treatment. It clearly defines when to explore the interpersonal and intrapersonal dimensions, and it gives the therapist a mandate that can extend into remote areas of a patient's life. The therapist establishes the relevance of these explorations by showing how the failure to employ the adaptive solution is linked to the interpersonal dimension, and how intrapersonal issues interfere with interpersonal functioning. Thus, the problem-centered orientation maintains a clear agreement about the goals of the therapy and establishes the relevance of therapeutic tasks.

The bond dimension of the alliance develops as a result of the therapist's respect for all family members and the therapist's focus on feelings. The model defines the expression and use of feelings as an important aspect of adaptive problem solving. The bridge to the interpersonal level is often the nonexpression of important feelings between system members. When the therapist inquires about with whom an individual shares his or her feelings, the underlying assumption is that this affective communication is an integral aspect of dealing with the problem. The therapist's attention to feelings and respect for the individual contribute to the development of a positive bond with each family member and with the family as a whole.

CONCLUSION

In the problem-centered model of interviewing, the therapist's task changes as the stages of the model unfold. After establishing agreement about the nature of the problem and the appropriate adaptive solution, the therapist first intervenes by educating the family and directing the appropriate behaviors to resolve the problem. If these efforts are not sufficient, the therapist assumes more of a referee role as the family is helped to interact and resolve their interpersonal issues. If the interpersonal issues are influenced by significant individual psychopathology, the family interacts less and the therapist becomes more centrally involved with the individual family members.

The therapist conducts the therapy so that it evolves through these stages as he or she tests hypotheses about the problem maintenance structure. The therapist must be able to propel the family system from one stage to another through techniques such as exploring the emotional access in the interpersonal system and exploring the transference origins of interpersonal issues. The therapist also must be alert to family reactions to the changes in his or her role (e.g., increases and decreases in directiveness), and must help the family process these changes so they do not interfere with the therapeutic task.

Finally, although the model was presented in a linear fashion, the reader is not obligated to move in the direction presented in this chapter. As intrapsychic and interpersonal issues are resolved, the therapist may become more active in helping the family make renewed attempts at implementing the adaptive solution. As adaptive solutions are effectively implemented, newer problems may emerge, leading the therapist again to pursue interpersonal and intrapsychic hypotheses and interventions.

REFERENCES

Anderson, C. M., Hogarty, G. E., & Reiss, D. J. (1980). Family treatment of adult schizophrenic patients: A psycho-educational approach. *Schizophrenia Bulletin, 6,* 490–505.

Bordin, E. S. (1979). The generalizability of the psychoanalytic concept of the therapeutic alliance. *Psychotherapy: Theory, Research and Practice, 16,* 252–260.

Catherall, D. R., & Pinsof, W. M. (1987). The impact of one's personal family life on the ability to establish viable therapeutic alliances. *Journal of Psychotherapy and the Family, 3*(2), 135–160.

Epstein, N. B., & Bishop, D. S., (1981). Problem-centered systems therapy of the family. In A. Gurman & D. Kniskern (Eds.), *Handbook of family therapy* (pp. 444–482). New York: Brunner/Mazel.

Epstein, N. B., Bishop, D. S., & Levin, S. (1978). The McMaster model of family functioning. *Journal of Marital and Family Therapy, 8,* 295–308.

Feldman, L. B., & Pinsof, W. M. (1982). Problem maintenance in family systems: An integrative model. *Journal of Marital and Family Therapy, 8,* 295–308.

Kaplan, H. S. (1974). *The new sex therapy.* New York: Brunner/Mazel.

Kaplan, H. S. (1979). *Disorders of sexual desire and other new concepts and techniques in sex therapy.* New York: Brunner/Mazel.

Kaye, K. (1984). *Family rules: Raising responsible children.* New York: Walker.

Minuchin, S. (1974). *Families and family therapy.* Cambridge, MA: Harvard University Press.

Pinsof, W. M. (1983a). Integrative problem-centered therapy: Toward the synthesis of family and individual psychotherapies. *Journal of Marital and Family Therapy, 9*(1), 19–35.

Pinsof, W. M. (1983b). *The marital-relational defocusing operation: The remote block determinant operation.* Unpublished manuscript. Center for Family Studies/The Family Institute of Chicago.

Pinsof, W. M., & Catherall, D. R. (1986). The integrative psychotherapy alliance: Family, couple, and individual therapy scales. *Journal of Marital and Family Therapy, 12*(2), 137–151.

Sluzki, C. E. (1978). Marital therapy from a systems theory perspective. In T. J. Paolino & B. S. McCrady (Eds.), *Marriage and marital therapy: Psychoanalytic, behavioral and systems theory perspectives* (pp. 366–394). New York: Brunner/Mazel.

11

Current Approaches to Therapy with Elderly Clients

Victor Molinari, PhD

Dr. Molinari is Director of Geropsychology at the Veterans Affairs Medical Center, Houston, TX, and Clinical Assistant Professor of Psychology in the Department of Psychiatry and Behavioral Sciences at Baylor College of Medicine, Houston, TX.

KEY POINTS

- The elderly constitute the fastest growing, yet most psychologically underserved, age group in the United States. Psychotherapy for the elderly requires specialized expertise and patience.

- General suggestions for working with elderly clients include: building a therapeutic alliance and a "shared world"; providing direct, problem-focused treatment with well-defined therapeutic goals; emphasizing the client's strengths; and dealing with current concerns rather than past failures.

- The psychological diagnosis of an elderly client may fall into four broad categories: recurrent functional impairment, late-life functional impairment, organic brain impairment, and minimal impairment.

- Barriers in providing services to the elderly include: aging stereotypes, therapeutic nihilism, the therapist's own aging concerns, avoidance of mortality issues, countertransference reactions, the therapist's fears of a devalued professional status associated with the unglam-orous status of geriatric clients, and lack of therapist training.

- Older adults are among the most rewarding clients; they are probably more likely than younger adults to express their gratitude directly to the therapist for the time devoted to making their lives better.

INTRODUCTION

Approximately 12% of the United States population is older than 65 years of age (Teri & Logsdon, 1992). In the next 40 years, the number of elderly will almost double, with the number of persons 85 years and older increasing most rapidly (Blazer, 1989). Although older adults have total prevalence rates for functional psychological problems similar to those of younger adults, they comprise only approximately 6% of clients treated in community mental health centers (Burns & Taube, 1990). Less than 3% of psychologists in private practice see older adults (Taube, Burns, & Kessler, 1984) and physicians are less likely to refer older patients to mental health professionals (Waxman, Carner, & Berkenstock, 1984).

It has been estimated that 80% of the elderly who require mental health services are underserved (Levenson & Felkins, 1979). Due to financial incentives for institutional rather than outpatient care, 85% of the elderly are treated for psychological problems on an inpatient basis (Gatz, Smyer, & Lawton, 1980). Nursing homes are a major destination for elderly mentally ill persons. Estimates indicate that 35%–85% of nursing home residents have mental health problems, but despite a growing base of knowledge, few receive proper treatment (Hinrichsen, 1990; Lichtenberg, 1994).

Unfortunately, geropsychiatric clients in mental health facilities routinely are administered psychotropic medication and are rarely recommended for psychotherapy, and there remains a dearth of psychologists trained to work with older adults (Gatz & Smyer, 1992; Teri & Logsdon, 1992). Such a state of practice is far from ideal, because researchers consistently have endorsed the view that, contrary to popular belief, *the elderly are indeed able to benefit from psychotherapy*. Nonetheless, professionals and lay people alike often harbor myths regarding mental illness in older adults; this constitutes a major barrier to the delivery of psychological care to this vastly overlooked group (see Table 11.1).

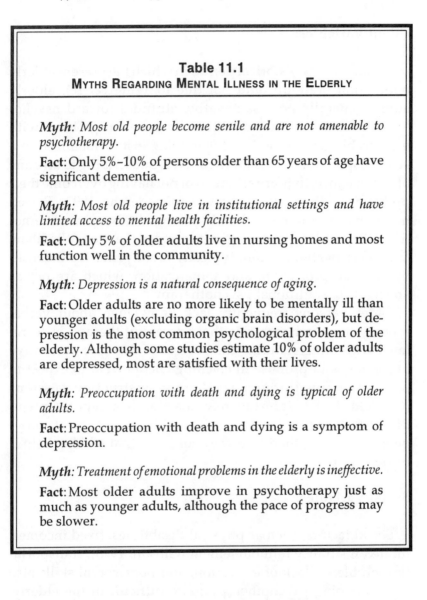

Table 11.1
MYTHS REGARDING MENTAL ILLNESS IN THE ELDERLY

Myth: Most old people become senile and are not amenable to psychotherapy.

Fact: Only 5%–10% of persons older than 65 years of age have significant dementia.

Myth: Most old people live in institutional settings and have limited access to mental health facilities.

Fact: Only 5% of older adults live in nursing homes and most function well in the community.

Myth: Depression is a natural consequence of aging.

Fact: Older adults are no more likely to be mentally ill than younger adults (excluding organic brain disorders), but depression is the most common psychological problem of the elderly. Although some studies estimate 10% of older adults are depressed, most are satisfied with their lives.

Myth: Preoccupation with death and dying is typical of older adults.

Fact: Preoccupation with death and dying is a symptom of depression.

Myth: Treatment of emotional problems in the elderly is ineffective.

Fact: Most older adults improve in psychotherapy just as much as younger adults, although the pace of progress may be slower.

WHY SUCH A LOW RATE OF PSYCHOTHERAPY IN THE ELDERLY?

Client, society, and therapist variables account for a low rate of psychotherapy in elderly clients.

Client Variables:

Because of the historical period in which the present elderly population grew up (and not due to aging *per se*), elderly adults generally possess negative attitudes toward psychological treatment. They often equate a mental problem with unalterable "craziness," and fear being institutionalized in a state hospital for the rest of their lives. Subscribing to an ethic of self-reliance, they are ashamed of not having overcome their problems on their own (Lebowitz & Niederehe, 1992). Raised in a home environment that discouraged talking about emotions, they are less psychologically minded (Lawton, Whelihan, & Belsky, 1980) and more typically favor primitive defenses like denial, projection, and somatization, which are not as amenable to traditional psychotherapy.

Older persons frequently lack knowledge about verbal therapy. Research suggests that successful therapy is correlated with understanding the process of therapy; innovative programs hold promise in teaching clients what to expect in psychotherapy through pretherapy instruction sessions (Garfield, 1978). Unfortunately, the elderly accept the prejudice that their problems are irreversible and a natural consequence of aging; therefore, they conclude that seeking help is futile.

Social Variables:

Social factors, such as physical disabilities, fixed incomes, limited insurance reimbursement (Gibson, 1973), transportation problems, lack of education, and poor verbal skills also make ongoing psychotherapy more difficult in the elderly. Perhaps the most significant social factor is the fragmentation of the mental health system, in which services adapted to the unique needs of the elderly are too few and disorganized to prevent them from "falling through the cracks." This lack of coordination has resulted in many chronically mentally ill elderly persons being "transinstitutionalized" from state hospitals to nursing homes.

Therapist Variables:

Perhaps the major reason why older persons do not receive psychotherapy is therapists' biases against providing care to the elderly (Table 11.2). Professionals often share society's negative stereotypes about the elderly (Gaitz, 1974). It is important to consider that older adults represent a *varied* age group (George, 1992) and cannot be pigeonholed into "grandpas in rocking chairs" or "Golden Girls."

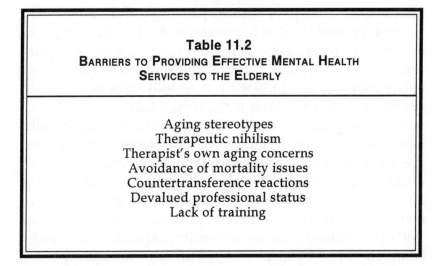

Table 11.2
BARRIERS TO PROVIDING EFFECTIVE MENTAL HEALTH SERVICES TO THE ELDERLY

Aging stereotypes
Therapeutic nihilism
Therapist's own aging concerns
Avoidance of mortality issues
Countertransference reactions
Devalued professional status
Lack of training

Also, in adults' later years, a pervasive therapeutic nihilism regarding the possibility of change seems to develop. This misconception began with Freud (1904), who theorized that an individual's character was fixed after age 5 and that it would be a far-too-long and arduous process to alter his or her personality after age 50. Jung (1933) disagreed and provided a much-needed antidote to Freud's pessimism. Jung believed that people were unable to attain wisdom until they had come to terms with the disowned masculine or feminine aspects of themselves and that this integration could be achieved only through the emotional openness acquired in the later years. Erikson (1963) postulated that the resolution of this final stage leads to mature knowledge and ego integrity.

It is important for therapists to scrutinize their beliefs about their clients' potential for change, because expectations affect outcome. If one expects limited results from psychotherapy, a self-fulfilling prophecy may result. Indeed, there is no good rationale for such discouragement, because research consistently has demonstrated that older clients improve just as much as younger clients (though often less quickly) with both cognitive-behavioral and interpersonal therapies (Thompson, Gallagher, & Steinmetz-Breckenridge, 1987).

Another therapist variable that may explain the lack of availability of psychotherapy to older clients is "gerontophobia"; that is, interaction with the elderly triggers unconscious fears of disability and dependence. Therapists must acknowledge and confront these issues in themselves before they can be addressed successfully with their elderly clients. A related inhibitor is the notion that the elderly will only talk of dying or actually die. In reality, they are usually more concerned with living and survival issues (Kastenbaum, 1985); the dread of helplessness is far more prominent than the dread of death. Therapists also may have strong countertransference reactions by which consultation with the elderly reawakens unresolved conflicts with parents (Butler & Lewis, 1991) and creates discomfort with role reversal. In other words, being an "expert" on mental health with an older person arouses ambivalence, competitiveness, and/or anxiety. Some gerontologists who are new to the field worry about not being valued by their colleagues because of the unglamorous status of geriatric clients. Such biases are perpetuated by the inadequate training with normal and abnormal older persons provided by typical doctoral programs in clinical and counseling psychology.

GENERAL GUIDELINES FOR PSYCHOTHERAPY WITH THE ELDERLY

• An evaluation of psychotherapeutic potential should

be performed *routinely* as part of an overall biopsychosocial assessment. Psychotherapy must be conducted within the context of a multidisciplinary treatment plan, including investigation of concomitant medical problems, possible need for and/or side effects of psychotropic medication, and arrangements for amelioration of stressful social conditions.

• A therapeutic alliance is crucial for successful therapy and is disrupted by mental health professionals with aging biases and stereotypes.

• Building a "shared world" can bridge the aging gap and set the stage for a facilitative therapeutic alliance. Younger mental health professionals should be open to revealing parts of themselves and emphasize common life experiences with their older clients as a way of making contact with this age group.

• Most elderly clients prefer direct, problem-focused treatment strategies with well-defined therapeutic goals. The need for structure is particularly critical during the early stages of therapy.

• Emphasis should be placed on the client's strengths. It is important to remember that elderly persons are survivors. Generally, it is best to support and fine-tune preexisting coping patterns, particularly when acute stresses are overwhelming.

• Deal with current concerns rather than past failures. Most elderly persons seek practical solutions rather than personality reconstruction. Mental health professionals must honor their wishes, particularly because research has indicated that concordance between mental health professional and client goals is predictive of successful treatment.

• Therapeutic flexibility is key. Mental health professionals working with the elderly must be eclectic in their treatment approach. The tremendous variability in cognitive ability, verbal skills, cultural heritage, physical well-being, social support, etc., of older clients necessitates that the mental health professional be familiar with all predominant therapeutic orientations and their application to older persons, ranging from the psychodynamic (Verwoerdt, 1981), to the cognitive-behavioral (Zarit, 1980), to the operant-behavioral (Hussian, 1981).

DIAGNOSIS AS AN AID TO SUCCESSFUL THERAPY

An accurate psychological diagnosis should yield a cognitive template for guiding the mental health professional in addressing the prominent therapeutic issues typical of those assigned specific diagnoses within their overall ego capacities and prognostic possibilities. The scheme presented in this chapter is adapted from Varner and Calvert's (1974) classification of psychological diagnosis in the elderly into four broad categories: (a) recurrent functional impairment, (b) late-life functional impairment, (c) organic brain impairment, and (d) minimal impairment. These divisions are not mutually exclusive, but they are offered as aids to facilitate the translation of geropsychological assessment into tactical treatment options.

Recurrent Functional Impairment:

Chronically impaired older adults suffer from what is known as "recurrent functional impairment." Such persons have suffered from mental disorders throughout their lives and simply have become older; aging persons with chronic schizophrenia or who suffer from alcoholism are examples. Major treatment strategies are similar to those implemented with younger clients with chronic problems. These strategies include: (a) stabilizing mental status via medical monitoring of physical problems (e.g., alcohol withdrawal) and administration of psychotropic medication (e.g., low-dose antipsychotic medication for patients with chronic schizophrenia or antidepressants, lithium [Lithane], and/or anticonvulsants for patients with mood disorders); and (b) planning a structured, low-stress discharge environment to prevent relapse. Psychotherapeutic techniques most often are supportive in nature (Goldfarb & Turner, 1953) and can be extremely important in the management of long-standing maladaptive behavior patterns by ensuring that a "concerned other" is available to counsel the client and family members during periods of crisis. Referral to support groups, such as Alcoholics Anonymous (AA) and the National Alliance for the Mentally Ill (NAMI), may be helpful to promote continued recovery.

Late-Life Functional Impairment:

The most common late-life psychological problem is depression. This category also includes bipolar and paranoid disorders. Elderly persons in this group have led relatively healthy lives psychologically, but have become stymied in attempting to negotiate aging milestones. Most of the time, a major loss or multiple losses have overwhelmed the person's capacity to cope. The death of a spouse (or adult children), retirement, decline in importance of the parenting role ("empty-nest" syndrome), physical debilitation, and decrease in social status (related to the generally low accord given to older people in Western society) can precipitate strong affective reactions. Certain character types are particularly prone to late-life depression: persons with passive-dependent personality orientations often become depressed after a "dominant" significant other dies, whereas those with obsessive-compulsive traits may become agitated when they recognize that due to medical disability, they are no longer able to control their lives as they could in the past.

A three-stage model can be used in conceptualizing psychotherapeutic approaches to clients with late-life psychological problems. First, most older clients usually are seen initially during a crisis situation when their problems have become severe. At these times, the immediate goal is symptomatic relief, typically accomplished via prescription of psychotropic medication and modification of precipitating anxiety-provoking circumstances (possibly necessitating hospitalization). During this period, dialogue with concerned family members is essential to identify contributing stressors, gain knowledge of "baseline functioning," and monitor progress.

Second, after acute symptomatology has been relieved, individual and family therapy should be instituted to address both interpersonal and intrapsychic dimensions of the problem. Brief, systemic interventions (Herr & Weakland, 1979) that target basic faulty communication patterns (Satir, 1983) and/or multigenerational issues (Duffy, 1986) can be powerful agents of change in this therapeutically unsophisticated age group.

Individual therapy should focus primarily on the personal meaning of the losses sustained and, in particular, the unacknowledged ambivalence toward recently deceased loved ones that acts as a stumbling block to the normal mourning process. Continuity always should be emphasized between younger (the past) and current (the present) selves. Empowerment to meet the challenges presented by this advanced stage of development (with psychological growing pains as one way of achieving peaceful resolution) should be highlighted. Self-psychological theory can be employed as an overarching organizing principle in understanding and working with the elderly during this intermediate stage (Lazarus, 1988).

The older person typically has suffered from a series of narcissistic blows (such as loss of a spouse), which often result in reduced access to resources of interpersonal nurturance, thereby resulting in diminished self-esteem. The purpose of therapy is to repair the sense of self by helping elderly clients integrate current life changes into an overall developmental perspective reflecting who they are, where they have been, and what goals to strive for in the future. Group therapy is uniquely suited to managing the self-psychological issues of older adults; it provides a ready-made forum for socialization that allows members to share ongoing aging concerns in a supportive atmosphere of peers.

Third, with remission of the presenting symptoms, treatment should concentrate on prevention of recurrence. The therapeutic goal in this stage is to construct viable strategies for replacing the losses suffered. Such strategies include: (a) referral to senior centers, church groups, and volunteer organizations to satisfy the twin needs of caring for others and being cared for in return; (b) fostering communication and stress reduction in the home environment; and (c) well-rehearsed plans for maintaining contact with mental health professionals via referral to outpatient clinics for at least a short-term follow-up.

Organic Brain Impairment:

Half of psychiatric inpatients seen in geropsychiatric clinics manifest significant cognitive impairment (Molinari, 1991), most often some form of chronic dementia. Traditional psychotherapeutic techniques can readily be tailored to aid in the adjustment of the elderly impaired person and family to the changed situation. It is unfortunate that there are professionals who still do not realize that *care merely begins after the diagnosis of dementia is made.* A thorough explanation of the etiology, progression, and management of the disease process is helpful in planning for the future, even though definitive solutions for changing specific disruptive behaviors of patients with dementia are the exception.

The major focus of interventions for family members should be to reduce their burden of care by encouraging them to accept the tragedy of the illness and providing information regarding respite care (i.e., temporary relief or "time out" from caregiving). Open discussion of nursing home placement should yield informal agreement among caregivers that with the progression of the disease, other living arrangements for the client should be considered to forestall guilt-ridden victimization of the entire family. Routine referral to Alzheimer's support groups should also be made as a way for family members to commiserate with peers.

Minimal Impairment:

The minimally impaired group consists of elderly persons who may be suffering from a transient situational disturbance not debilitating enough to warrant a psychiatric diagnosis or who simply may experience a lack of meaning in their old age. Meaninglessness and monotony can be managed therapeutically. Gerontologists agree that there is usually a psychological need for older persons to pass on a shared legacy of personal value to the next generation which, in a sense, immortalizes them. Butler (1963) proposed that the onset of old age triggers an evaluative form of reminiscence — the life review — leading to an intimate examination of one's personal history. A therapeutic life review group can be beneficial in identifying a meaningful legacy by placing the life course into perspective and helping members accept their lives without recrimination. The group context fosters interpersonal validation, allowing older adults to approach the future with a fresh sense of identity and appraisal of the paths they wish to travel in their remaining time (Birren & Deutchman, 1991; Molinari & Reichlin, 1984–1985). A syllabus for a life review group is presented in Table 11.3 (Carlisle & Molinari, 1980).

Another group that falls into the category of minimally psychologically impaired are those who are seriously ill or dying. Although counseling dying clients is not the specific province of geropsychologists, and although the typical geropsychiatric client is not overly concerned with dying, knowledge of the dying process is important when he or she is grappling with impending death and wishes to talk with someone about his or her fears. Given the conspiracy of silence that too often surrounds a terminal diagnosis, discussions with a therapist may be the only opportunity a person has to process feelings, resolve "unfinished business," and make final decisions.

Although many people erect similar defenses and progress through the stages of dying documented by Kübler-Ross (1974), there is no sequence of stages culminating in acceptance and no "right way" to die (Feifel, 1990). Because dying is a uniquely personal experience, terminally ill patients implement the same defense mechanisms to manage this last monumental stress as they have employed previously to deal with other anxiety-provoking events in their lives. It is the therapist's role to accompany dying patients in their concluding days if they so desire, to bear witness to their last struggles, and *not* to preprogram therapy to fit an idealized version of the perfect death. At the patient's request, referral to a hospice program can be made; after death, bereavement counseling for surviving family members is an appropriate measure.

Table 11.3
SYLLABUS FOR A LIFE REVIEW GROUP

Session 1 — Leader introduction
Discussion of the uses of reminiscence and its effect on one's self-concept

Session 2 — Family history
Describe the family members who have influenced you the most

Session 3 — Developmental stages
Make an outline of your life, dividing it into significant periods

Session 4 — Life crises
Describe the major crises in your life, and how you handled them

Session 5 — Experiences with death
Relate examples of personal encounters with death and your present concerns with dying

Session 6 — Meaning of life
Describe the development of your life goals from past to present in relation to the current meaning of your life

---

CASE VIGNETTES

Mr. M, age 60, was referred for psychotherapy by home health nurses who were trying unsuccessfully to teach him how to take care of his stoma after a colostomy. A few months earlier, he had undergone surgery for bladder cancer. Because of the operation, Mr. M was unable to return to work at the barbershop he had owned for the past 30 years. He was impotent as well. During this same period, his wife divorced him after a long separation, and she was awarded the barbershop in the settlement. Mr. M's five children, all of whom appear to have sided with his wife, rarely visit him.

Since the surgery and divorce, Mr. M has complained of general fatigue but denies depression. He has become isolated in his trailer home and has discontinued steady contact with old friends. The nurses report that Mr. M talks a great deal about his fundamentalist religion but cannot seem to learn how to care for his stoma on his own. Although he complains of concentration problems and forgetfulness, mental status examinations reveal neither significant memory deficits nor psychosis. He was diagnosed with an adjustment disorder accompanied by depressed mood. He had no significant alcohol or drug history.

Mr. M is a prime example of a client who falls into the late-life impairment category. It is easy to see how someone could become depressed with such an unfortunate confluence of losses. Within the span of a year, Mr. M lost his physical health, was divorced from his wife of many years, became alienated from his children, retired from his job, and withdrew from his friends.

The major treatment goal was to allow him to experience the impact of these losses gradually within a supportive context so he could emotionally access his masked depression and thus be motivated to replace the losses. His positive premorbid adjustment bode well for slow but steady progress. Referral to a peer-support ostomy group prompted him to share his experiences regarding loss of physical integrity. The psychotherapist viewed Mr. M's difficulty with stoma care as an indirect way of maintaining the contact with others Mr. M so desperately craved but could not directly accept in this time of need. The therapist explored with Mr. M the possibility of new relationships with women within the parameters of Mr. M's religious framework as a way of untying a destructive knot with his ex-wife. The therapist advised him to meet with his children individually to discuss his relationship with them independent of his relationship with their mother. Finally, the therapist encouraged Mr. M to attend adult education classes in mechanics as a means of maintaining productivity at home and replacing his beloved barbershop work.

Therapy also might have been taken in other directions. A relaxation exercise class could have been offered to Mr. M as an aid in reducing the anxiety attendant on the limitations imposed by his medical problems. A structured cognitive-behavioral treatment program challenging his belief that his losses were irreplaceable could have been tried. Also, formal family therapy conceivably could have been conducted with those of his adult children who were motivated to improve their filial bond. As with all psychotherapy clients, the therapeutic alliance was of paramount importance for Mr. M and was nurtured by careful listening and nonjudgmental suggestions for change.

Five differences in psychotherapy with older clients are highlighted in this example. First, a slower initial pace was required because therapy was new to Mr. M, and he did not understand what was appropriate content for therapeutic sessions. With unconditional positive regard assured, he gradually grew more confident and began exploring his feelings. Second, he had to learn about the linkage between his life stressors and depression before his general fatigue could be interpreted as a psychological reaction to his changed circumstances; somatization is often a main defense in the elderly. Third, the major themes revolved around losses: wife, children, body integrity, sexual potency, and profession. Fourth, more emphasis was placed on current problem areas than on early family relationships and basic personality change. Finally, a medical intervention (penile implant operation to allow sexual functioning) and a social intervention (referral to the stoma support group) were necessary to supplement psychological techniques in abetting socialization.

*   *   *

Mr. C, age 67, was admitted to the geropsychiatric ward of the hospital because of forgetfulness, disorganized thinking, and inability to perform simple tasks. He had begun experiencing memory problems 3 years previously, and these had become increasingly worse. Medical and neuropsychological evaluation strongly supported the diagnosis of Alzheimer's disease. Mr. C also had been hospitalized many times before for alcoholism, which caused significant tension in his 40-year marriage. Mr. C had been working as a highly-paid insurance executive but was forced to retire due to his cognitive decline.

A year ago, his memory became so bad that he could not be left in the house alone, and his wife quit her job as a realtor to take care of him. The resulting loss of incomes caused them to file for bankruptcy, sell their home, and live on a very tight budget.

Mr. C has two adult daughters and one teenage son; the latter lives with him and refuses to believe that his father has dementia. Mr. C's wife says that she may not be able to manage him in their new apartment any longer. Mr. C often is disoriented in the hospital and cannot understand why he is not back at home.

This case illustrates how both individual and family work are critical for those diagnosed with organic brain impairment. The therapist proposed a variety of psychological services for Mr. C and his family to help them handle his inexorable decline. Respite care was immediately proposed to the wife as a way for her to gain strength to make some difficult decisions affecting the entire family. She was encouraged to arrange in-home, day center, or institutional care for relief in his day-to-day management. In addition, she was scheduled for individual sessions to grieve the psychological death of her husband as she once knew him. To this end, she was also referred to an Alzheimer's disease family support group, where she was validated in her decisions to seek more help from her children and to broach the idea of nursing home placement with them if his memory deteriorated further.

The therapist set up family meetings with Mr. C, his wife, and children to help them process their feelings about Mr. C's decline and ultimately confront the denial system of his son by having him face the obvious intellectual problems so apparent in his father's conversation during the session. Mr. C was included in these meetings so that he could play a part in the decision-making process and express his desires about his long-term care. When Mr. C became agitated and attempted to leave the locked ward, he was given as-needed medication by the treating psychiatrist but was also talked to about how scary it must be to have one's mind malfunction and not be secure in one's own home. Although Mr. C's therapy was supportive due to his more advanced dementia, intensive psychotherapy with a self-psychological focus for cases of early-stage dementia has been reported (Sadavoy, 1991).

Mr. C was discharged; however, his progressive mental decline necessitated nursing home placement 6 months later. The client's family continued to avail themselves of the support group, where affirmation consistently was given that they were not abandoning him and that they would now spend quality time with him in the nursing home setting.

CONCLUSION

The elderly constitute the fastest growing, yet most psychologically underserved, age group. Psychotherapy for the elderly requires specialized expertise and patience. The pace of therapy is usually slower because of the client's (and sometimes the mental health professional's) unfamiliarity with the task at hand and because of the variety of sensory impairments that are a normal part of the aging process. However, psychotherapy can be a uniquely rewarding experience for both client and therapist. Older adults are probably more likely than younger adults to express their gratitude directly to the therapist for the time devoted to making their lives better. Just as the client learns new ways to cope with the hazards of aging, the mental health professional can also be enriched by the older client's wealth of life experiences, which, in the hands of a caring and skilled professional, can be transformed into a legacy of wisdom to be passed on to future generations.

REFERENCES

Birren, J. E., & Deutchman, D. (1991). *Guiding autobiography groups for older adults: Exploring the fabric of life.* Baltimore: The Johns Hopkins University Press.

Blazer, D. (1989). The epidemiology of psychiatric disorders in late life. In E. W. Busse & D. G. Blazer (Eds.), *Geriatric psychiatry* (pp. 235–260). Washington, DC: American Psychiatric Press.

Burns, B., & Taube, C. A. (1990). Mental health services in general medical care and nursing homes. In B. S. Fogel, A. Furino, & G. Gottlieb (Eds.), *Protecting minds at risk* (pp. 63–84). Washington, DC: American Psychiatric Press.

Butler, R. (1963). The life review: An interpretation of reminiscence in the aged. *Psychiatry, 26,* 65–74.

Butler, R., & Lewis, M. (1991). *Aging and mental health: Positive psychosocial approaches.* St. Louis: C. V. Mosby.

Carlisle, A., & Molinari, V. (1980, March). *Life review.* Paper presented at the TRIMS Seventh Annual Research Forum, Houston.

Duffy, M. (1986). The techniques and contexts of multigenerational therapy. In T. L. Brink (Ed.), *Clinical gerontology: A guide to assessment and intervention* (pp. 347–362). New York: Haworth Press.

Erikson, E. H. (1963). *Childhood and society* (2nd ed.). New York: W. W. Norton.

Feifel, H. (1990). Psychology and death: Meaningful rediscovery. *American Psychologist, 45*(4), 537–543.

Freud, S. (1904). On psychotherapy. In J. Strachey (Ed.), *The complete psychological works of Sigmund Freud* (vol. 7, pp. 257–268). London: Hogarth Press.

Gaitz, C. M. (1974). Barriers to the delivery of psychiatric services to the elderly. *Gerontologist, 14,* 210–214.

Garfield, S. L. (1978). Research on client variables in psychotherapy. In S. L. Garfield & A. E. Bergin (Eds.), *Handbook of psychotherapy and behavior change* (pp. 191–232). New York: John Wiley & Sons.

Gatz, M. & Smyer, M.A. (1992). The mental health system and older adults in the 1990s. *American Psychologist, 47* (6), 741–751.

Gatz, M., Smyer, M. A., & Lawton, M. P. (1980). The mental health system and the older adult. In L. W. Poon (Ed.), *Aging in the 1980s: Psychological issues* (pp. 5–19). Washington, DC: American Psychological Association.

George, L. K. (1992). Community and home care for mentally ill older adults. In J. Birren, R. B. Sloane, & G. D. Cohen (Eds.), *Handbook of mental health and aging* (pp. 793–813). San Diego: Academic Press.

Gibson, R. W. (1973). Insurance coverage for treatment of mental illness in later life. In E. W. Busse & E. Pfeiffer (Eds.), *Mental illness in later life* (pp. 179–198). Washington, DC: American Psychiatric Press.

Goldfarb, A., & Turner, H. (1953). Psychotherapy of aged persons, II: Utilization and effectiveness of "brief" therapy. *American Journal of Psychiatry, 109,* 916–921.

Herr, J., & Weakland, J. (1979). *Counseling elders and their families: Practical techniques for applied gerontology.* New York: Springer.

Hinrichsen, G. (1990). *Mental health problems and older adults*. Santa Barbara, CA: ABC-CLIO, Inc.

Hussian, R. A. (1981). *Geriatric psychology: A behavioral perspective*. New York: Van Nostrand Reinhold.

Jung, C. G. (1933). *Modern man in search of a soul*. New York: Harcourt Brace Jovanovich.

Kastenbaum, R. (1985). Dying and death: A life-span approach. In J. E. Birren & K. W. Schaie (Eds.), *Handbook of the psychology of aging* (2nd ed., pp. 619–643). New York: Van Nostrand Reinhold.

Kübler-Ross, E. (1974). *Questions and answers on death and dying*. New York: Macmillan.

Lawton, M., Whelihan, W., & Belsky, J. (1980). Personality tests and their uses with older adults. In J. Birren, R. B. Sloane, & G. D. Cohen (Eds.), *Handbook of mental health and aging* (pp. 537–553). Englewood Cliffs, NJ: Prentice-Hall.

Lazarus, L. (1988). Self psychology – Its application to brief psychotherapy with the elderly. *Journal of Geriatric Psychiatry, 21,* 109–125.

Lebowitz, B., & Niederehe, G. (1992). Concepts and issues in mental health and aging. In J. E. Birren, R. B. Sloane, & G. D. Cohen (Eds.), *Handbook of mental health and aging* (pp. 3–26). San Diego: Academic Press.

Levenson, A., & Felkins, B. (1979). Prevention of psychiatric recidivism. *Journal of the American Geriatrics Society, 27,* 536–540.

Lichtenberg, P. (1994). *A guide to psychological practice in geriatric long-term care*. New York: Haworth Press.

Molinari, V. (1991). Demographic and psychiatric characteristics of 390 consecutive discharges from a geropsychiatric inpatient ward. *Clinical Gerontologist, 10*(2), 35–45.

Molinari, V., & Reichlin, R. E. (1984–1985). Life review reminiscence in the elderly: A review of the literature. *International Journal of Aging and Human Development, 20,* 81–92.

Sadavoy, J. (1991, May/June). Psychodynamic perspectives on Alzheimer's disease and related dementias. *The American Journal of Alzheimer's Care and Related Disorders & Research*, pp. 12–20.

Satir, V. (1983). *Conjoint family therapy* (3rd ed.). Palo Alto, CA: Science and Behavior Books.

Taube, C. A., Burns, B. J., & Kessler, L. (1984). Patients of psychiatrists and psychologists in office-based practice: 1980. *American Psychologist, 39*, 1435-1447.

Teri, L. & Logsdon, R. G. (1992). The future of psychotherapy with older adults. *Psychotherapy, 29* (1), 81-87.

Thompson, L., Gallagher, D., & Steinmetz-Breckenridge, J. (1987). Comparative effectiveness of psychotherapies for depressed elders. *Journal of Consulting and Clinical Psychology, 55*(3), 385–390.

Varner, R., & Calvert, W. R. (1974). Psychiatric assessment of the aged: A differential model for diagnosis. *Journal of the American Geriatrics Society, 22*(6), 273–277.

Verwoerdt, A. (1981). *Clinical geropsychiatry* (2nd ed.). Baltimore: Williams & Wilkins.

Waxman, H. M., Carner, E. A., & Berkenstock, G. (1984). Physicians' recognition, diagnosis, and treatment of mental disorders in elderly medical patients. *Gerontologist, 24*, 593-597.

Zarit, S. (1980). *Aging and mental disorders: Psychological approaches to assessment and treatment.* New York: The Free Press.

12

Power Imbalances in Therapeutic Relationships

Michael L. Perlin, JD

Dr. Perlin is Professor of Law at the New York Law School, New York, NY.

KEY POINTS

- Because therapeutic relationships take place behind closed doors, the rest of society remains somewhat in the dark as to what actually goes on in therapy and what impact the underlying power imbalances have over what transpires.

- The three most common areas of litigation arising from boundary violations caused by power imbalances are: improper treatment, improper sexual conduct, and perceived violations of confidentiality. Surveys suggest that 10%–17% of therapists have engaged in such behavior with their clients.

- Confidentiality cases must be viewed through two different prisms: cases that arise from a mental health professional's failure to maintain secrecy regarding a disclosure, and those that stem from an inquiry into the professional's duty to protect others as a result of information given by the client that clearly indicates danger to a third party.

Most legal decision making is best explained by a study of the types of simplifying heuristics that frequently lead to distorted and systematically erroneous decisions. An examination of the way that "ordinary common sense" unconsciously animates decision makers is also helpful.

Source: Perlin, M. L. (1991). Power Imbalances in therapeutic and forensic relationships. Behavioral Science and Law, 9. Copyright (c) 1991 John Wiley and Sons, Ltd. Reprinted by permission of John Wiley & Sons, Ltd.

INTRODUCTION

Public issues are often at the center of the forensic relationship power struggle. Some of the more common examples include the publicized insanity acquittal, the hearing on the dangerousness of a death penalty defendant, and the operational impact of the implementation of the right to refuse treatment on an institutionalized population. However, these are largely missing in the therapeutic relationship.[1] Therefore, perhaps it becomes easier to gloss over the underlying power imbalances that must be reconciled in the traditional, dyadic relationship between therapist and client.

THERAPEUTIC RELATIONSHIPS

In his monumental work *The Powers of Psychiatry*, Robitscher was clear in his critique of the alleged neutrality or value-freedom of the therapeutic relationship: a whole "constellation of values—personal, economic, political, philosophical, therapeutic—determines the treatment relationship,"[2] and it is "foolish" for mental health professionals to claim that their disciplines are "objective and value-free."[2] Robitscher continued to state that "the purpose of the therapeutic encounter is to permit one person to have enough effect on another person to change behavior and personality, and such a situation is invariably value-laden. The values that psychiatrists represent to their patients and for society are the most influential expressions of the great authority that psychiatry exerts."[3]

Halleck saw the power issue even more specifically; he argued that by participating in individual psychotherapy, a client "regularly experiences either a gain or a loss of power in relation to his family or friends,"[4] and that the "vectors" in the therapeutic endeavor that favor conformity "tend to be the most powerful."[5]

Halleck and Robitscher were engaging primarily in a social critique rather than a legal one (although they both acknowledged the degree to which behavioral decisions by mental health professionals led to legal outcomes and implicated legal standards).[6] However, their concerns still help direct our thinking on this topic. Issues of power permeate the therapeutic relationship, albeit in more subtle ways than they infect the forensic relationship.

Because the therapeutic relationship is a private one and generally takes place behind closed doors (in direct opposition to the media frenzy that sometimes accompanies forensic decision making),[7] the rest of society remains somewhat in the dark as to what actually goes on in therapy and as to what impact the underlying power imbalances have over what transpires. For better or worse, one major source of data is that of the reported case law: what happens when the therapeutic relationship is perceived as being infected so severely that a party resorts to litigation.

LITIGATION AND THE MENTAL HEALTH PROFESSION

Notwithstanding the general perception of a "litigation explosion" (a perception that is deeply flawed on a variety of important levels),[8] the reality is that the incidence of civil malpractice suits against mental health professionals remains substantially lower than rates for other medical specialties[9] — a variance that is reflected in the comparatively "minuscule" increases in insurance rates in the mental health professions as compared with other branches of health care.[10]

Many reasons have been offered for this low rate: the general reluctance of the tort law to provide remedies for emotional injuries; the difficulty of proving the applicable standard of care and the existence of a causal relationship between the breach of the standard and the alleged injury; the stigma that clients fear might result from making their psychiatric history public; reluctance to sue as a result of a client's emotional tie to his or her therapist and/or the client's feeling that psychotherapy could not succeed without his or her full cooperation; the inability on the part of many clients either to formulate clear expectations for the result of their treatment or to assess the "success" of their results; the ability of trained mental health professionals to deal therapeutically with client hostility and thus avoid a suit; the frequency with which many clients see mental health professionals; and the fact that the fields of psychiatry, clinical psychology, and counseling remain somewhat enigmatic to a significant percentage of the trial bar.[11]

Important data are emerging as to why some persons choose to sue over the "violation of expectations"[12] that leads to malpractice litigation. Recent empirical studies suggest that the decision to file suit is correlated positively to a client's assertiveness, to the client's ability to engage in strategic formulations, and to the involvement and discernment of a "broad audience network" (actors external to the relationship between dissatisfied clients and health professionals). It is correlated negatively to factors such as the client's evaluation (prior to the precipitating grievance) of the health professional's competence, to the health professional's concern for the client's "state in life," and, interestingly, to the patient's degree of knowledge about the work of both the health and legal professionals (i.e., clients with greater knowledge about either profession are less likely to sue).[13]

Some significant external evidence exists suggesting that this "most favored nation"[14] status is now changing. In recent years, the law has become generally more receptive to allegations of emotional injury, former clients have openly and candidly discussed their treatment experiences, the "explosion" in litigation on behalf of *institutionalized* mentally ill patients has sensitized judges and litigators to some of the underlying substantive issues, and more has been learned about what happens empirically when certain treatments are employed.[15] However, many explanations for the lower relative rate of litigation can still be traced to the power imbalances inherent in the therapeutic relationship: the stigma resulting from publicizing a "failed" therapy encounter; the impact of the transference phenomenon on reluctance to sue; the feelings of patient-generated self-blame for therapy "failures"; and the skill with which many mental health professionals can deftly sidestep hostility by shifting the focus of therapeutic encounters.[16]

. Still, important cases involving therapeutic relationships have been litigated. It is likely that the public's use of the available heuristic reasoning[17] significantly inflates perceptions of both the frequency and the precedential impact of such cases. For both empirical and instrumental reasons, it is important that these areas of litigation be examined in an effort to evaluate the extent to which they are permeated by issues of power imbalance.

Three specific problems may stem from the sort of boundary violation[18] that accompanies power imbalance: litigation based on improper treatment (including drug reactions)[19]; litigation based on improper sexual conduct and/or attempts to manipulate clients financially[20]; and litigation that arises from perceived violations of confidentiality, especially with regard to the type of "third-party" protection or warning that was present in the *Tarasoff* case.[21]

Improper Treatment:

It should be intuitive that the improper administration of medication is a "potential mine field."[22] Beyond the problems posed by neurological side effects, such as tardive dyskinesia,[23] liability issues can arise in a variety of medication-related settings, including:

Absence of an adequate history, physical examination, and laboratory examination prior to treatment; prescription of a drug where it is not indicated; prescription of the wrong dosage; prescription of medication for inappropriately short or long time periods; failure to recognize, monitor, or treat side effects or toxicity; failure to abate the possibility of drug reactions or interactions; and failure to consult with the necessary experts.[24]

Although there have been few decisions in this area,[25] the scant litigation that has been reported reflects some of the issues inherent in power imbalances. For example, there are cases of physicians who prescribed a 50-day supply of diazepam (Valium) without taking a medical history or checking the patient's medical records,[26] who failed to change a prescription following an observation of side effects and the onset of self-destructive behavior on the part of the client,[27] or who prescribed addictive drugs to help the client see the nature of his or her addictive personality.[28] It is not clear whether the physicians' actions stemmed simply from sloppy medical practice ("negligence" in the true sense of the word) or from a failure to take the client's individual needs into account.

These cases all have a common pattern: the defendant (perhaps employing "typification"[29]) places the clients into certain categories and prescribes a similar regimen for all.[30] Such a pattern reflects precisely the kind of power imbalance about which Robitscher and Halleck have warned.[31]

Sexual Boundary Violations:

Sexual misconduct cases[32] are probably the most pernicious because although there is no question that such behavior by a therapist is "always unethical,"[33] surveys suggest that between 10% and 17% of therapists have engaged in such behavior with their clients.[34,35] Three well-publicized cases are *Roy v Hartogs*,[36] *Zipkin v Freeman*,[37] and *Landau v Warner*.[38] In *Roy v Hartogs*,[36] the court upheld a damage award to a client whose therapist engaged in sexual intercourse with her based on the rationale that it was a legitimate part of therapy. In *Zipkin v Freeman*,[37] an award was upheld when the therapist persuaded his client to swim with him in the nude, leave her husband, and invest her money in business ventures that he controlled. In

Landau v Warner,[38] a verdict was similarly affirmed when after explaining the transference phenomenon[39] to a client who had told him she had fallen in love with him, the therapist began to date the client and discussed the possibility of vacationing together. In these three instances — as well as others less notorious[40] — the client remained vulnerable and susceptible to the influence and suggestion of the therapist.[41]

As revelations of similar improper sexual relations increase, and as we confront the reality that the vast majority of therapists self-report a feeling of sexual attraction to their clients,[42] a proliferation of "sexual misconduct" litigation can be expected. In virtually every instance, the power imbalances inherent in the therapeutic relationship will be at the core of the litigation.

Breached Confidentiality:

Confidentiality cases must be seen through two different prisms: (a) cases that arise from a breach of a mental health professional's failure to maintain secrecy regarding a disclosure made to him or her directly by a client (about the client),[43] and (b) those that stem from an inquiry into the professional's duty to protect others as a result of information given by the client that clearly indicates danger to a third party. The latter is referred to as the *Tarasoff* exception.[44]

The first grouping of cases implicates statutory rights (in those jurisdictions in which there is an operative therapist-client privilege),[45] contractual rights,[46] and constitutional rights (where the right to privacy is given such content).[47] The right to confidentiality is not absolute. In addition to *Tarasoff* cases (where there is a judicially or legislatively imposed duty to warn a third party of potential danger),[48] there are exceptions inherent in the forensic relationship.[49] These involve cases in which the client places his or her mental status affirmatively into the arena of litigation,[50] and in cases in which a conflict exists between confidentiality and a police-power statute (such as one governing civil commitment or reporting of child abuse).[51] Nevertheless, the policy's rationale rests finally on a power issue: disclosure of confidential communications might well "deter persons from seeking needed assistance, or from making the full disclosure on which diagnosis and treatment depend."[52]

The *Tarasoff* paradigm actually more closely parallels the issues raised in considering forensic relationships. Because courts and legislatures have carved out a confidentiality exception, the question remains: *how will therapists respond to the externally imposed duty to breach confidentiality?* Various sensitive solutions have been suggested. For instance, Roth and Meisel listed five guidelines to govern *Tarasoff* situations: (a) prudence to avoid being "stampeded" into giving unnecessary warnings; (b) provision of information to the client regarding the limits of confidentiality prior to the entry into the therapeutic relationship; (c) the use of various "social and environmental manipulations" prior to being forced to compromise confidentiality (such as bringing third parties into the therapeutic setting); (d) obtaining the client's permission (whenever possible) prior to disclosure of confidential information and disclosing such information in the presence of the client; and (e) assessing any such intervention in light of its potential impact on future therapy and in light of the likelihood that it will be successful in preventing future violence.[53] Again, these suggestions implicitly reflect the problems raised by power imbalances in the therapeutic/forensic relationship.

CONCLUSION

It is necessary to acknowledge some extraordinarily important additional truths.[54] Courts are suspicious of and generally reject psychodynamic explanations of interpersonal behavior as being inherently dissonant with the "free will" basis of the criminal justice and tort systems.[55] Most legal decision making can best be explained by a study of the types of simplifying heuristics that frequently lead to distorted and systematically erroneous decisions through ignoring or misusing rationally useful information[56] and an examination of the way that "ordinary common sense" unconsciously animates decision makers.[57]

Judges are profoundly teleological in their use of social science and behavioral evidence in their decision making — a factor that tends to further debase and trivialize scientific research, data, and discourse.[58]

Jurors are overwhelmingly ambivalent about *all* the underlying concepts: the role of mental health expert testimony in the court process; mental disability as an animating explanation for behavior; the efficacy of therapy; and the proper balance that must be struck between professional autonomy, public safety, and privacy. *Jurors'* decision making similarly reflects the use of heuristic reasoning devices and "ordinary common sense."[59]

As a result of these conflicts and ambivalences, legal decision makers exhibit cognitive dissonance (the reinterpretation of information and experience that conflicts with their internally accepted or publicly stated beliefs so as to avoid the unpleasant state that such inconsistencies produce)[60] in the way they deal with the substantive issues under consideration.

We must consciously "unpack the myths"[61] and "strip the facade"[62] from the stereotypical ways that vivid, heuristic evidence is presented[63] — in legal forums, in mental health forums, and in public forums — to consider the power imbalance issues that underlie each of these relationships. This must be done consciously and openly if we are to illuminate and attempt to resolve the core questions that concern all of us.

REFERENCES

1. *See generally,* Perlin, *Power Imbalances in Forensic Relationships,* 3B
Ethics in Psychother. 3 (1995).

2. J. Robitscher, *The Power of Psychiatry* 399 (1980).

3. *Id.* at 400.

4. S. Halleck, *The Politics of Therapy* 33 (1971).

5. *Id. at* 33-34.

6. *See, e.g.,* S. Halleck, *supra* note 4, at 139-46; J. Robitscher, *supra* note 2,
at 401-05; J. Robitscher, *Pursuit of Agreement: Psychiatry and Law* 16-34
(1966).

7. On the impact of the media on the shaping of insanity defense
jurisprudence, *see* Perlin, *Unpacking the Myths: The Symbolism Mythology
of Insanity Defense Jurisprudence,* 40 Case W. Res. L. Rev. 599, 617 n. 76,
621-22 n. 101 (1989-90), and sources cited; *see generally,* M. L. Perlin, *The
Jurisprudence of the Insanity Defense* (1994).

8. *Compare* Barton, *Behind the Legal Explosion,* 27 Stan. L. Rev. 567 (1975),
and Manning, *Hyperlexis: Our National Disease,* 71 Nw. U. L. Rev. 767
(1977) (setting out myths), to Galanter, *Reading the Landscape of Disputes:
What We Know (And Think We Know) About Our Allegedly Contentious and
Litigious Society,* 31 U.C.L.A. L. Rev. 4, 38-39 (1983); Felstiner, Abel &
Sarat, *The Emergence and Transformation of Disputes: Naming, Blaming,
Claiming...,* 15 Law & Soc'y Rev. 631, 652 (1984); Rottman, *Tort Litigation
in the State Courts: Evidence From the Trial Court Information Network,* 14 St.
Ct. J. 4 (Fall 1990) (setting out reality).

9. *See* 3 M.L. Perlin, Mental Disability Law: Civil and Criminal §12.02,
at 3-4 (1989), citing Slawson, *The Clinical Dimension of Psychiatric Malpractice,* 14 Psychiatric Annals 358, 363 (1984); *see also,* Slawson, *Psychiatric
Malpractice: A State-wide Survey,* 6 Bull. Am. Acad. Psychiat. & L. 58
(1978). *See generally* M.L. Perlin, Law and Mental Disability §3.01, at 398–
402 (1994).

10. *See* Bonnie, *Professional Liability and the Quality of Mental Health Care,*
16 L., Med. & Health Care 229, 229 (1988). For an overview of relevant
issues, *see* Herzog, *The Reform of Medical Liability: Tort Law or Insurance,*
38 Am. J. Compar. L. 99 (1990).

11. 3 M.L. Perlin, *supra* note 9, §12.02, at 4-5; *see generally*, Fishalow, *The Tort Liability of the Psychiatrist*, 4 Bull. Am. Acad. Psychiat. & L. 191 (1975); Taub, *Psychiatric Malpractice in the 1980s: A Look at Some Areas of Concern*, 11 L., Med. & Health Care 97 (1983); Klein & Glover, *Psychiatric Malpractice*, 6 Int'l J. L. & Psychiat. 131 (1983).

12. *See* M. Silberman, "Law as Process: A Value-Added Model of the Mobilization of Law," paper presented at the annual meeting of the American Sociological Association (1977), manuscript at 3, as cited in May & Stengel, *Who Sues Their Doctors? How Patients Handle Medical Grievances*, 24 Law & Soc'y Rev. 105, 106 (1990).

13. *Report of the Task Force on the Role of Psychology in the Criminal Justice System*, in J. Monahan, ed., *supra* note 5, at 1, 5. Monahan's inquiry is considered carefully in Lyon & Levine, *Ethics, Power, and Advocacy: Psychology in the Criminal Justice System*, 6 Law Hum Behav 65 (1982).

14. *See* Perlin, *Institutionalization and the Law*, in Psychiatric Services in Institutional Settings 75, 76 (Amer. Hosp. Ass'n, ed. 1978).

15. 3 M.L. Perlin, *supra* note 9, §12.02, at 6-7; *see also*, B. Furrow, Malpractice in Psychiatry (1980); Wettstein & Appelbaum, *Legal Liability for Tardive Dyskinesia*, 35 Hosp. & Commun. Psychiat. 992 (1984); Wettstein, *Psychiatry and the Law*, in Textbook of Psychiatry 1059 (J. Talbott, R. Halers & S. Yudofsky, eds. 1988); Wettstein, *Psychiatric Malpractice*, in 8 Review of Psychiatry 392 (A. Tasman, R. Hales & A. Frances, eds. 1989).

16. On the correlative question of the duties that can be imposed on patients in the context of therapeutic relationships *see* Beahrs, *Legal Duties of Psychiatric Patients*, 18 Bull. Am. Acad. Psychiat. & L. 189 (1990).

17. *I.e.*, concrete and vivid information about a specific case overwhelms the abstract data upon which rational choices are usually made. *See* Rosenhan, *Psychological Realities and Judicial Policies*, 10 Stan. Law. 10, 13-14 (1984); Perlin, *Are Courts Competent to Decide Competency Questions? Stripping the Facade from* United States v. Charters, 38 U. Kan. L. Rev. 957, 987 n. 197 (1990) (Perlin, *Charters*); *see generally*, Perlin, *Psychodynamics and the Insanity Defense: "Ordinary Common Sense" and Heuristic Reasoning*, 67 Neb. L. Rev. 3, 12-14 (1990) (Perlin *OCS.*).

18. The boundaries of client-therapist relationships are discussed in 1 The Techniques of Psychoanalytic Psychotherapy 206-08, 581 (R.D. Langs ed. 1973).

19. *See, e.g.*, Wettstein, *Tardive Dyskinesia and Malpractice*, 1 Behav. Sci. & L. 85 (1983).

20. *See, e.g.*, Coleman, *Sex in Power Dependency Relationships: Taking Unfair Advantage of the "Fair Sex,"* 53 Alb. L. Rev. 95 (1988).

21. *See, e.g.*, Note, *The Psychotherapist's Calamity: Emerging Trends in the Tarasoff Doctrine*, 1989 B.Y.U. L. Rev. 261.

22. 3 M. L. Perlin, *supra* note 9, §12.10, at 34.

23. *See id.* §12.11, at 37-39.

24. Wettstein, *supra* note 19, at 89.

25. *See* Klein & Glover, *supra* note 11, at 135.

26. *Watkins v. United States*, 589 F. 2d 214 (5th Cir. 1979).

27. *Hale v. Portsmouth Receiving Hosp.*, 44 Ohio Misc. 90, 338 N.E. 2d 371 (Ct. Cl. 1975).

28. *Rosenfeld v. Coleman*, 19 Pa. D. & C. 2d 635 (C.P. 1959).

29. *See* Perlin, *OCS, supra* note 17, at 29-30, discussing the self-fulfilling prophecies inherent in typification; *see generally*, Van Zandt, *Commonsense Reasoning, Social Change, and the Law*, 81 Nw. U. L. Rev. 894, 913 (1987).

30. Similar "I always do it this way" issues are raised in Mills, *Psychiatric Malpractice*, Fair Oaks Hosp. Psychiat. Newsl. (Vol. 7, Issue 7, Sept. 1990), at 1, 3, and in Schuchman & Wilkes, *Dramatic Progression Against Depression*, N.Y. Times (Magazine, Part 2) (Oct. 7, 1990), at 12.

31. *See* J. Robitscher. *supra* note 2; S. Halleck, *supra* note 4.

32. *See* 3 M.L. Perlin, *supra* note 9, §12.09, at 28-34.

33. Klein & Glover, *supra* note 11, at 138.

34. *See, e.g.*, B. Furrow, *supra* note 15, at 34 (10%); R.J. Cohen, Malpractice: A Guide for Mental Health Professions 88-89 (1979) (same); *Dresser v. Board of Medical Quality Assurance*, 130 Cal. App. 3d 506, 181 Cal. Rptr. 797, 800 (1982) (17%).

35. *See* Coleman, *supra* note 20, at 96.

36. 81 Misc. 2d 350, 366 N.Y.S. 2d 297 (Civ. 1975), *modified* 85 Misc. 2d 891, 381 N.Y.S. 2d 587 (Sup. 1976).

37. 436 S.W. 2d 753 (Mo. 1968).

38. 105 Sol. J. 1008 (C.A. 1961).

39. *See Decker v. Fink*, 47 Md. App. 202, 422 A. 2d 389, 391 (1980): Inherent in the transference neurosis is the development of a strong dependence by the patient upon the analyst and an extraordinary faith and trust in him, which may develop into a love relationship and which can deprive the patient of her independent judgment and ability to distinguish the reality of her interaction with the analyst and vice versa. The "transference neurosis" is explained and discussed in R. Balsam & A. Balsam, *Becoming a Psychotherapist: A Clinical Primer* 64-73 (1974).

40. *See also, e.g., Anclote Manor Found. v. Wilkerson*, 263 So. 2d 256 (Fla. Dist. App. 1972); *Cotton v. Kambly*, 101 Mich. App. 537, 300 N.W. 2d 627 (1980); *Mazza v. Huffaker*, 61 N.C. App. 170, 300 S.E. 2d 833 (1983); *Andrews v. United States*, 732 F. 2d 366 (4th Cir. 1984); *Matter of Schroeder*, 415 N.W. 2d 436 (Minn. App.), *rev. den.* (1988); *Block v. Ambach*, 140 A.D. 2d 814, 528 N.Y.S. 2d 204 (1988), *aff'd* 73 N.Y. 2d 323, 537 N.E. 2d 1181, 540 N.Y.S. 2d 6 (1989).

41. *Decker*, 422 A. 2d at 391. *See also*, Note, *Patient-Therapist Sexual Relations: Professional Services Rendered? A Case Comment on Doe v. Swift*, 14 Law & Psychol. Rev. 87 (1990).

42. Solursh & Solursh, *Sex and Therapy*, Psychiat. News (Oct. 5, 1990), at 31 (letter to the editor).

43. *See* 3 M. L. Perlin, *supra* note 9, §12.37, at 105-09.

44. *See id.*, §§13.05-13.21, at 134-84.

45. *See, e.g.*, Smith, *Medical and Psychotherapy Privileges and Confidentiality: On Giving With One Hand And Removing With the other*, 75 Ky. L. Rev. 473 (1986-87); D. Shuman, Psychiatric and Psychological Evidence §§10.01-10.12, at 223-52 (1986).

46. *See* Eger, *Psychotherapists' Liability for Extrajudicial Breaches of Confidentiality*, 18 Ariz. L. Rev. 1061, 1065-77 (1976).

47. *Cutter v. Brownbridge*, 183 Cal. App. 3d 836, 228 Cal. Rptr. 545 (1986).

48. See *Tarasoff v. Board of Regents of Univ. of Cal.*, 17 Cal. 3d 425, 551 P. 2d 334, 131 Cal. Rptr. 14 (1976). *See generally*, Perlin, Tarasoff *and the Dilemma of the Dangerous Patient: New Directions for the 1990s* , 16 Law & Psycholog. Rev. 29 (1992); M.L. Perlin, *supra* note 10, §3.19, at 473–488.

49. *See* Perlin, *supra* note 1.

50. *See, e.g., In re Lifschutz*, 2 Cal. 3d 415, 467 P. 2d 557, 84 Cal. Rptr. 829 (1970); *Caesar v. Mountanos*, 542 F. 2d 1064 (9th Cir. 1976).

51. *See, e.g., Commonwealth ex rel. Platt v. Platt*, 266 Pa. Super. 276, 404 A. 2d 410 (1979) (commitment); Miller & Weinstock, *Conflict of Interest Between Therapist-Patient Confidentiality and the Duty to Report Sexual Abuse of Children*, 5 Behav. Sci. & L. 161 (1987). On the impact of an AIDS diagnosis on the right to confidentiality, *see e.g.*, Note, *AIDS: Establishing a Physician's Duty to Warn*, 21 Rutgers L.J. 645 (1990); Weiss, *AIDS: Balancing the Physician's Duty to Warn and Confidentiality Concerns*, 38 Emory L.J. 299 (1989).

52. *Simek v. Superior Court*, 117 Cal. App. 3d 169, 172 Cal. Rptr. 564, 569 (1981).

53. Roth & Meisel, *Dangerousness, Confidentiality, and the Duty to Warn*, 134 Am. J. Psychiat. 508, 509-511 (1977). For an alternative methodology, *see* Appelbaum, *Tarasoff and the Clinician: Problems in Fulfilling the Duty to Protect*, 142 Am. J. Psychiat. 425, 426-27 (1985). For other alternative solutions, *see* 3 M. L. Perlin, *supra* note 9, §13.20, at 67 n. 422 (1994 pocket part) (listing sources).

54. *See generally*, Perlin & Dorfman, *Sanism, Social Science, and the Development of Mental Disability Law Jurisprudence*, 11 Behav. Sci. & L. 47 (1993).

55. *See generally*, Perlin, *supra* note 7, at 673-88.

56. *See generally*, Perlin, *OCS, supra* note 17, at 12-22; Saks & Kidd, *Human Information Processing and Adjudication: Trial By Heuristics*, 15 Law & Soc'y Rev. 123 (1980-81).

57. *See generally*, Sherwin, *Dialects and Dominance: A Study of Rhetorical Fields in Confessions*, 136 U. Pa. L. Rev. 729 (1988); Perlin, *OCS, supra* note

17, at 22-39; *see also,* Newman, *A Tale of Two Cases: Reflections on Psychological and Institutional Influences on Child Custody Decisions,* 34 N.Y.L. Sch. L. Rev. 661, 669 (1989).

58. Perlin, *OCS, supra* note 17, at 61-69; Appelbaum, *The Empirical Jurisprudence of the United States Supreme Court,* 13 Am. J. L. & Med. 335, 341 (1987); *see generally,* Perlin, *Pretexts and Mental Disability Law: The Case of Competency.,* 47 U. Miami L. Rev. 625 (1993).

59. Perlin, *OCS, supra* note 17, at 39-53; Gunn, *An English Psychiatrist Looks At Dangerousness,* 10 Bull. Am. Acad. Psychiat. & L. 143, 147 (1982).

60. Perlin, *Morality and Pretextuality, Psychiatry and Law: Of "Ordinary Common Sense," Heuristic Reasoning, and Cognitive Dissonance ,* 19 Bull. Am. Acad. Psychiat. & L.; 131 (1991); *see generally,* L. Festinger, A Theory of Cognitive Dissonance (1957).

61. *See* Perlin, *supra* note 7; M.L. Perlin, *supra* note 7.

62. *See* Perlin, *Charters, supra* note 17.

63. *See id.;* Perlin, *Competency, Deinstitutionalization, and Homelessness: A Story of Marginalization,* 28 Hous. L. Rev. 63 (1991).

13

Therapeutic Approaches to Erotic Transference

Glen O. Gabbard, MD

Dr. Gabbard is Callaway Distinguished Professor at the Menninger Clinic and Training and Supervising Analyst at the Topeka Institute for Psychoanalysis, Topeka, KS.

KEY POINTS

- *Erotic transference* is a term that refers to a mixture of tender, erotic, and sexual feelings a client experiences for his or her therapist that form part of a positive transference.

- A correct interpretation of the erotic transference will frequently reduce the desire and resistance inherent in transference love.

- The therapist's countertransference reactions to the client's erotic transference feelings may represent countertransference narrowly, as a reactivation of a relationship in the therapist's past; broadly, as an identification with a projected aspect of the client; or as a combination of both.

- Erotic transference is a resistance and a communication. Instead of being simply taken at face value, it should be explored through the client's associations, dreams, and memories for all its multiple meanings, some of which may be unconscious.

- When therapists find themselves sexually aroused by their clients or are the object of a client's intense sexual desire, consultation with a colleague is advised.

A "SEXIST" BIAS

Despite the pervasiveness of the phenomenon of erotic transference, many therapists do not receive adequate training in
the effective and therapeutic management of transference
feelings. Historically, a subtle (or not-so-subtle) sexism has
pervaded psychotherapy training programs. One female psychiatric resident who was struggling with a male client's
sexual feelings toward her took the problem to her psychotherapy supervisor, an analyst. He responded by scratching
his head and replying, "I don't know what you girls do about
this problem."

Because the vast majority of erotic transference reports in
the literature, from Freud to the present, have been of female
clients who have fallen in love with their male therapists or
analysts, male supervisors have sometimes inadvertently pro-
moted among their male supervisees a casual, denigrating
attitude toward female clients who develop an erotic transference. One male resident who was beginning psychotherapy
training told his male supervisor he was uncertain about how
to approach his first psychotherapy client. His supervisor
informed him, "It's really very simple. Do you know how to
seduce a woman?" The supervisor went on to draw an analogy
between "hooking" the client in a psychotherapy process and
seducing a woman. This unprofessional attitude typifies an
unfortunate historical trend to "enjoy" the erotic transference
rather than to analyze and understand it.

EROTIC TRANSFERENCE DEFINED

Because the term *erotic transference* is used to describe a number of different transference developments, a clear definition
is relevant to a discussion of its management. Person (1985)
provided a succinct definition that applies to psychotherapy
as well as to psychoanalysis:

The term *erotic transference* is used interchangeably with the term *transference love*. It refers to some mixture of tender, erotic, and sexual feelings that a patient experiences in reference to his or her analyst and, as such, forms part of a positive transference. Sexual transference components alone represent a truncated erotic transference, one that has not been fully developed or is not fully experienced.

NEUROTIC VS. BORDERLINE CONTENT

In neurotic clients, erotic transference usually develops gradually and in an atmosphere of considerable shame and embarrassment. Sexual longings for the therapist are often experienced as ego dystonic, and the client knows that the fulfillment of these wishes would be inappropriate.

Borderline clients may develop a subtype of erotic transference that Blum (1973) has termed *the eroticized transference*. In contrast to ordinary transference love, the client in the throes of an eroticized transference makes a tenacious and ego syntonic demand for sexual gratification. Because of their ego impairments, borderline clients experience blurring of their internal and external realities and they view their expectation of sexual consummation with their therapist as reasonable and desirable. Their seeming obliviousness to the crossing of symbolically incestuous boundaries may stem from a childhood history of being victimized in actual sexual seductions by parents or parental figures (Blum,1973; Kumin, 1985-86).

RISKS VS. THERAPEUTIC WINDOWS

The spectrum of transference that ranges from the erotic to the eroticized is aptly described by Person (1985) as "both gold mine and minefield"; such transferences can set the scene for devastating countertransference acting out. Sex between therapist and client has severely stigmatized the mental health professions, has ruined the careers of a number of psychotherapists, and has caused severe psychological damage in the clients who have been its victims (Gabbard,1989; Pope, 1986). Surveys reveal as many as 10% of all male therapists have engaged in such behavior (Gabbard, 1989), so it cannot be dismissed as an occasional aberration of only the seriously disturbed therapist. Many of these therapists appear to be seeking a cure for themselves as well as to be making a desperate attempt to cure their clients (Twemlow & Gabbard, 1989).

The "gold mine" aspect of erotic transferences is that they provide the therapist with an in vivo recapitulation of a past relationship in the present situation of the transference relationship. Such clients demonstrate the contributions they bring to similar relationships outside the therapeutic situation. Thus, a client's problems with love and sexuality can be examined and understood as they develop in a safe relationship in which that client will not be exploited or abused. To gain insight into the experience without being destroyed in the process demands that the therapist adhere to four principles of technique (see Table 13.1).

Table 13.1
**STEPS IN THE THERAPEUTIC MANAGEMENT OF
EROTIC TRANSFERENCE**

1. Examination of countertransference feelings

2. Nonexploitive acceptance of erotic transference as important therapeutic material to be understood

3. Assessment of the multiple meanings of the transference in its function as a resistance to the deepening of the therapeutic process

4. Interpretation of connections between transference and both current and past relationships

---

EXAMINATION OF COUNTERTRANSFERENCE FEELINGS

The therapist's countertransference reactions to erotic transference feelings in the client may represent countertransference narrowly, as a reactivation of a relationship in the
therapist's past; broadly, as an identification with a projected
aspect of the client; or as a combination of both (Kumin, 1985-
86; Sandler, 1976). The client may well represent a forbidden
but sexually arousing object from the therapist's past, but the
therapist's desire for the client may also be linked to the actual
incestuous desire of a parental figure from the client's oedipal
phase of development. The first step in monitoring countertransference, therefore, is for the therapist to assess the relative weight of his or her own contributions versus those of the
client. Therapists who attempt to manage erotic transference
in intensive psychotherapy without a personal treatment experience, however, will be at a serious disadvantage. Several
countertransference patterns are related to erotic transference.

Seeing Erotic Transference Where None Exists:

Common in male trainees treating attractive female clients
is a countertransference pattern in which the trainee sees
erotic transference where none exists. Male therapists may
react to their own sexual arousal by projectively disavowing it
and instead seeing it in their clients, whom they label as
"seductive." In those circumstances, the trainee who is pressed
for details about why the client is seductive, or why she is
sexually interested in him, is often at a loss to present convincing evidence. Because of anxieties about his own sexual feelings, he has avoided them, much as the hysterical client attempts to avoid her sexual feelings.

Although such avoidance may simply reflect the therapist's
"beginner's anxiety" about having sexual feelings in psychotherapy, it may also be a repetition of the client's father's
response to his own sexual arousal in the presence of his
daughter (Gorkin, 1985). If beginning therapists ignore these

feelings, they unconsciously act them out by making phallic, "penetrating" interpretations too often and too soon — a common pitfall of the new therapist.

Cold Aloofness:

A second countertransference reaction is cold aloofness in response to the client's confessions of erotic longings for the therapist (MacKinnon & Michels, 1971). To control any sexual countertransference reactions to the client's feelings, the therapist may become more silent, less empathic, and more distant. Such "strait jacketing" of all emotions helps rigidly maintain control of sexual impulses that seem threatening.

Anxiety:

A third common countertransference reaction is anxiety, which arises from the fear that sexual feelings, either in the client or therapist, will get out of control. That anxiety may lead the therapist to divert the conversation from the client's expressions of love or sexual arousal or to interpret such feelings prematurely as "resistance," a digression from the therapeutic task. When a male therapist inappropriately tells his female client that he will not allow the therapy to be sidetracked by her feelings for him, he forces her to concentrate on the problems outside therapy that brought her to treatment. Such an anxious attempt to eliminate erotic transference feelings may give the female client the message that sexual feelings are unacceptable and possibly disgusting, a view that often mirrors her own feelings. The therapist's own underlying disgust may relate to the covert message in intense erotic transference that therapy is useless — that only sex or "love" can cure (Gorkin, 1985).

Self-gratification:

In the fourth countertransference pattern, which may be more insidious than the others, therapists encourage and foster erotic feelings for their own gratification. Such therapists, who listen with voyeuristic delight to the details of their client's sexual fantasies, may have been drawn to the profession because they long to be idealized and loved. Still, underneath that wish they may gain sadistic pleasure by arousing their clients' futile sexual wishes. The pattern can often be traced to the therapist's childhood interactions, in which he or she felt aroused by the opposite-sex parent only to be frustrated. By practicing psychotherapy, such individuals may be trying to reverse that childhood situation. Therapists must be aware of their own desires in the therapeutic relationship. As Kumin (1985-1986) noted, "Both the analyst's capacity and incapacity to interpret accurately the client's wishes in the transference require an appreciation of not only what and whom the client desires but also what and whom the analyst desires." Kumin has also suggested the desires of the therapist for the client may present a more formidable resistance than the client's desires for the therapist. Numerous psychotherapy processes have become stalemated in the throes of intense erotic transference because the therapist has been too busy basking in the glow of sexual feelings.

NONEXPLOITATIVE ACCEPTANCE OF EROTIC TRANSFERENCE AS IMPORTANT THERAPEUTIC MATERIAL

After the therapist has carefully analyzed countertransference feelings, he or she must convey to the client that sexual or loving feelings are acceptable in the therapeutic experience. The therapist may make an educational comment such as, "In psychotherapy, you are likely to experience a broad range of feelings—hate, love, envy, sexual arousal, fear, anger, and joy—all of which must be dealt with as acceptable topics for discussion and as carriers of important information for the therapy." Although it is true that erotic transference may serve as resistance to the emergence of other material in the process of therapy, it is a technical error to immediately interpret such feelings as resistance. To understand what is being repeated from the past, the erotic transference must be allowed to develop fully.

Freud (1958) first used the term *acting out* to describe a client's tendency to repeat in action something from the past rather than to remember and verbalize it. Therapists may tell clients that the feelings that develop in therapy will provide important information about those that develop elsewhere, both past and present. If a client insists on gratification of the transference wishes, the therapist can point out that not gratifying the wishes can lead to a better understanding of what happens in other relationships. The therapist should remember that erotic transference may be intensely unpleasant for the client, just as it may be for the therapist, not only because of the frustration it brings but also because it may be embarrassing. Perhaps the therapist may wish to communicate an empathic understanding of the client's shame: "I know it is difficult and painful for you to have these feelings without being able to gratify them, but if we can explore them together we may be able to help you understand more fully the problems that brought you here."

ASSESSMENT OF THE MULTIPLE MEANINGS OF THE TRANSFERENCE IN ITS FUNCTION AS A RESISTANCE

Erotic transference is a resistance in the sense that something is being repeated rather than remembered and verbalized. Resistance should not be equated, however, with something bad that must be removed immediately, as beginning therapists often perceive it to be. As stated earlier, erotic transference is also an important communication that should be understood. Like all other mental phenomena, erotic transference is determined by the principle of multiple function. It should not be taken simply at face value but rather should be explored through the client's associations, dreams, and memories for all its multiple meanings, some of which may be unconscious. For example, a male client's erotic transference to a female therapist may represent passive homosexual longings, even though the therapist is of the opposite sex (Torras de Bea, 1987). Because erotic transference must also be understood in terms of its function at a particular moment in therapy, the therapist must assess what preceded its development and what follows its flourishing.

Therapist Envy—A Case Study:

One male client began his therapy session with his male therapist by saying that he had been helped enormously in the previous session by the explanations the therapist had given. After commenting on how much the therapist's interpretation had helped him at work, the client began to contradict what he had just said by maintaining that his relationships were deteriorating. As he continued to talk, he revealed that he had been having sexual fantasies about the therapist and that he believed the therapist could only help him by ejaculating semen into his rectum to make him more masculine.

The therapist pointed out that the client was devaluing the help of the insights that he had received in the previous session by holding onto a magical belief that a sexual liaison was the only way to obtain help. The client acknowledged that he needed to devalue the therapist's help because he felt so inferior to him, who he said was "on Mount Olympus." The therapist then explained that the client's envy had increased as he was helped, so he had sexualized the transference to devalue the help. In other words, if the therapist's insights were not particularly effective or useful, there was much less to envy. In response, the client said that his liberating feelings of having been helped had alternated with feelings of humiliation because he was forced to acknowledge that the therapist knew something the client did not know, which made him feel vulnerable.

In this example, the client's erotic transference was a way to defend against his envy of the therapist's competence by devaluing it. Sexualization in the transference may be a way to defend against other feelings as well.

Defense Against Loss — A Case Study:

A male client was seeing his female therapist for the last time prior to her departure at the end of her residency training program. He told her that he had seen a movie the night before in which a female psychiatrist had kissed one of her male clients. He observed that the client had seemed to benefit from the therapist's affection, and he asked his therapist if she might do the same with him. After an initially anxious reaction to the request, the therapist asked if the unexpected request might be related to the termination of the therapy. The client responded that he would rather not think about that subject. The therapist then pointed out to the client that his wish to sexualize their relationship might be a defense against facing the grief associated with termination.

Sexualizing the end of a relationship is a common phenomenon, both in therapy and in life in general, serving to avoid the mourning process connected with loss of an important figure. In the vignette described above, the client's wish to become physically involved with his therapist was also a way to deny the definitive nature of termination: a kiss might lead to a beginning, rather than an ending.

Therapists who view transference love as a natural and understandable response to their enormous sexual appeal are overlooking the darker side of erotic transference. One of the many stories told about Karl Menninger illustrates this dilemma: A depressed and hysterical 40-year-old woman was hospitalized at the Menninger Clinic for over a year with essentially no improvement in her condition. During her hospitalization, she developed an intense and intractable eroticized transference toward her male psychotherapist, so Dr. Menninger was asked to consult on the case because of the therapeutic stalemate that had been reached. Throughout much of the interview, the client repeatedly commented on her great love for her therapist. After listening to her protestations of love for several minutes, Dr. Menninger reportedly said, "You know, if you really loved him, you would get better for him."

Dr. Menninger was addressing the hostility that often lies just beneath the surface of a client's transference love. Indeed, erotic transferences frequently mask considerable aggression and sadism, even to the extent that an erotic transference might be considered a form of negative transference (Kumin, 1985-86). A client's demands for crossing of sexual boundaries may be so tormenting, especially in instances of the eroticized variant typical of borderline clients, that the therapist dreads each session. The therapist may feel used and transformed into a need-gratifying object whose only function is to fulfill the client's inappropriate demands (Frayn, 1986).

Controlling the Therapist—A Case Study:

Ms. A, a 24-year-old homosexual histrionic client functioning at a borderline level of ego organization, had a history of sexual abuse by male relatives. She formed an intense eroticized transference to her female therapist almost immediately. She flirted with her provocatively in the sessions by touching the therapist's foot lightly with her own foot and asking, "Does this make you nervous?" Ms. A steadfastly maintained that her therapist could only get to know her if the therapist slept with her. She also demanded to know her therapist's sexual orientation. Although the therapist frustrated the client's wish to destroy their professional relationship by transforming it into a sexual one, the client continued her efforts at seduction, regularly bringing to the sessions and reading aloud explicit sexual fantasies about her therapist that she had written.

Needless to say, the client's expression of such fantasies made the therapist feel uncomfortable and anxious—as well as controlled. If she interrupted the fantasies, she felt that she was revealing her discomfort and disapproval of the client's transference feelings. If she remained silent, she felt that she was colluding in an exhibitionist-voyeur pairing. Finally, however, the client revealed some of the underlying aggressive feelings that were masquerading as eroticized transference. She commented to the therapist, "You know I'm aware of still wanting to piss you off. Probably force you into rejecting me. Make you hate me. Am I succeeding? I really want you to like me. But since I know that's out of the question, I'll just drive you away."

To a large extent, Ms. A had induced a paralysis in the therapist, who was made to feel cruel and sadistic by frustrating the client's wishes. A consultation helped the therapist understand that she was being controlled by a projective identification process, so the normal, professional limits of psychotherapy seemed ruthless and unreasonable. In other words, a cold, depriving object from the client's past had been projected into the therapist, who unconsciously identified with that projected material. Moreover, her own anger at the client for her relentless control of the therapy also contributed to her feelings that any intervention would appear cold and ruthless.

As the psychotherapy continued, it became more clear that the overt sexual wish was only the tip of an iceberg. During one session, Ms. A reported a dream in which she was in a high-tech office. There was a machine that could translate the client's thoughts, so that she did not have to tell them to her therapist. The client acknowledged that her longings for the therapist were not truly sexual, but rather a wish for her therapist to really know her intimately. The therapist eventually helped Ms. A to see that her wish for sex was really a wish for merger — a wish that her therapist would know her thoughts without her having to voice them. This regressive longing to return to the mother-infant symbiotic state is often a powerful component of erotic or eroticized transferences in the female client-female therapist dyad. The sexualized wish may be preferable to the more threatening wish for merger.

THE CONNECTIONS BETWEEN TRANSFERENCE AND CURRENT AND PAST RELATIONSHIPS

A correct interpretation of the erotic transference will often reduce the desire and resistance inherent in transference love (Kumin, 1985–86). To avoid premature interpretation, the therapist may need silently to formulate the interpretation to help with countertransference desires even before revealing the interpretation to the client. The timing of transference interpretation is a matter of judgment, but a rule of thumb is avoidance of interpreting erotic transference until the underlying linkages to past relationships and to current extratransference relationships approach conscious awareness. The therapist can point out connections between the transference feelings and past relationships, as well as between the transference and current extratransference relationships. By noting that transference love is a repetition of an event from the past — and asking the client if the situation is reminiscent of past situations — the therapist can lay the groundwork for interpretive interventions.

> Ms. B was a 26-year-old married female client with a diagnosis of hysterical personality disorder. She was seen twice weekly by a male therapist in expressive-supportive psychotherapy with a predominantly expressive emphasis. She began psychotherapy with complaints of anorgasmia, headaches, constant marital difficulties, fear of "standing on her own two feet," feelings of being unloved and unwanted, and a generalized concern that she was too dependent. Midway through the second year of treatment, the following exchange occurred during one session. (The actual transcript of a psychotherapy session that follows illustrates some of the technical approaches to interpreting erotic transference.)
>
> *Client*: My husband and I haven't been getting along. We don't see each other much, and when we do, we argue. I wanted to make you a buddy again today, but when I walked in, something changed. I don't know what to say today. I'd like to get

real mad at you, but I don't know why. Probably because I need attention and my husband's not giving me any. When I don't have anything to say, it's usually because I have feelings for you — I had butterflies just now when I said that. There are two kinds of feelings I get in here — one is when I feel that you're like my dad and I want you to cradle me and give me the pat on the back. The other is when I want you to hold me real tight. . . . (client stops)

Therapist: You had a feeling just now that stopped you in mid-sentence. What was it?

Client: I don't want to say it. It's ridiculous. (With great hesitation) I can't just come in here. . . and look at you. . . and think, "I want to make love with you." I can't feel that way. That's not me.

Therapist: To think that you could have sexual feelings is so unacceptable to you that you cannot own the feelings as yours?

Client: I'm just not like that. Not even with my husband. My subconscious wants to hang on to you and hold you tightly, but my conscious mind wants to pretend I don't have the feelings. I'd rather go back to just having the feeling that you were like my dad and I need a pat on the back.

Therapist: It's particularly unacceptable for you to have sexual feelings for someone that you also view as a dad. I wonder if the same thing happened as a little girl in your relationship with your father.

Client: I was always very special to my dad. When he walked me down the aisle and gave me away at the wedding, he told me that I was always his favorite of his three daughters. I shouldn't be talking like this. I have to go out and get in the car with my husband and spend the evening with him, but my thoughts are going to be about you.

Therapist: It sounds like there is a similarity between your attachment to me and your attachment to your dad in that both make it difficult for you to invest emotionally in your husband.

In the above discourse, the therapist draws a connection between the client's erotic transference and her feelings for her father. Sexual feelings are forbidden in both relationships, because she sees them as incompatible with her otherwise paternal view of the therapist and her father. After linking the transference feelings to the client's past relationship with her father, the therapist connects those longings to her difficulty with her husband, a current extratransference relationship.

SEEKING CONSULTATION

The approach to erotic transference outlined in this chapter provides a conceptual framework that may assist the psychiatrist in understanding and managing a potentially disconcerting clinical situation. However, when therapists find themselves sexually aroused by their clients, or are the object of a client's intense sexual desire, consultation with a colleague is advised. Poets have known for centuries that desire may cloud judgment. A colleague's objective feedback may help a therapist steer a truer course through the turbulent seas of erotic feelings in therapeutic relationships.

REFERENCES

Blum, H. P. (1973). The concept of erotized transference. *Journal of the American Psychoanalytic Association, 21,* 61-76.

Frayn, D. H. & Silberfeld, M. (1986). Erotic transference. *Canadian Journal of Psychiatry, 31,* 323-327.

Freud, S. (1958). *Remembering, repeating and working-through (further recommendations on the technique of psychoanalysis II)* (Vol. 12). London: Hogarth Press.

Gabbard, G. O. (Ed.). (1989). *Sexual Exploitation in Professional Relationships.* Washington, DC: American Psychiatric Press.

Gorkin, M. (1985). Varieties of sexualized countertransference. *Psychoanalytic Review, 72,* 421-440.

Kumin, I. (1985-86). Erotic horror: Desire and resistance in the psychoanalytic situation. *International Journal of Psychoanalytic Psychotherapy, 11,* 3-20.

MacKinnon, R. & Michels, R. (1971). *The psychiatric interview in clinical practice.* Philadelphia: Saunders.

Person, E. S. (1985). The erotic transference in women and in men: Differences and consequences. *Journal of the American Academy of Psychoanalysis, 13,* 159-180.

Pope, K. S. & Bouhoutsos, J. C. (1986). *Sexual intimacy between therapists and patients.* New York: Praeger.

Sandler, J. (1976). Countertransference and role-responsiveness. *International Review of Psychoanalysis, 3,* 43-47.

Torras de Bea, E. (1987). A contribution to the papers on transference by Eva Lester and Marianne Goldberger and Dorothy Evans. *International Journal of Psychoanalysis, 68,* 63-67.

Twemlow, S. W. & Gabbard, G. O. (1989). The lovesick therapist. In Gabbard, G. O. (Ed.), *Sexual Exploitation in Professional Relationships.* Washington, DC: American Psychiatric Press.

FOR FURTHER READING

Gabbard, G. O. (1994). On love and lust in erotic transference. *Journal of the American Psychoanalytic Association, 42,* 385-404.

Gabbard, G. O. (1994). Sexual excitement and countertransference love in the analyst. *Journal of the American Psychoanalytic Association, 42,* 1083-1106.

14

On the Efficacy of Psychotherapy

Henry M. Bachrach, PhD

Dr. Bachrach is Clinical Professor of Psychiatry, New York Medical College at St. Vincent's Hospital and Medical Center of New York, N.Y.

KEY POINTS

- A brief history of theories on the efficacy of psychotherapy is reviewed.

- Factors to be considered in the evaluation of the effectiveness of psychotherapy include: the clinical condition being treated, the type of psychotherapy in relation to clinical conditions, the suitability of the client for the treatment, the client's readiness to undertake psychotherapy, the experience and skills of the therapist, and how well the therapist and the client are matched.

- This chapter discusses the efficacy of various modalities: psychoanalysis, psychoanalytically

oriented psychotherapy and related expressive psychotherapies, cognitive psychotherapy, and combination therapy.

- The more favorable the client's level of overall functioning (ego strength), the more likely it will be that the client will achieve substantial therapeutic benefit from most forms of psychotherapy.

- With careful diagnostic evaluation and treatment prescription based on considerations of indications and suitability for a given form of psychotherapy, the odds for significant therapeutic benefit improve substantially.

INTRODUCTION

June 1952:

Basing his conclusion on a selective review of formal research studies, British experimental psychologist Hans J.
Eysenck (1952) stuns the psychiatric world with the statement
that there is no empirical evidence to demonstrate that psychotherapy has any significant, measured effectiveness. However, his review seems to have had more impact on the academic than clinical community; clinicians still continue to
recommend and practice psychotherapy and clients still continue to claim they derive substantial benefits.

Eysenck never did state that psychotherapy was not effective; he only stated there was no evidence from his logical
positivist perspective to demonstrate that it did. Therefore,
the null hypothesis that clients treated by psychotherapy
improve more than untreated clients was not disconfirmed.

August 1956:

American psychologist Donald Cartwright (1956) challenges
Eysenck's conclusion in the same journal and raises questions
about the selection of studies and the rendering of the evidence. New formal studies of the efficacy of psychotherapy
and the predictability of outcomes are under way at The
Menninger Foundation and at the University of Chicago.

1957–1970:

Empirical studies of psychotherapeutic processes and outcomes capture the imagination of academic psychiatrists and
psychologists. A groundswell of formal research emerges.
Most of the research, however, is limited in that it draws upon
the work of relatively inexperienced therapists (e.g., residents, graduate students) treating select populations in academic settings. Concerned with the direction that the research
is taking, Keissler (1966) echoes past clinical wisdom in the

search for a more cogent paradigm. He writes that questions about the efficacy of psychotherapy can only be posed meaningfully in terms of (a) what kinds of patients benefit, (b) in what kinds of ways, (c) when what kinds of therapies, (d) are applied by what kinds of therapists.

Keissler's formulation of the question goes back to Oberndorf's (1943) pioneering research on psychoanalytic outcomes, but it seems that it needs to be stated every decade or so. Still, before 1970, the times or technology were not quite ripe for such a formulation. To pool resources, a small group of clinically informed researchers begin to meet annually, forming the national Society for Psychotherapy Research. The American Psychological Association convened three interdisciplinary conferences on psychotherapy research. The results of the more informed Menninger (Kernberg et al., 1972) and Chicago (Fiske, Cartwright & Kirtner, 1964) studies began to provide reliable, formal, empirical evidence to demonstrate the efficacy of psychotherapy for some clients. Nevertheless, debates continued. A new large-scale, methodologically rigorous, multivariate, predictive study began at the University of Pennsylvania Medical Center.

1970–1980:

New forms of therapy germinating during the 1960s come into their own (e.g., cognitive therapy, behavior therapy) and their efficacy begins to be compared with that of more traditional psychodynamic approaches. Luborsky, Singer, & Luborsky (1975) review the growing literature on comparative studies and conclude that all forms of therapy yield equal benefits: there is no empirical evidence to demonstrate that one form of therapy provides more therapeutic benefit than another for clients as a general class — the quality of benefit cannot, however, be addressed by the available research. (Clinicians still continue to make differential diagnoses and treat different kinds of clients differently.) Garfield and Bergin's thousand-page *Handbook of Psychotherapy Research* (1978/ 1986) is now in its second revision. At the sunset of the decade,

Smith, Glass, and Miller (1980) apply an ingenious statistical method ("meta-analysis") to pool the results of all controlled studies. On the basis of 475 "controlled" studies of "psychotherapy" involving well over 25,000 "patients," they conclude:

> The results show unequivocally that psychotherapy is effective. . . At the end of treatment [the patient] is better off than 80% of those who need therapy but remain untreated. In absolute terms, the magnitude of therapeutic effect is greater than most interventions in social science. Not only is psychotherapy effective on the average, but there is scant evidence of negative or deterioration effects of psychotherapy.

Smith, Glass, and Miller's review is not without its own difficulties, for in their desire to be both comprehensive and rigorous, most of the studies that they included in their review tended to be clinically naïve, based upon the work of novice therapists and unrepresentative of the everyday world of clinical practice.

1980–1990:

In this decade, informed clinical practice begins to inform research. Questions about the general efficacy of psychotherapy no longer seem to be compelling or even interesting. Recognition that empirical research had not much influenced clinical practice largely because it did not correspond to the world of informed practice now seems as if it had always been self-evident. The National Institute of Mental Health now consents to support only studies of informed practice, germane to serious clinical problems, where it can be demonstrated that the particular kind of therapy being studied is actually being administered at a requisite level of skill (e.g., as assessed through treatment manuals applied to tape records of actual treatments).

A major, multicenter collaborative investigation comparing the efficacy of cognitive, interpersonal, and psychopharmacologic treatment of dysthymic disorder is under way (Klerman et al., 1974), though its findings are somewhat equivocal be-

cause most of the treatments, including psychopharmacologic, were not administered consistent with research criteria
(Prien et al., 1984). Nonetheless, cognitive, interpersonal, and
imipramine therapy seemed equally effective, especially in
regard to combining psychotherapy with pharmacotherapy in
treating dysthymic disorder.

Psychoanalysts also begin to publish outcome studies using
research methodologies consistent with the level of their data,
and the findings from nearly a dozen studies involving more
than 1000 clients all tend to converge on the finding that most
suitably selected clients treated by psychoanalysis functioning within a nonpsychotic range of illness achieve substantial
therapeutic benefits (Bachrach et al., 1991). The final account
of the Menninger Project (Wallerstein, 1986) and the Penn
Project (Luborsky et al., 1988) are now in and suggest most
clients carefully selected as suitable candidates for psychotherapy derive substantial benefits, though it is not easy to
predict at the beginning of treatment who among the seem-
ingly suitable candidates will benefit, and to what degree
(Bachrach et al., 1991, Luborsky et al., 1988; Wallerstein, 1986).

Questions about the effects of client-therapist matches are
now being considered. In an age of increasing accountability,
clinicians and researchers share concerns. All seem to conclude that the once-ambitious questions posed by earlier investigators were premature or ill-conceived. The accumula-
tion of knowledge proceeds by a focus upon small, manageable questions where there exist means of finding answers. No
one research model or method, be it the model of experimental
psychology, psychoanalysis, or hermeneutics, is equally well
suited to all questions. Answers to questions about the efficacy
of psychotherapy must come from many perspectives, from
the level of clinical observation of the consulting room to
formal research strategies. The decade ends with the question
of which therapy for whom and for what?

1990–present:

The Diagnostic Specificity and Treatment Planning series

emerges. Despite its limitations, the DSM series brings a measure of reliability to classification. Increasingly, the relationship between the type of therapy, administered by whom, for what kind of client, experiencing what manner of psychopathology, commands center stage. The decade begins with a decided focus upon the relationship between the indications for a particular form of treatment, the client's suitability for a given form of treatment, and the demonstrated effectiveness of these treatments for the psychopathology of individual clients. The gap between actual clinical practice and formal research narrows as clinicians are now actively engaged in the research enterprise. However, the field is still not prepared overall to conduct formal studies meeting meaningful criteria for effective outcome research (especially in relation to the comparative efficacy of different treatments), in part because effective and applicable methods of assessing of treatment processes and outcomes have not yet been brought to the point of sophisticated clinical specificity and meaningfulness. The development of such methods remains one of the main challenges to the field in the new decade. Systematic, rigorous individual case studies clustered according to target questions appear as one promising methodology.

THE EVALUATION OF EFFICACY

Many factors should be carefully considered in the evaluation of efficacy. These factors include: the clinical condition being treated, the type of psychotherapy in relation to clinical conditions, and the suitability of the client for the treatment.

The Clinical Condition Being Treated:

Psychotherapy is not a panacea for all psychopathology. Its effectiveness can only be evaluated in terms of the extent to which one might reasonably expect a given clinical condition to be ameliorated at a given state of knowledge. For example,

some conditions, such as autism, are not known to be systematically amenable to any form of treatment. Other conditions,
such as certain schizophrenias, may be arrested or stabilized
by pharmacologic and/or psychotherapeutic means, although,
as in diabetes, the fundamental condition is not known to be
alterable. Other conditions, such as certain borderline disorders, may be amenable with difficulty while others, such as
certain depressive states, may be readily amenable. Viewed in
this light, the matter of efficacy becomes a question of the
extent of reasonably expectable influence rather than cure, and
the degree and quality of change in comparison to what can be
achieved by other treatment methods. If a given form of
psychotherapy results in the improvement of a given clinical
condition more than other forms of treatment for the same
condition, it would certainly be regarded as effective. If, however, it is shown to be helpful, but not as helpful as other forms
of treatment for that condition, the degree of efficacy would
have to be viewed in another light.

The Type of Psychotherapy in Relation to Clinical
Conditions:

Insofar as we understand incompletely both the pathogen-
esis and the action of different forms of psychotherapy, one
can evaluate only the efficacy of a particular kind of psychotherapy in relation to a specific clinical condition or class of
conditions. To speak of efficacy in general terms is about as
meaningful as speaking about the efficacy of education or
surgery. The key questions are: "What kind?" "For what?"
"When?" and so on.

The Suitability of the Client for the Treatment:

Broadly speaking, all forms of treatment present tasks to
clients. Implicitly or explicitly, they require clients to do certain things, and assume that clients have the ability to do these
things. Some cognitive-behavioral therapies, for example, re-

quire clients to construct precise hierarchies of conditions surrounding the appearance of symptoms. They assume clients will have the capacity for precision and be able to construct such hierarchies; if clients cannot do so, they cannot be considered suitable candidates for this form of treatment. Another modality, psychoanalysis, assumes that clients are able to respond with self-observation and candor rather than action in the face of strong feeling. Clients unable to do so are therefore not suitable candidates for psychoanalysis.

In general, all forms of psychotherapy require that clients be able to participate actively in the treatment process and, to some extent, entertain the idea that their lot, at least in part, is a product of their attitudes, desires, perceptions, values, etc. Therefore, no matter what the indications are for any given form of treatment, the efficacy of that treatment also depends upon the client's ability to engage in the treatment procedures. But since there are many different kinds of people, treatment prescriptions must take into account who the client is, how he or she sees the world, and what his or her natural proclivities are for dealing with problems. Obvious as these points may be, they are often overlooked.

The efficacy of a particular form of psychotherapy for a given clinical condition can therefore only be meaningfully evaluated if the client possesses the requisite capacities and abilities to engage in the treatment effort, that is, the tasks implicit to the treatment method. As in sculpting, one can only work with the substance and grain of the marble; to go against the grain is to invite misfortune. In clinical terms, going against the grain of the marble may mean incomplete diagnosis, an errant treatment prescription, or limitations of experienced and technical skill.

A DEFINITION OF PSYCHOTHERAPY

Psychotherapy may be defined as a clinical procedure governed by systematically conceptualized and specified rules of technique, rationally derived from a systematic body of knowledge regarding psychopathology and the human condition. Its means of influence are verbal, and its aim is to ameliorate psychological stresses, symptoms, and/or conflicts.

From this definition, it follows that simply talking to clients, *per se*, or counseling them, helpful as this may sometimes be, should probably not be regarded as psychotherapy. The main forms of psychotherapy today include cognitive therapy, cognitive-behavioral therapy, psychoanalytically oriented therapy, and psychoanalysis. These categorizations are only generic, and each in turn also subsumes a variety of approaches. Psychotherapies may also be classified according to their degree of expressiveness or supportiveness — that is, the extent to which techniques aim toward modifying or strengthening attitudes, defenses, and coping styles.

EFFICACY AND THE PRESCRIPTION FOR PSYCHOTHERAPY

As has been suggested, the efficacy of any clinical procedure, including psychotherapy, can be meaningfully considered only in the broader context of where its administration is and is not indicated. In relation to the prescription for a particular modality of psychotherapy, it has proven especially useful to make distinctions between indications for the form of psychotherapy and the client's suitability in terms of psychological makeup and resources.

About the only general statement one can make about the prescription for psychotherapy is that the higher the client's overall level of psychological function (i.e., ego strength), the more likely the client will be able to benefit from most forms of psychotherapy (Garfield & Bergin, 1986). The more impaired the client, the more guarded the prognosis. This is only to state the somewhat obvious proposition that the more effective resources people have and the more effectively they have been able to make use of their developmental learning opportunities, the more likely they will be to make productive use of the opportunities provided by psychotherapy. This is well illustrated by the finding of the Menninger Foundation Psychotherapy Research Project. Clients initially misdiagnosed as having severe impairments in ego functioning and placed in supportive psychotherapy achieved substantial benefits, at times close to the levels achieved by clients of high ego strength treated by the most expressive form of psychotherapy. Clients initially misdiagnosed as having high levels of ego strength and placed in the more expressive forms of psychotherapy did poorly and sometimes deteriorated (Horwitz, 1974).

SOME SPECIFIC MODALITIES

Psychoanalysis:

Psychoanalysis continues to be the most therapeutically ambitious and demanding form of psychotherapy. It is therefore indicated only for conditions generally refractory to less demanding approaches and in areas where it has proven its mettle. It is never indicated for transient, situational, or relatively minor conditions. It is probably the treatment of choice for seriously consequential disorders of intrapsychic conflict such as character neuroses and characterological anxiety or depressive states. Common indications include the character neuroses, including masochistic and narcissistic personality disorders, and major impairments of interpersonal or vocational functioning deriving from intrapsychic conflict, i.e., difficulties in forming lasting, intimate relations with persons of the opposite sex or the recurrent undermining of opportunities for advancement and success.

Even though a wide range of persons may experience such difficulties, psychoanalysis is generally suitable only for persons functioning within a neurotic range of ego weakness and whose character attitudes and values are given to autoplastic modes of coping. Such persons are typically psychologically minded, seeking treatment to change something about themselves, with good ego strength, relatively mature object relations, and capacities for response to stress by thought more than action.

Psychoanalysis has clearly been shown to yield high levels of therapeutic benefits for disorders of intrapsychic conflict among clients functioning within a neurotic range of ego weakness (Erle, 1979; Erle & Goldberg, 1984; Wallerstein, 1986; Weber, Bachrach, & Solomon, 1985). The clinical literature and general clinical lore also suggest that among suitable clients treated by psychoanalysis the levels of therapeutic benefit and their resilience are higher than in similar clients treated by psychotherapy. Few formal comparative investigations of this distinction have been undertaken, but a mounting body of formal research that tends to support the clinical wisdom has emerged (Wallerstein, 1986; Weber et al., 1985). Psychoanalysis is clearly contraindicated for clients functioning within a psychotic range of ego weakness and for most clients functioning within a borderline range (Bachrach & Leaff, 1978).

Psychoanalytically Oriented Psychotherapy and Related Expressive Psychotherapies:

These are indicated for a wider range of conditions than psychoanalysis proper and for a broader range of clients. In its many variants (from short-term expressive psychotherapy to longer-term approaches) it can be indicated for transient disturbances, symptomatic affect states, and more circumscribed characterological conditions. It may also be indicated where psychoanalysis is indicated, but when the client's level of ego functioning, attitudes, or reality circumstances do not permit psychoanalysis. Expressive and supportive psychotherapies are generally regarded as helpful in the treatment of borderline personality organization, depending on the client's psychological resources, though adjunctive procedures (e.g., hospital management, pharmacotherapy) may also be required. Expressive psychotherapy is generally contraindicated if used alone or as the primary treatment method for client's functioning within a psychotic range of ego weakness. Formal research studies show that most clients suitable for expressive psycho-therapy achieve considerable therapeutic benefit, especially for anxiety disorders, certain affective disorders, and for de-limited characterological difficulties (Kernberg et al., 1972; Luborsky et al., 1980).

Cognitive Psychotherapy:

Cognitive therapy is a relatively recent approach to psycho-therapy pioneered by Ellis (1962) and Beck (1976). Although there are many varieties of cognitive therapy (lately it has also been combined with elements of behavioral therapies into what is termed cognitive-behavior therapy), it is generally indicated for some depressive and anxiety disorders that im-pinge upon interpersonal and vocational functioning and for certain disorders of self-esteem (Beck, 1976; Garfield & Bergin, 1986). Because of the premium that these approaches place upon rationality and precision of thought, they are generally suitable mainly for persons with autoplastic modes of coping and with ideational, precise cognitive styles, such as obses-sive-compulsive personalities. These approaches are not indi-cated in the full treatment of borderline, psychotic, or major characterological conditions. The above recommendations re-garding indications and circumstances of suitability for cogni-tive therapy have received substantial support from formal research (Garfield & Bergin, 1986).

Miscellaneous Other Therapies:

There is a wide range of other forms of psychotherapy currently being employed, especially as an outgrowth of the Human Potential Movement (e.g., Gestalt therapy, Primal Scream therapy), about which indications and suitability has not been systematically investigated. These approaches vary in their degree of expressiveness and supportiveness. Gener-ally, however, it would seem they are contraindicated in severe borderline or psychotic conditions.

Combination Therapy:

Many therapies are also employed in combination. For example, some reports have indicated that pharmacotherapy in combination with cognitive and/or psychoanalytic psychotherapy in the treatment of depression and schizophrenia may be more effective than either method used alone (Garfield & Bergin, 1986). Behavioral treatments have shown merit in the treatment of simple phobias, inhibitions, and stress-related conditions and are also being employed in combination with other approaches. Although it is generally accepted today that pharmacotherapy is indicated in the treatment of major affective disorders and psychoses, successful treatment of these conditions by variations of long-term psychoanalytic psychotherapy has been reported. Little is understood about these reports; treatments and their effectiveness may be specific to the qualities and resources of the client, the special talents of the therapist, and the suitability of the personal match between client and therapist.

GENERAL CONCLUSIONS REGARDING THE EFFICACY OF PSYCHOTHERAPY

By this time, a substantial clinical and formal research literature has developed to support the view that most clients wisely chosen for specific forms of psychotherapy achieve substantial therapeutic benefit. At the same time, this literature shows that though clients benefit as a class, it is not possible to predict with absolute accuracy which of those carefully selected clients will benefit to what extent. Substantial literature also exists on the kinds of clients not likely to benefit from most forms of psychotherapy (Baekeland & Lundwall, 1975).

Some argue that the relative unpredictability of therapeutic outcomes among carefully selected clients is a function of the limitations of current diagnostic methods. Others, such as

Freud, have argued that it is not possible to obtain all the necessary information regarding a client's suitability in initial assessment, and that the human condition and the psychotherapeutic interactions are so complex that full predictability will never be possible. Some general conclusions may, however, be drawn:

1. The more favorable the client's level of overall functioning (ego strength), the more likely it is that the client will achieve substantial therapeutic benefit from most forms of psychotherapy.

2. A client's readiness to undertake psychotherapy is a key factor in determining its effectiveness. One's readiness to undertake psychotherapy may vary with circumstances and with different points in one's life.

3. With careful diagnostic evaluation and treatment prescription based upon considerations of indications and suitability for a given form of psychotherapy, the odds for significant therapeutic benefit improve substantially.

4. The experience, special talents, and skills of the therapist, and the suitability of the match between client and therapist, are significant influences.

5. With the present state of knowledge, it is difficult to be as precise as one might like about the specific indications and conditions of suitability for the particular modalities of psychotherapy. In the final analysis, much still depends upon the clinical circumstances of each case.

REFERENCES

Bachrach, H., & Leaff, L. (1978). Analyzability: A systematic review of the clinical and quantitative literature. *Journal of the American Psychoanalytic Association, 26,* 881-920.

Bachrach, H., et al. (1991). On the efficacy of psychoanalysis. *Journal of the American Psychoanalytic Association , 39,* 871-913.

Baekeland, F., & Lundwall, L. (1975). Dropping out of treatment: A critical review. *Psychological Bulletin, 82,* 738-783.

Beck, A. (1976). *Cognitive therapy and the emotional disorders.* New York: International University Press.

Cartwright, D. (1956). Effectiveness of psychotherapy: A critique of the spontaneous remission argument. *Journal of Consulting and Clinical Psychology, 20,* 403-404.

Ellis, A. (1962). *Reason and emotion in psychotherapy.* New York: Lyle Stuart.

Erle, J. B. (1979). An approach to the study of analyzability and analysis: The course of forty consecutive cases selected for supervised analysis. *Psychoanalytic Quarterly, 48,* 48-84.

Erle, J. B., & Goldberg, D. A. (1984). Observations on the assessment of analyzability by experienced analysts. *Journal of American Psychoanalytic Association, 32,* 715-732.

Eysenck, H. (1952). The effects of psychotherapy: An evaluation. *Journal of Consulting and Clinical Psychology, 16,* 319-324.

Fiske, D., Cartwright, D., & Kirtner, W. (1964). Are psychotherapeutic changes predictable? *Journal of Abnormal Social Psychology, 69,* 413-426.

Garfield, S., & Bergin, A. (1986). *Handbook of psychotherapy research: An empirical analysis.* New York: John Wiley & Sons. (Originally published in 1978.)

Horwitz, L. (1974). *Clinical prediction in psychotherapy.* New York: Jason Aronson.

Keissler, D. (1966). Some myths about psychotherapy research and the search for a paradigm. *Psychological Bulletin, 65,* 110-136.

Kernberg, O., et al. (1972). Psychotherapy and psychoanalysis: Final report of the Menninger Foundation Psychotherapy Research Project. *Bulletin of the Menninger Clinic, 36,* 1-275.

Klerman, G., et al. (1974). Treatment of depression by drugs and psycho-therapy. *American Journal of Psychiatry, 131,* 186-191.

Luborsky, L., Singer, B., & Luborsky, L. (1975). Comparative studies of psychotherapy: Is it true that "everyone has won and all must have prizes?" *Archives of General Psychiatry, 32,* 995-1088.

Luborsky, L., et al. (1980). Predicting the outcome of psychotherapy: Findings of the Penn Psychotherapy Project. *Archives of General Psychiatry, 37,* 471-481.

Luborsky, L., et al. (1988). *Who will benefit from psychotherapy?* New York: Basic Books, Inc.

Oberndorf, C. (1943). Results of psychoanalytic therapy. *International Journal of Psychoanalysis, 24,* 107-114.

Prien, R., et al. (1984). Drug therapy in the prevention of recurrences in unipolar and bipolar affective disorders: Report of the NIMH Collabora-tive Study Group comparing lithium carbonate, imipramine and a lithium carbonate-imipramine combination. *Archives of General Psychiatry, 41,* 1096-1104.

Smith, M., Glass, G., & Miller, T. (1980). *The benefits of psychotherapy.* Baltimore, MD: Johns Hopkins University Press.

Wallerstein, R. (1986). *Forty-two lives in treatment: A study of psychoanaly-sis and psychotherapy.* New York: Guilford Press.

Weber, J., Bachrach, H., & Solomon, M. (1985). Factors associated with the outcome of psychoanalysis and psychotherapy: Final report of the Columbia Psychoanalytic Center Research Project. *International Journal of Psychoanalysis, 12,* 127-141.

FOR FURTHER READING

Gabbard, G. (1994). *Psychodynamic psychiatry in clinical practice: The DSM-IV edition.* Washington DC: American Psychiatric Press.

Hartocollis, P. (1977). *Borderline personality disorders.* New York: International Universities Press.

Talley, P., et al. (1994). *Psychotherapy research and practice.* New York: Basic Books.

Name Index

A

Ackerman, A. B., 123, 141
Ackerman, Nathan W., 8, 146, 161
Adler, Alfred, 6, 11, 12, 101, 144
Alexander, F., 66, 78
Alexander, Franz, 6, 10
Alexander, R., 83, 93
Allen, Frederick H., 9
Allen, Martin G., 100, 101, 103, 107, 118
Alson, A., 109, 120
Anderson, C., 48, 61
Anderson, C. M., 177, 190
Andolfi, Maurizio, 146, 161
Ansbacher, H. L., 48, 61
Aristotle, 100
Auerbach, A., 87, 95
Azim, F. A., 87, 92, 96

B

Bachrach, Henry, 253, 259, 263, 264
Baekeland, F., 261, 263
Balint, E., 83, 93
Balint, M. P., 83, 93
Barber, J., 86, 94
Barlow, J. M., 31
Bateson, Gregory, 145, 153, 161, 162
Baum, M. S., 123, 141
Beavin, J. H., 154, 164
Beck, A., 260, 263
Beckham, E. E., 91, 93
Belsky, J., 196, 212
Bergin, A., 251, 257, 260, 261, 263
Berkenstock, 194
Bettleheim, Bruno, 6
Beutler, L. E., 91, 93
Bienvenu, J., 91, 96
Binder, Jeffrey L., 86, 87, 88, 91, 92, 93, 95, 97
Bion, W. R., 28, 30, 102
Birren, J. E., 204, 210
Bishop, D. S., 182, 190
Blazer, D., 194, 210

Bloch, D., 161, 162
Bloch, S., 103, 109, 119
Blum, H. P., 233, 246
Bordin, E. S., 187, 190
Boscolo, Luigi, 146
Boszormenyi-Nagy, Ivan, 147, 162
Bouhoutsos, J. C., 246
Bowen, Murray, 155, 156, 159, 160, 162
Bowlby, John, 144, 162
Bransford, J. D., 18, 27, 30
Bugental, Elizabeth K., 45
Bugental, James F. T., 38, 45
Burns, B., 194, 210
Burns, B. J., 213
Burrow, Trigant, 101
Butcher, J. N., 80, 95
Butler, R., 198, 204, 210
Butler, S. F., 91, 95

C

Callanan, P., 123, 128, 138
Calvert, W. R., 200, 213
Carlisle, A., 204, 210
Carner, 194
Carroll, M. R., 123, 138
Cartwright, Donald, 250, 251, 263
Catherall, Donald R., 166, 167, 187, 188, 190, 191
Ceccin, Gianfranco, 146
Coffman, E. W., 123, 141
Conyne, R. K., 123, 138, 141
Cook, E., 122, 139
Cooley, Charles, 100
Cooper, A., 91, 94
Corey, G., 122, 123, 125, 127, 128, 135, 138
Corey, M., 122, 123, 127, 128, 135, 138
Corsini, R. J., 103, 119
Crits-Christoph, P., 86, 87, 90, 91, 92, 93, 94, 95
Crouch, E., 103, 109, 119
Curtis, J. T., 90, 91, 97

J

Jackson, Don D., 145, 149, 153, 154, 155, 161, 162, 163, 164
Joffe, R., 115, 120
Jones, E., 80, 95
Jordan, L., 73, 78
Joyce, S. A., 87, 92, 96
Jung, Carl, 3, 6, 197, 212

K

Kantor, D., 147, 162
Kaplan, H. S., 168, 177, 190
Kastenbaum, R., 198, 212
Kates, W., 107, 119
Kaye, K., 177, 190
Keissler, D., 250, 264
Keith-Spiegel, P., 123, 140
Kelly, George A., 25, 30, 44, 45
Kelman, H. C., 103, 115, 119
Kernberg, O., 251, 260, 264
Kessler, L., 194, 213
Kirby, P. C., 123, 132, 140
Kirtner, W., 251, 263
Kleinman, Arthur, 4, 16
Klerman, G., 252, 264
Kline, W. B., 141
Knapp, S., 133, 139
Korn, R., 58, 61
Koss, M. P., 80, 95
Kottler, J., 126, 139
Krasner, B. R., 147, 162
Kubler-Ross, Elizabeth, 204, 212
Kumin, I., 233, 235, 237, 241, 246

L

Labov, W., 19, 30
Lakin, M., 135, 140
Lamb, D. H., 133, 139
Langs, R., 29, 30
Langs, R. D., 225
Lawton, M., 196, 212
Lawton, M. P., 194, 211
Lazarus, L., 202, 212
Lazell, Edward, 101
Le Bon, Gustave, 100, 101
Leaff, L., 259, 263
Lebowitz, B., 196, 212
Leddick, G. R., 123, 138
Levenson, A., 194, 212
Levin, S., 190

Lewin, Kurt, 101
Lewis, M., 198, 210
Lichtenberg, P., 194, 212
Lidz, Theodore, 155
Loar, Lynn, 78
Locke, N., 113, 119
Logsdon, R. G., 194, 213
Luborsky, L., 251, 253, 260, 264
Luborsky, Lester, 86, 87, 90, 91, 95
Lugo, M., 18, 31
Lundwall, L., 261, 263
Lyddon, W., 55, 61
Lynch, S. K., 133, 140

M

McCallum, M., 87, 92, 96
McConnell, S. G., 126, 141
McCorkle, L., 58, 61
McCullough, L., 91, 96
MacKinnon, R., 236, 246
Madanes, Cloe, 146
Mahler, C. A., 130, 140
Major-Kingsley, S., 123, 141
Malan, D. H., 82, 83, 84, 85, 86, 91, 95, 96
Mann, J., 103, 119
Mann, James, 83, 84, 96
Marsh, L. Cody, 101
Martin, D., 139
Maslow, Abraham, 11, 15
May, Rollo, 37, 45
Meloy, R., 49, 52, 53, 61
Menninger, Karl, 58, 61, 82, 96, 240, 241
Mesmer, 100
Michels, R., 236, 246
Miller, T., 252, 264
Mintz, J., 87, 93
Minuchin, Salvador, 146, 161, 163, 177, 190
Molinari, Victor, 203, 204, 210, 212
Moreno, Jacob, 101
Moreno, J. L., 144, 163
Morran, D. K., 123, 138, 141
Mullan, H., 100, 101, 115, 119

N

Nacht, Sacha, 14, 16
Nathans, S., 90, 97
Nichols, N., 144, 147, 153, 158, 160, 163
Niederehe, G., 196, 212
Nixon, G., 87, 96

Subject Index

A

Acting out, 53, 238
Adolescents, 103, 108, 118
Aged,
    See Elderly
AIDS, disclosure by patient with, 133
Alcoholics, 57, 108
Alcoholics Anonymous, 201
Alcoholism, 151, 200
    See also Substance abuse
Alcoholism therapists, 58
Alliance, therapeutic, 166, 187-188,
    199
Aloofness, countertransference
    reaction, 236
Alzheimer's, support groups, 203, 209
American Association of Counseling
    and Development, 122
American Association for Marriage
    and Family Therapy (AAMFT),
    126, 144
American Counseling Association, 126
American Group Psychotherapy
    Association, 122
American Psychological Association
    (APA), 122, 123, 125, 126, 251
Anticonvulsants, 200
Antidepressants, 200
Antipsychotics, 200
Anxiety, countertransference reaction,
    236
Arguments, avoiding with clients, 69-
    70
Association for Specialists in Group
    Work (ASGW), 122, 124, 125,
    126
Assumptions, 24
Attention
    evenly-suspended, 26, 28-30
    free-floating, 26, 28-30

B

Basic Assumption groups, 102
Batterers, 60

Behavior therapy, 7, 251
Behaviorism, 6, 7
Bipolar disorder, 201
Birth order, 159
Block determinants, 169
Blocks
    behavioral, 170
    interpersonal, 170
        resolving, 181-182
            case dialogue, 182-183
    intrapersonal
        resolving, 183-185
            case dialogue, 185-187
    problem-solving, 170
Body language, 155
Bowenian family therapy, 155-161
    techniques, 159-161

C

Catatonia, 108
Causality, defined, 148
Change
    case study, 36-37
    considerations for therapists
        dealing with resistance to, 43
    fear of, 33-44
    is to kill or to die, 44
    kind of a suicide, 44
    therapeutic, when it occurs, 83
    viewed as realignment, 5-6
Child, schizophrenic, 145
Child Guidance movement, 145
Children, 103, 118
    birth order of, 159
Choice, 41
    humans have, 38
Circular thinking, 148
Clients
    See also Patients
    with alcohol problem, 57
    court-ordered, 64
    dangerous, 135
    difficult, 47-60

Contributors

Paul L. Adams, MD
Emeritus Professor of Child Psychiatry, University of Texas Medical Branch, Galveston, TX, and Visiting Professor of Child Psychiatry, University of Tennessee Center for Health Sciences, Memphis, TN. He maintains a private practice in Louisville, KY.

Martin G. Allen, MD
Clinical Professor of Psychiatry, Department of Psychiatry, Georgetown University School of Medicine; in private practice, Washington, D.C.

Henry M. Bachrach, PhD
Clinical Professor of Psychiatry, New York Medical College at St. Vincent's Hospital and Medical Center of New York.

Jeffrey L. Binder, PhD, ABPP
Member of the Core Faculty of the Georgia School of Professional Psychology, Atlanta, GA.

Elizabeth K. Bugental, PhD
Formerly Assistant Director of Inter/Logue and now serves as a board member and consultant to several community agencies.

James F. T. Bugental, PhD
Rockefeller (Teaching) Scholar at the California Institute of Integral Studies, Emeritus Professor of the Saybrook Institute, and Emeritus Clinical Faculty of the Stanford University Medical School.

Donald R. Catherall, PhD
Executive Director, The Phoenix Institute, Chicago, IL.

Alan Forrest, EdD
Professor of Counselor Education at Radford University, Radford, VA, and a licensed professional counselor in private practice.

Stanley C. Feist, PhD
Emeritus Professor of Psychology, The State University of New York College of Technology, Farmingdale, NY.

Frederic Flach, MD
Adjunct Associate Professor of Psychiatry, Cornell University Medical College, New York; Attending Psychiatrist at Payne Whitney Clinic of The New York Hospital and St. Vincent's Hospital and Medical Center, New York.

Glen O. Gabbard, MD
Callaway Distinguished Professor at the Menninger Clinic and Training and Supervising Analyst at the Topeka Institute for Psychoanalysis, Topeka, KS.

Jim Gumaer, EdD
Professor of Counselor Education at Radford University, Radford, VA, and a licensed professional counselor in private practice.

George A. Harris, PhD
Psychologist in private practice in Kansas City, MO; formerly a therapist in vocational rehabilitation and corrections.

Lynn Loar, PhD, LCSW
Educational Coordinator of the San Francisco Child Abuse Council, San Francisco, CA.

Victor Molinari, PhD
Director of Geropsychology at the Veterans Affairs Medical Center, Houston, TX, and Clinical Assistant Professor of Psychology in the Department of Psychiatry and Behavioral Sciences at Baylor College of Medicine, Houston, TX.

Michael L. Perlin, JD
Professor of Law at the New York Law School, New York, NY.

Fraser N. Watts, PhD
Employed at the Medical Research Council's Applied Psychology Unit, Cambridge, England.

For information on other books in the
Hatherleigh Guides series, call the
Marketing Department at Hatherleigh
Press, 1-800-367-2550, or write:
Hatherleigh Press
Marketing Department
420 E. 51st St.
New York, NY 10022